# THE MURDERS THAT MADE US

# THE MURDERS THAT MADE US

## HOW VIGILANTES, HOODLUMS, MOB BOSSES, SERIAL KILLERS, AND CULT LEADERS BUILT THE SAN FRANCISCO BAY AREA

BOB CALHOUN

Published by ECW Press
665 Gerrard Street East
Toronto, Ontario, Canada M4M 1Y2
416-694-3348 / info@ecwpress.com



Editor for the Press: Michael Holmes
Cover design: Michel Vrana

PRINTED AND BOUND IN CANADA

LIBRARY AND ARCHIVES CANADA CATALOGUING IN PUBLICATION

Title: The murders that made us : how vigilantes, hoodlums, mob bosses, serial killers, and cult leaders built the San Francisco Bay Area / Bob Calhoun.

Names: Calhoun, Bob, author.

Identifiers: Canadiana (print) 20200383493 | Canadiana (ebook) 20200383868

ISBN 978-1-77041-549-2 (softcover)
ISBN 978-1-77305-684-5 (ePUB)
ISBN 978-1-77305-685-2 (PDF)
ISBN 978-1-77305-686-9 (Kindle)

Subjects: LCSH: Murder—California—San Francisco Bay Area—Case studies. | LCSH: Murder—Social aspects—California—San Francisco Bay Area—History. | LCSH: Murder—California—San Francisco Bay Area—History. | LCSH: San Francisco Bay Area (Calif.)—History.

Classification: LCC HV6534.S37 C35 2021 | DDC 364.152/3097946—dc23

PRINTING: MARQUIS 5 4 3 2 1

*To my dad, Leo, for showing me around the neighborhood that was while driving through streets that weren't there.*

# CONTENTS

*"If one must be murdered, it be far more satisfactory, from many standpoints, to be murdered in San Francisco."*

— RUSSEL CROUSE,

*NEW YORK TIMES*, AUGUST 3, 1947

INTRODUCTION

# A SHORT HISTORY OF THE ONGOING END OF SAN FRANCISCO

San Francisco is over. You missed it. This ain't the Summer of Love. Punk is dead. Die, yuppie scum. Die, techie scum. Fuckin hipsters.

But San Francisco has always been over. It ended about 20 years before you got here—no matter when that was. If you grew up here, it ended sometime before you turned 21, and you had to hear your older sister tell you how you're just tromping through the ruins of the real San Francisco that she was lucky enough to be around for.

My mother used to go to El Patio, this jazz club over on Market and South Van Ness in the 1950s. She danced to Pérez Prado and the Dorsey Brothers when they blew through town. Bill Graham took it over in 1968 and turned it into the Fillmore West. Grateful Dead and Santana played there, and Allen Ginsberg read poetry from its stage.

"The hippies took it over and ruined everything," my mother said, lamenting the downfall of El Patio and the San Francisco she knew. She and my dad hightailed it out of the city and moved to Redwood City. There weren't any hoppin' jazz clubs in the burbs, but they did get a swimming pool out of the deal. You had those kinds of options when you were fleeing the city because the rent was too damned low instead of the other way around. But to the baby boomers, the Summer of Love with all the brown acid you could OD on and venereal crabs you could catch was what made San Francisco what it was, and if you missed that, you missed San Francisco. The city was over. Dan White and Jim Jones stuck a fork in it in 1978. It was done.

My parents escaped the hippie ruination in the '60s. I returned to the city looking for that sort of thing. I saw Dead Kennedys at the Farm in the '80s, and I wrestled Macho Sasquatcho in a concrete nightclub in SOMA in the 1990s (not-so-humblebrags, I know), but I still feel like I missed the better, crazier, wilder San Francisco that had been—that I was way too late.

This isn't to say that other cities don't inspire the same kind of nostalgia that San Francisco does. Vanishing New York will match every defunct diner and shuttered dive bar that Vanishing SF can throw at you. Chicago also mourns its closed-down watering holes (along with a heartbreaking number of public schools). But San Francisco seems to hold this idea that a more real version of itself existed sometime before you got there, poured into its very concrete and seeping out of the wood of its old Victorians. The city that was is the city that is, inseparable but kept apart by the chasm of time.

In Alfred Hitchcock's *Vertigo* (1958), when Tom Elmore as smarmy shipping magnate Gavin Elster (yes, his name is Gavin) hires Scottie Ferguson (Jimmy Stewart) to tail his wife, Madeleine (Kim Novak), he tells Ferguson, "The things that spell San Francisco to me are disappearing fast." The mid-20th century San Francisco that Elster bemoans is the city that my mother longed to return to, 10 years before Ken Kesey, Jerry Garcia, and Grace Slick showed up and wrecked the damned El Patio. The city that was is also made seemingly more authentic by its crimes, or "who shot who in the Embarcadero, August 1879," as Ferguson's long-suffering gal pal Midge (Barbara Bel Geddes) puts it. And the San Francisco that was with its criminal past giving it gravitas becomes a malevolent force in *Vertigo*, possessing and obsessing Madeleine and Ferguson until the film's climax in a centuries-old mission adobe.

"One final thing I have to do, and then I'll be free of the past," Ferguson says as he drives Madeleine through redwood trees that have lived on this Earth for thousands of years. "I have to go back into the past once more, just once more, for the last time."

The sad thing for him is that he can't. None of us can.

Twenty-two years earlier, the opening title card of MGM's *San Francisco* (1936) informed us that San Francisco "dreams of the queen city she was—splendid and sensuous, vulgar and magnificent." That city was completely leveled by the 1906 earthquake and the pillars of flame that followed it. In the film, buildings shake apart via special effects that complete a Sodom and Gomorrah narrative. The city we live in today is the one that Clark Gable, Jeanette MacDonald, and Spencer Tracy pledge to rebuild as they march towards the camera,

Lobby card for the 1936 film *San Francisco*, old Hollywood's celebration of the city that was.

singing "Battle Hymn of the Republic." The final shot of the film shows the smoldering ruins of San Francisco fading into the 1930s-era financial district—a shot Scorsese pays homage to at the end of *Gangs of New York* (2002).

The total destruction caused by the quake goes a long way towards explaining why San Francisco is a city preoccupied with its own demise, but these musings over Vanishing San Francisco predate 1906. Bret Harte, one of early California's great scribes along with Mark Twain and Ambrose Bierce, tells us you pretty much had to come over on a tall ship with Richard Henry Dana to see the real San Francisco.

In "Bohemian Days in San Francisco," published in the *Saturday Evening Post* in 1900, Harte recalls a city of houses with floors made from wooden tobacco crates and roofs that were nothing more than cloth tarps. If you thought (as I did) that things were rough in front of Taqueria Cancun on 18th and Mission in the 1990s, that scene had nothing on "the weird stories of disappearing men found afterward imbedded in the ooze in which they had fallen and gasped their life away" or that "one Sunday when a Chinaman was stoned to death by a crowd of children returning from Sunday-school." If you weren't there for that, you're just a goddamned poseur.

In "The Mission Dolores," published in 1863, Harte waxes like the *San Francisco Chronicle*'s "A Changing Mission" series from 2014, only with more racism: "The Mission Dolores is destined to be the 'The Last Sigh' [sic] of the Native Californian," Harte writes. "When the last Greaser [sic] shall indolently give way to the bustling Yankee, I can imagine he will, like the Moorish king, ascend to one of the mission hills to take his last lingering look at the hilled city.

"I miss those black-haired women, with swaying unstable busts," Harte writes, speculating on a future San Francisco bereft of Latinas. Guess what, Bret? They're still here and, unfortunately, still being pushed out by today's version of bustling Yankees, with blockchains filled with crypto. Change itself seems to never change.

San Francisco scribe Bret Harte in 1872, dreaming of the lost San Francisco of 1851.

In August 2015, Jeremy Lybarger, editor of the *SF Weekly*, invited me to contribute a true crime column for the paper's website. After several weeks of presenting the Bay Area's murders and scandals of the past, I started to see a narrative of the metropolitan region itself through the crimes that were committed here. As I arranged my criminal history of the Bay Area into a loose chronology, I found that I wasn't just telling stories of the prominent citizens who met bad ends but also about the "people you've never heard of," as Jimmy Stewart's Scottie Ferguson says in *Vertigo*. The assassinations of *Chronicle* publisher Charles de Young, Mayor George Moscone, and Supervisor Harvey Milk are here, side by side with Spanny Lopez, the carnation grower who was hacked up and left behind a Market Street movie theater. The kidnapping of newspaper heiress Patty Hearst or the attempts to assassinate President Ford are only pages from the stories of LeRoy Carter Jr., nine-year-old Michael Nguyen, and all the other people you've never heard of who got killed and dumped in Golden Gate Park—there are so many of those that they get their own chapter.

There isn't a corner of this city that hasn't been touched by crime. San Francisco was founded by genocidal missionaries and modernized by vigilantes who hung people from the roof of a brick building on Sacramento and California Streets. Many of our mayors have been hucksters, and our cops are often corrupt. What Midge (again with the *Vertigo*) calls "the juicy stories" are intertwined with the histories of art movements, lost neighborhoods, suburban migrations, the struggle for LGBTQ+ rights, the Summer of Love, and political fortunes.

Joan Didion—who's made a pretty good career out of explaining California to New Yorkers—wrote that "all narrative was sentimental" in her essay "The White Album," a meditation on the 1960s that springs from buying a dress for Manson Family member Linda Kasabian. Didion connects the dots between buying a white dress on the morning that JFK was shot to Roman Polanski spilling red wine on it four years later. Polanski marries Sharon Tate, who is stabbed to death during the Manson Family's murderous raid on her home on August 9, 1969. On July 27, 1970, Didion buys another dress for Kasabian to wear during her testimony on the murders at Sharon Tate Polanski's house on Cielo Drive in Benedict Canyon. Didion also warns, "all connections were equally meaningful, and equally senseless." I blow past this admonition here but can't quite ignore it.

As I formed a cohesive narrative from what Didion would call the "shifting phantasmagoria" of San Francisco's criminal past, I hit upon the awful truth that crime held as much nostalgia for me as the dive bars being torn down for luxury condos. So here is my true crime history of San Francisco, equal parts revulsion and sentiment, where the city we long to return to has far too many skeletons in its closet. It begins not with shootings on the Embarcadero in 1879 but with a brutal murder on San Bruno Mountain overlooking the Bay in 1959—a murder my own mother was once suspected of.

CHAPTER 1

# MY MOTHER, THE MURDER SUSPECT

My mother, Jackie Calhoun, only talked about the murder sparingly. Her hushed tones when she did stood in sharp contrast to how she spoke of everything else. Tales of a fight at the laundromat over the dryers, or that time the doctor threw a pen at her hypochondriac friend, were retold often and in excruciating detail. My mother loved to gossip, and though the murder was her juiciest story by far, it was different. It was serious.

The details of the murder that she told me were muddled in my memory by the names of friends and acquaintances she knew before I was born. From what I remember, a friend of the family's was shot in his truck by some crazy woman he picked up somewhere. He called her either a "stupid fool" or a "stupid bitch," depending on the telling. That my mom could know this little detail didn't make sense, because the murder took place in the suburban woods somewhere on the Bay Area peninsula.

But there was one other detail of the murder that really stuck in my mind. My mom spoke of growing suspicion among her clique

Courtesy of Bob Calhoun

Author Bob Calhoun's mother, Jackie Calhoun, in front of the house at 330 Guttenberg Street in the early 1950s.

of suburbanites as the murder investigation dragged on unsolved for months.

"You started to suspect everybody—friends, neighbors," she said. "You didn't know who to trust. You wondered who could've done it."

I always meant to write an article, or even a novel, out of all that backyard paranoia, but I never thought of asking my mom to retell the story of the murder until it was too late. She passed away in October 2009 after cancer had shrunk her down to almost nothing. My last conversations with her were about the hallucinations brought on by her steady supply of painkillers, or my pleading with her to drink her damned Ensure. I've never tasted Ensure, but it must be horrible. Elderly people would rather die than drink it.

During those final days, I never asked my mom about the murder, or about anything else for that matter. I didn't get the story of how she moved to San Francisco from Oklahoma in the 1940s; divorced my dad in the '70s; or that time in the '50s when she went to the Black Cat, a seminal gay bar, with my dad and uncle, and all the men hit on them and ignored her. I know these stories well enough to tell you about them, but I only have recollections of her recollections, usually delivered from her favorite chair as she lit a smoke. Details are scant and murky.

My dad, Leo Calhoun, is in good health, but he's pushing 80. I asked him about the murder while we were having lunch at a Peruvian restaurant in Redwood City, a once working-class Bay Area suburb that's being gobbled up by Silicon Valley.

"Do you remember the murder that my mom used to talk about?" I asked. "I think it happened back when you both lived in the Redwood City hills, or maybe it was South San Francisco. I got the impression it happened out in the woods somewhere, but not too far out there."

"August Norry," he answered, letting the victim's name hang in the air for a while before elaborating.

The murder happened when my mom and dad lived on Guttenberg Street in Crocker Amazon, not far from where I live today. My dad pronounces it "gut-ten-burg," like a punch in the gut, instead of "goo-ten-burg," like the Bible. August Norry was dumping some lawn clippings on Mount San Bruno, a hillside covered with eucalyptus trees on the southern edge of San Francisco. Norry ran into a young woman with a gun. She asked him if he was up for a little target practice. He said yes, not realizing he was the target. She shot him several times for no reason at all. My dad gave me the names and places that I didn't have before, but then he dropped a bomb.

"You know, your mother was questioned in the murder investigation," he said. "She matched the suspect's description. A blonde was seen leaving the scene of the murder in Norry's car. Your mother was blonde, and we lived next door to the Norrys back then."

"They were looking for someone who was having an affair with him," he added.

This was a shock to say the least. My mother never mentioned being braced by homicide dicks. I'd remember that. Anyone would remember that. I pressed my dad for more details. He didn't really have any. He came home from work one day, and my mom said that she'd been questioned for about an hour or so.

"Now when we went to Augie's memorial on Mission Street, you could see binoculars or camera lenses being poked through the blinds of the office across the street from the funeral home," my dad recalled. "They were watching everyone."

Details were now less scant, but maybe even murkier. I put my skills as a researcher and journalist to piecing together the story of the murder the way I should have when my mom was still alive. I dug through online newspaper archives, yellowing clipping files kept by local historical societies, and aging spools of microfilm in the hopes that I'd be able to figure out why my mom chose to soft-pedal this story.

August Norry had an Errol Flynn mustache and a mess of dark, slicked-back hair in the one headshot I could find of him that kept cropping up on lurid crime websites. He was a former Arthur Murray dance instructor and a one-time minor league pitching prospect.

"He had all kinds of trick pitches," my dad recalled during a later phone conversation, "but he couldn't get the major league hitters out with his fastball."

After failing in a tryout with the San Francisco Seals, Norry became a self-employed gardener mowing lawns at the Lake Merced Golf Club not far from his home in Daly City, which he shared with his new bride, Darlene. On Monday, February 2, 1959, Norry made the papers in the worst possible way when his "bullet-torn, blood-spattered automobile" was found "abandoned on a lonely 'lover's lane,'" according to the *San Mateo Times*. The car was ditched on the 300 block of Peoria Street in Daly City, eight blocks from my parents' house.

The next day, the *San Mateo Times* headline blared "POLICE HUNT BLONDE IN MULTIPLE SHOT MURDER" with the kind of overwhelming typeface usually reserved for things like the bombing of Pearl Harbor. Crowding the paper's masthead into a corner was a gruesome photo of Norry's corpse lying in a patch of weeds on the downward slope of Mount San Bruno. A bullet wound is clearly visible in Norry's cheek even with the low-resolution reproduction. In the lower right-hand corner, way below the fold, a much smaller headline reads, "Trio of Rock 'N' Roll Fame Die in Crash." August Norry almost pushed the deaths of Buddy Holly, Ritchie Valens, and the Big Bopper—the day the music died—to page five.

Norry was shot 18 times with a .38 Special, a six-shooter. That means the killer emptied the revolver once, reloaded, kept shooting, and reloaded again. On the day of the shooting, a "good-looking blonde" driving a car that looked like Norry's almost ran over a 12-year-old kid playing on the hillside. "We have information that there was another woman involved in Norry's life," San Mateo County sheriff Earl Whitmore told reporters. Whitmore added that "the blonde woman might be married," and there was the "remote possibility" that "Norry was slain by an avenging husband." While the eyewitness description led the police to my mother, they were also figuring my dad for the crime.

Norry was murdered on Sunday and found on Monday. On Tuesday, Sheriff Whitmore and Daly City police questioned Darlene Norry for several hours. August was 28. Darlene was 20. They had been married for only 18 months. The couple was expecting their first child. Police inspectors found a paperback on child-rearing titled *The First Year of Life* in the back seat of Norry's blood-soaked sedan. The whole thing was incredibly sad.

Sheriff's inspectors Eugene Stewart and William Ridenour continued the search for the blonde "revenge slayer." On Wednesday, February 4, 1959, they questioned a 19-year-old blonde waitress who "was found drunk in a Daly City residence that wasn't her own." They cleared the drunken waitress and then questioned more blondes. One of those blondes was Jacqueline Faye Calhoun, age 24. Ten years later, she'd be my mother.

Did my mom offer Stewart and Ridenour coffee when they came knocking on her door? Was she cordial or hostile? Either way, she must've been scared—probably more scared than she'd ever been in her life, before or since, except maybe when she was diagnosed with cancer. My older sister, Danielle, was just seven months old at the time. Had my mom put her down for a nap, or did she cry through the entire interview, providing my mom with a living, screaming alibi? Either way, my sister's existence probably helped cross my mom off the suspect list.

The wood-shingled house on Guttenberg Street where my mother was interrogated straddles the border between the Daly City suburbs and San Francisco's Crocker Amazon neighborhood. My grandmother lived there with my mom while my dad was away in the Air Force. When my dad got back from fixing radios in South Korea in 1957, my grandmother moved to downtown San Francisco to party down at El Patio. (You go, Grandma.) My grandmother on my father's side lived just up the block in a house that now has in front of it a broken-down truck so old that it looks like she left it there. Growing up with divorce and custody battles, I find it hard to imagine both sides of my family ever being so close.

A block away, Guttenberg dead-ends at the incline of the mountain where Norry became a human target. Up the street from my parents lived Charles and Rose Norry, August's parents. Charles Norry was a hard-looking man with an uneven bowl haircut. He was a union beer bottler and coach of the minor league baseball team that August pitched for. My dad was a batboy with the team in the 1940s and even traveled with the team for a game at San Quentin. My mother's younger brother, Dan Williams, briefly dated the woman who later married Bob Norry, August's younger brother. The histories of my family and the Norrys were once intertwined.

The murder investigation dragged on for six weeks. My mom always made it sound like six months because it probably felt that way. The killer was finally announced with more banner headlines on April 16, 1959. Her name was Rosemarie Diane Bjorkland. Her friends called her Penny. Blonde and 18, she lived in her parents' house on Oliver Street in Daly City, four blocks parallel to the houses on Guttenberg Street. The inspectors probably passed by her block on their way to grill my mother.

The sheriffs tracked her down through the cheap, homemade bullets she used called wadcutters. She bought them from an auto mechanic out in Colma, the Bay Area's suburban necropolis. The mechanic tried to tell the cops that a box of bullets had been stolen out of his car. The cops leaned on him. His story fell apart. He gave up Penny. She was arrested on April 14, a Tuesday. Sheriff Whitmore sweet-talked a confession out of her at "a quiet family restaurant" in San Carlos called the Doll House. Penny had the meatloaf, with strawberry shortcake for dessert.

"For about a year, or a year and a half, I've had the urge to kill someone," she said. "I wanted to see if I could commit a murder and not have it on my conscience."

She could.

"I've felt better ever since I killed him," she confessed. "It's like a burden has been lifted off of me."

The papers dubbed her with names worthy of a pulp fiction villain. She was the "Urge Killer" or the "Blonde Murderess." The story was

Bob Campbell / ©*San Francisco Chronicle* / Polaris

Rosemarie "Penny" Bjorkland rips off her shades for the cameras as she's escorted through the Redwood City courthouse by an unnamed deputy.

strange enough to get picked up by papers as far away as Moberly, Missouri, and Pottstown, Pennsylvania. The *San Francisco Chronicle* devoted nearly a full-page spread to a celebrity-style profile of Bjorkland with glamor shots flanked by lingerie ads. The *Times Tribune* out of Palo Alto called her "plump and pretty."

Sometime after her confession, law enforcement officials drove Bjorkland to the same hillside where she obliterated Norry so she could reenact the crime. Inspector Stewart filmed Bjorkland as she pretended to shoot an imaginary version of Norry. According to several newspaper accounts, Bjorkland told sheriffs that Norry called her a "stupid fool" after she pumped the first shot into his gut, although the *Examiner* quoted her as saying "stupid ----," lending validity to both of my mom's versions of events.

Bjorkland hadn't arranged to meet with Norry on the day of the murder, but they did know each other. About a month before the murder, Penny found Norry dumping lawn clippings on the hill where she later killed him. He took her to a drive-thru burger joint before returning her home. She gave him her phone number. He never called her. Norry didn't try anything with Penny either time he met her, but he was playing it real close to the line.

After months of generating headlines while awaiting trial, Penny Bjorkland was found guilty of first-degree murder and sentenced to life in prison on August 6, 1959. "This was a willful, wanton killing," Superior Court judge Frank B. Blum declared. Bjorkland served just seven years of her sentence before being released and fading into obscurity. At 25 years old, she was still young. She might've gone on to marry, have kids. A public figure page on Facebook (that likely isn't maintained by her) has 69 likes with people leaving comments on how they'd love to meet her.

About a week after my mother died, I was going through voicemails. There was one from her, asking when I was coming to see her. She sounded so weak. I had to crank the volume just to make

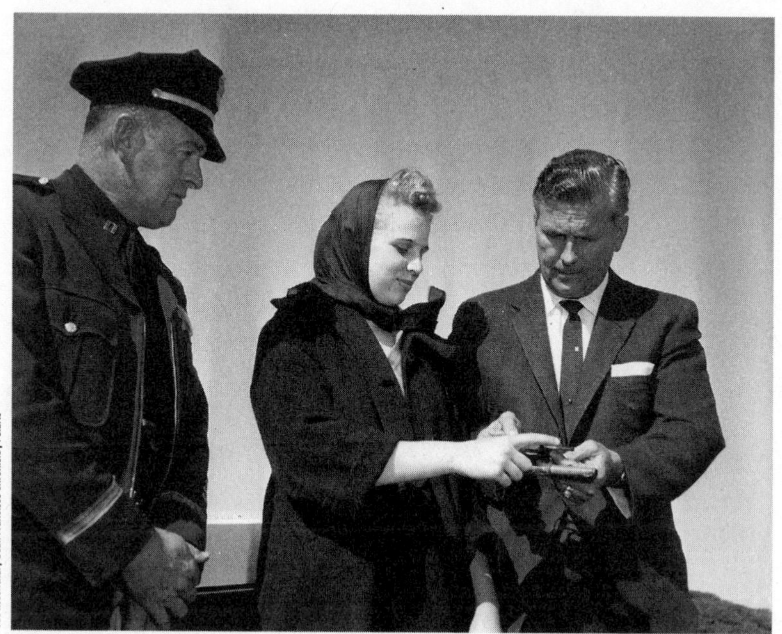
Joe Rosenthal / ©San Francisco Chronicle / Polaris

Rosemarie "Penny" Bjorkland (center) returns to the scene of the slaying of August Norry on San Bruno Mountain and shows the murder weapon to San Mateo County sheriff Earl B. Whitmore (right) while an unnamed police officer looks on.

out what she was saying. I hit the delete key without thinking, only to feel a wave of guilt seconds later. That was the last time I would hear my mother's voice, and I erased her just to make space on a hard drive.

The newspapers told me the story of August Norry and Penny Bjorkland bathed in hyperbole, but they didn't tell me the story that I was really after—the story of my mother during that police questioning in 1959 and the weeks of suspicion afterwards. I attempted to find that story in court records and police reports, but they had all been purged. Details of death sentences and lives ruined had been tossed in a dumpster somewhere, just to make space. Crime isn't usually something we get sentimental over.

My dad and my uncle are some of the only people left who remember the murder. I've gotten their stories and unearthed little pieces of family history that I never asked of my mother. I took notes and asked questions this time. I thought the mid-20th century would always be with us, just in the rearview mirror, but it's not anymore. It's getting to be so long ago.

## CHAPTER 2

# VIGILANCE!

### THE HOUNDS

Flakes of gold were found by a New Jersey carpenter in the American River near Sutter's Mill in the Sacramento Valley on January 24, 1848. John Sutter, the Swiss immigrant who owned the mill where he enslaved several Hawaiians, wanted to keep the discovery quiet, but word got out. By 1849, San Francisco's then natural harbor was clogged with ships filled with gold-hunters from the eastern United States, Australia, China, Chile, and Peru. The 49ers, as they came to be called, ditched their ships in the bay and hightailed it inland in hopes of striking it rich. Many of the ships were sunk near the shore, covered in sludge, and used to form the highly unstable landfill that the 58-story Millennium Tower is sinking into today.

Even with people streaming from the tent cities of San Francisco to the gold fields, the population of the city shot from 400 to 25,000 in 1849. In the power vacuum created by a major port city springing up almost overnight, a gang of military men called the Hounds set themselves up as the city's de facto police force.

The Hounds were headquartered in a tent saloon they dubbed Tammany Hall and often paraded through the muddy streets wearing what the *Weekly Alta California* described as "fantastic or ridiculous dresses." As the Hounds became quasi-official, they changed their name to the San Francisco Society of Regulators, but were still little more than a protection racket with drums and bugles. At first, San Francisco's emerging business community was happy to pay the Hounds to shake down recently arrived Chileans, but soon the gang was shaking down the businessmen who were already paying them. With what passed for prominent San Franciscans already fed up with them, the Hounds finally went too far on Sunday, July 15, 1849.

After a day of conducting drunken military drills in the East Bay, Hounds leader Samuel Roberts came home and caught Felice Alvarez in her room with Leopold Bleckschmidt and another German man. Roberts believed he had forced Alvarez, a Chilean prostitute, into an exclusive relationship, but she had other ideas. Roberts flew into a rage and dragged Bleckschmidt into the street, beat him unconscious with a club, and slashed his face with his riding spur. Still raging, Roberts then gathered up his Regulators and attacked the Chilean encampment. The Regulators came down on everyone who spoke Spanish or looked like they might. Men were shot, women were raped, and tents were ransacked. The Regulators snatched sacks of gold dust and auctioned off the Chileans' other belongings to passersby on the streets. Several Chileans escaped into the bay on boats.

"In every direction were heard the cries and shrieks of women and children, mingled with the oaths and demoniac laughter of reckless and impious men," the *Weekly Alta California* reported. Historian Stanton Coblentz later exclaimed the raid was "a spectacle of madness, a scene reminiscent of wartime horrors!"

On the following day, Sam Brannan, W.D.M. Howard, and several other men with streets now named after them held a meeting at Portsmouth Square (in what is now Chinatown). They organized a police force and an instant court system to take down the Hounds.

Roberts and 20 of his men were arrested and tried, but nothing much came of it beyond the spectacle of the trial itself. Despite being sentenced to 10 years hard labor, most of the Hounds were freed a short time later.

The surviving Chileans saw little difference between the vanquished Hounds and those who replaced them. They had a word for these men who took it upon themselves to enforce order if not the law. They called them "vigilantes."

The Jon B. Lovelace Collection of California Photographs in Carol M. Highsmith's America Project, Library of Congress, Prints and Photographs Division

"Vigilante Days," painted by Anton Refregier in 1943, shows the city's bloody beginnings. Commissioned by the Depression-era Works Progress Administration, the mural adorns the walls of the Rincon Annex Post Office near the Embarcadero at 101 Spear Street, not far from where the vigilantes once strung people up from buildings.

## THE SYDNEY DUCKS

By 1850, San Francisco was built on wooden tobacco crates and lit by oil lamps. Not surprisingly, things burned down—a lot. Instead of seeking rational explanations, the city's newspaper of record drummed up anti-immigrant conspiracy theories.

"It is a well known fact that some of the most desperate scoundrels of England who have been serving the Queen in Sydney are in this city, and would stick at nothing in the attempt to obtain money by any diabolical crime," the *Daily Alta California* decried in a January 24, 1850, article blaming Aussies for an alleged wave of "incendiarism," or arson, that was blazing through the city. Yes, Aussies.

The *Alta California* continued to hammer on "the transported felons of Great Britain" for over a year. A February 25, 1851, editorial warned, "Our citizens are at their mercy, and their mercy is such as the wolf gives the lamb."

White American xenophobia went beyond the racial lines of today and extended to white people from anywhere but the continental United States. Making the reporting of the time more confusing to the modern reader, the phrase "Native Americans" referred to white people from the East Coast, and not the Ohlone or Miwok peoples. Australians were often called English or British.

Even though only a few Australian immigrants in California were convicts from the Botany Bay penal colony, the dime-store-novel prose that passed for newspaper reporting back then reported the Aussies had formed a secret society of thugs called the Sydney Ducks. In addition to almost every murder and robbery in Northern California, San Franciscans were led to believe the Sydney Ducks burned down buildings in order to loot the charred wreckage. While this seems like a hard way to rob someone, American citizens who had only been in California for a year or two were moved to combat this imagined secret society by forming an order of their own.

After the beating and robbery of Charles J. Jansen in his Montgomery Street store on February 19, 1851, an angry mob of thousands assembled at the plaza in front of City Hall. Police had two Australian men in custody who kind of met the description of the suspect in the case—an escaped convict called "English" Jim Stuart, who had killed the sheriff of Auburn. The problem was neither man in custody was English Jim. Both were totally innocent.

Sam Brannan, a Mormon elder who collected tithe money from Mormon miners without ever passing it along to his church, addressed the mob. Still pissed off about the light sentences handed out to the Hounds, Brannan didn't care about the guilt or innocence of the accused in this case. Brannan reasoned that even if these Aussies didn't rob Jansen, they had to be guilty of something.

"I am very much surprised to hear people talk about grand juries, or recorders, or mayors," Brannan said. "I am tired of such talk. These men are murderers, I say, as well as thieves. I know it and I will die or see them hung by the neck."

"I want no technicalities," he added, calling for execution without a trial. "Such things are devised to shield the guilty."

William Tell Coleman, a distant relative of George Washington blessed with the handsomeness of Daniel Day Lewis in *Last of the Mohicans*, managed to calm the crowd down from instant executions. He was still a-okay with forgoing due process, just as long as everyone was dignified and organized about it. The resulting show trial ended up with a hung jury even without the meddlesome interference of defense attorneys. Enraged over so many jurors voting for acquittal, the mob bum-rushed the courthouse to get the prisoners.

"Benches, desks and railings were broken to pieces," the *Alta California* reported. "The prisoners would certainly have been taken from the room had not the company of Washington Guards, who had been parading during the day, rushed in with fixed bayonets, and mounting the desks and benches drove the people away."

The two innocent men were left in the custody of the city jail and eventually set free, but the vigilantes pressed forward. By June 1851, the mob of February had organized into the Vigilance Committee with its own secret signals and motto: "Let justice be done, though the heavens may fall." With the bloodthirsty Brannan at the helm, there would no longer be any trials.

## LET EVERY HONEST CITIZEN BE A HANGMAN AT ONCE

On June 11, Brannan and his vigilantes were set to hang John Jenkins from the flagpole in Portsmouth Square given to the city by the people of Portland, Oregon. Unlike the men mistaken for English Jim, Jenkins had been caught fleeing a robbery, so his guilt was unambiguous. However, the vigilantes had opposition by this time. State Senator David Colbreth Broderick, a political fixer who made his fortune by selling $10 gold coins cast from $8 worth of gold, returned from Sacramento and was shocked to find what San Francisco had become. He went to the scene of the impending execution flanked by a team of his loyal henchmen. With the rope around Jenkins's neck, Broderick and his men grabbed onto Jenkins to try and wrest him free while Brannan and his men pulled at the other end of the rope in a macabre tug-of-war. Fighting for due process, Broderick's men were soon joined by actual city police and some concerned Australians, but there were too many angry men on the other side.

"A long pull and a strong pull and a pull together," Brannan shouted to encourage the vigilantes. "Let every honest citizen be a hangman at once!"

Brannan's cheerleading did the trick, and the vigilantes were finally able to hoist Jenkins from an old adobe building although he had probably already been strangled to death during the struggle. Jenkins's body dangled over Portsmouth Square for several hours until 7 a.m. when it was cut down. The corpse was taken to "the dead house in City Hall yard" where it was put on further display and "seen by a large number of persons," according to the *Alta California*. "Rarely have we seen a finer, more muscular frame than his."

Even with Broderick's bare-knuckled opposition to mob rule, the Vigilance Committee took control of the city's streets. Vigilante patrols turned away ships with immigrants they deemed undesirable. A Frenchman was stomped to death by a mob for speaking with a foreign accent. Buildings and ships were searched with scant provocation.

The patrols finally caught English Jim Stewart and hung him without incident from the mast of a ship in the harbor on July 11, 1851. While this seemed like a great victory for the vigilantes at the time, it confirmed that they had tried to hang the wrong men in the first place. Attendance at committee meetings declined after that, and Brannan had trouble collecting membership dues. The group disbanded after just 100 days. Dissolution due to lack of interest was hardly the kind of moral reawakening that Broderick had hoped for. He feared that vigilantism would return to San Francisco, and he was right.

But a future Vigilance Committee would not have Sam Brannan to lead it. Mormon elder Parley P. Pratt arrived in San Francisco around July 1851 and was horrified by Brannan's involvement with the vigilante movement. Pratt disfellowshipped Brannan from the Mormon Church for "unchristian like conduct, neglect of duty, and for combining with lawless assemblies that commit murder and other crimes." Pratt later called Brannan "a corrupt and wicked man."

Brannan founded the town of Calistoga in 1861 and hoped to make its hot springs into the tourist attraction they would eventually become. He failed at this, and was even shot at by townspeople angered over his attempts at gentrification. He later moved to Mexico, battled alcoholism, and died penniless in Escondido, California, on May 5, 1889.

## JOSEFA

The Fourth of July celebrations in Downieville were extra raucous in 1851. California had just gained statehood on September 9, 1850, so the small mining town at the north fork of the Yuba River in the Sierras pulled out all the stops. What began with parades and a speech from the state's first governor ended with the lynching of Josefa Segovia, the only hanging of a woman in California state history.

After a full day of guzzling mining camp swill, Joe Cannon and a few other drunks were out banging on doors around Downieville. Cannon—sometimes referred to as Fred or Jack—was well liked in the mining town, and was described in an 1882 history of Plumas, Lassen, and Sierra Counties as "a Scotchman of magnificent physical strength and herculean proportions." At some point in the night, Cannon and his pals burst through the door of Josefa Segovia, a proud Mexican woman around 25 years old who lived in her adobe home with her partner or common-law husband, Jose. Jose was out dealing monte at a local gambling house, and Segovia managed to fend off Cannon and his gang before they could rape her. Cannon returned early in the morning. Some accounts say he wanted to apologize, but others say he came back to finish what he started. Either way, Segovia was having none of it. She pulled a bowie knife out from under her blouse and drove the blade clear through Cannon's sternum, killing him instantly.

With many miners still celebrating out in the streets, the news of the stabbing went around almost instantly. Segovia took refuge at Craycroft's gambling house. The gamblers who knew her tried to protect her, but the gold diggers threatened to tear down the saloon if they didn't give her up. Segovia was soon dragged out into the street. A show trial was held right there on the spot. A San Franciscan lawyer offered a defense of the woman and stood on a barrel to be heard over the mob. "The crowd kicked the barrel from under him, threw him about and ordered him out of town," William McDonald told the Oakland *Tribune* in 1922. McDonald, then 92, was the last surviving witness to the incident.

A doctor who examined Segovia told the crowd that she was three months pregnant, but the drunk miners didn't care. "The doctor was given just two hours to get out of town," McDonald recalled. "When the time was up, he was nowhere to be found."

The mob sentenced her to death by hanging. Just four years earlier, she was a Mexican citizen on Mexican land, but now she had only two hours to live while the men born across a continent built a scaffold on the Jersey Bridge over the Yuba River. When Segovia returned to be hung, "she did not exhibit the least fear," according to the *Daily Alta California*. After she climbed the steps of her gallows, Segovia handed her Panama hat to a large miner known as Oregon. When asked if she had anything to say, she said, "Nothing, but I would do the same thing again if so provoked." She also asked that her remains be "decently taken care of." She then placed the rope around her own neck and reportedly said, "Adiós, señores," before a pistol was fired to

HANGING OF THE MEXICAN WOMAN.

**Artist's impression of the the lynching of Josefa Segovia in the Gold Rush town of Downieville in 1851, from William Downie's *Hunting for Gold*, published 1893.**

signal the men to cut the lashings. Segovia's body dropped four feet, but McDonald recalled rumors that her neck didn't snap from the fall.

"Her friends might have saved her had they taken her down immediately," McDonald said.

The execution of Segovia without anything even close to due process was condemned almost immediately. The *Daily Alta California*, which had been totally in the tank for the vigilantes back in San Francisco, called it "a blot upon the history of the State" on July 14, 1851. In more recent years, the killing has been placed within a wave of anti-Mexican violence during the Gold Rush. It is doubtful that Segovia would have been hung had she been white.

A plaque dedicated to Segovia's memory near the bridge where she was hung refers to her only as "Juanita" even though records of the time give her full name. Adding further desecration, her skull was later stolen from her grave and used in initiation ceremonies by a Sierra City men's club. Segovia's ghost reportedly still haunts the southeast corner of the Jersey Bridge, beckoning to the living on foggy nights.

## CHAPTER 3

# THE FOURTH ESTATE

### THE DAILY DRAMATIC CHRONICLE

Early San Francisco had its hoodlums, lynch mobs, and bands of masked men who garroted citizens in the streets. Just as violent a class of people, however, were the city's newspaper publishers who settled libel disputes with hot lead instead of lawyers. On May 15, 1856, just after 5 p.m., the ongoing war of words between James King of William, publisher of the *San Francisco Bulletin*, and *Sunday Times* proprietor James P. Casey ended in a shootout on the corner of Montgomery and Washington Streets in front of a joint called Phil's Oyster Saloon. King of William died from his wounds on May 20, and Casey was hung by vigilantes from a gallows built out from a roof on Sacramento Street two days later.

The Second Vigilance Committee and the militias that sprung from the killing of King of William ran the city like a police state and kept on hanging people without trials. However, it disbanded with a big self-congratulatory parade in August 1856, so it provided no deterrent to future acts of publisher-on-publisher violence by the

Library of Congress

**Before Salesforce Tower, the San Francisco Chronicle Building on Market Street dominated the city's skyline.**

time brothers Gustavus, Charles, and Michael de Young launched the *Daily Dramatic Chronicle* in 1865. The de Youngs wove a mythology for themselves as being the descendants of French aristocrats from New Orleans. In reality, their father, Meichel De Jong (or De Jongh), was a Dutch Jewish immigrant whose bank failed in the 1830s and who afterwards sold dry goods and made tortoise-shell jewelry. Meichel suffered a stroke on a Mississippi River steamboat and died, so the brothers, their mother, Amelia, and their five sisters moved from St. Louis to San Francisco in 1854.

Charles and Michael had learned the newspaper trade as typesetters for Rabbi Julius Eckman's *Weekly Gleaner* before they launched their *Chronicle*, a paper that they built up through various degrees of larceny. Unable to afford their own telegraph line, Charles hung

Courtesy of UC Berkeley, Bancroft Library

Charles de Young, the violent and larcenous founder of the *San Francisco Chronicle.*

around the Western Union office where he learned enough Morse code to horn in on the other papers' wire transmissions. He was there on April 15, 1865, when the news that President Lincoln had been shot came in. Charles rushed back to his office and had three editions of the *Chron* out on the street with the breaking news hours before their competitors. The other papers never recovered from this early act of info hacking.

After rebranding as the *Daily Morning Chronicle*, Gustavus mysteriously disappeared from the masthead of the family's tabloid in 1868 to be replaced by "Charles de Young & Co," the "& Co" being Michael. This was a step up since only Charles's and Gustavus's initials were included on previous editions. Within its first decade, the paper now known as the *San Francisco Chronicle* boasted (in every sense of the word) the largest circulation of any newspaper west of the Mississippi River with a winning combination of light gossip and populist takedowns of local movers and shakers. While the *Examiner* still breaks stories and fills downtown newspaper bins as a free tabloid, the *Chron* is the undisputed victor of the old newspaper wars that were often as violent as such a martial descriptor would suggest.

## THE HAUNTED CHURCH

The Emmanuel Baptist Church of Capp Street was cursed from the start. In 1878, the church moved from a rented hall on 22nd and Folsom to more permanent digs at 22nd and Capp. A short time later, the church's first pastor, Reverend Charles Hughes, slashed his own throat with a straight razor. His replacement chose a more common method of suicide and shot himself in the head. Two ministers. Two suicides. You'd think that Mission residents would've burned the place to the ground after that and called it a day, but the church kept going.

The third pastor, Isaac Milton "I.M." Kalloch, was young and politically connected. His father, Isaac Smith "I.S." Kalloch, a minister himself, was a higher-up in the powerful Workingmen's Party, which had won almost every seat on the Board of Supervisors on the strength of its really ugly anti-Chinese campaign. Rampant racism made the elder Kalloch a favorite to win the mayoral race of 1879.

But Charles and Michael de Young backed another candidate and started slinging the mud in the *Chron*'s editorial pages. In August 1879, the *Chron* ran a story "severely animadverting upon the character and moral standing" of I.S. Kalloch's dead father. It was on. Kalloch responded by calling the de Youngs "bastard progeny, born in the slums and nursed in the lap of a prostitute" during a speech at the Metropolitan Hotel.

Now this whole de Young "Mama was a whore" rumor came from an 1874 story in the competing *San Francisco Sun*. After the *Sun* ran the rumor, Charles de Young shot it out with the *Sun*'s editor on Market Street. The newspapermen managed to miss each other, but a young boy was shot in the leg. The *Chronicle* sent the kid $100 and nobody went to prison. Five years later, Kalloch not only read from the story but threatened to reprint it in the Workingmen's Party newsletter.

On August 23, 1879, Charles de Young went by carriage to the Metropolitan Church where Kalloch was addressing a gathering. He sent a messenger to get Kalloch. When Kalloch emerged from the church, de Young put one shot in his chest and another in his hip, making this a Victorian era drive-by. As de Young tried to escape, a crowd of people overturned his carriage and pulled him out. "He was dreadfully kicked and bruised," according to a wire story. De Young got himself arrested just to survive. The *Chronicle* had to station armed guards around its offices to keep mobs from trashing the place.

"The city is intensely excited," the *Deseret News* of Salt Lake City reported. "There was never a time when San Francisco was more angry."

Kalloch survived the shooting and won the mayoral race. Charles de Young was released on bail and hid out back east until things died down. But when he came back to San Francisco, he published a pamphlet bashing Kalloch all over again. De Young just kept at it. Until I.M. Kalloch, the son and pastor of the cursed church, stormed the *Chron*'s offices on April 23, 1880, and shot Charles five times, dead.

I.M. Kalloch was acquitted in March 1881 in a trial where several witnesses were jailed for perjury. Mayor I.S. Kalloch was indicted for

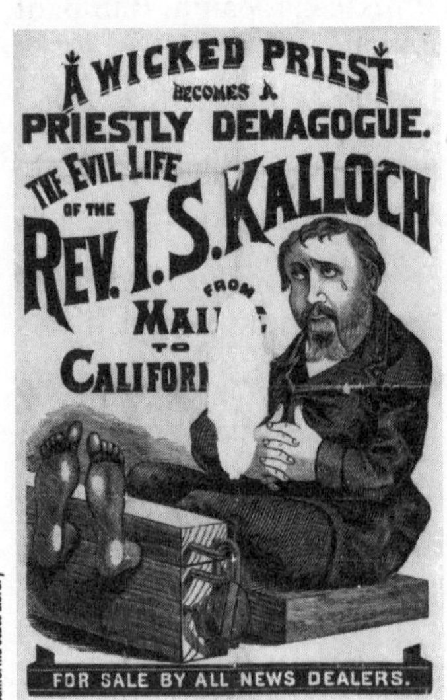


California State Library

A pamphlet slandering mayoral candidate I.S. Kalloch, likely distributed by *Chronicle* publisher Charles de Young.

taking bribes in 1882, but beat the case and served out his full term. Charles de Young was downplayed if not erased entirely from civic and family histories. His brother Michael took over the paper and became part of a shooting scandal of his own barely three years later.

Emmanuel Baptist Church hit a gruesome trifecta with two suicides and a murder, but even with three deaths in less than three years, the little church somehow endured.

The congregation moved to a new building on Bartlett Street between 22nd and 23rd in 1890, and things stayed quiet for nearly five years. When the Reverend John George Gibson took over the church in 1894, his predecessor didn't even have blood on his hands. But the curse came back, and this time it was bloodier than ever.

On Saturday, April 13, 1895, a group of church ladies was decorating the pulpit for the next day's lavish Easter Sunday celebrations when one of them found the blood-drenched body of a young woman in a small library storeroom.

"The girl had been assaulted and her remains had been cut and hacked," the *Spokesman-Review* of Spokane, Washington, later reported. The victim had also "been gagged by the assailant" with "a part of her underclothing" that was jammed down her throat "with a sharp stick."

At first, the churchwomen thought the body was 21-year-old Blanche Lamont, a popular member of the congregation who had been missing for 10 days. However, the body was later identified as that of Minnie Williams, a woman who liked the church enough to journey from Alameda by ferry for services. Lamont only stayed missing for another day before a search of the church grounds uncovered her body at the top of a rickety staircase in the church's ominous bell tower. She was "stripped of her clothing with her hands clasped upon her breast," according to the *Chron*. Unlike Williams, Lamont was not mutilated beyond "the marks of fingers that had been pressed deep into the tender flesh" and the damage done by 11 days of decomposition. The cursed church could now add a double homicide to its litany of misfortunes.

Police quickly arrested W.H.T. "Theodore" Durrant, a medical student and superintendent of Emmanuel Baptist's Sunday school, who was identified by several eyewitnesses as the last man seen with both victims. Durrant denied killing the two women, but Williams's purse was found in Durrant's coat during a search of his house. A pawnbroker later testified that Durrant had tried to sell him one of Lamont's rings days after her disappearance. Durrant's two-month trial moved a lot of newsprint as the *Chron* and *Examiner* used it to boost readership during the early days of their century-long rivalry. Durrant himself received bags of fan mail, much of it from female admirers. While Durrant captivated the public, his

El. Emanuel Baptist Church, Bartlett Street, between 22nd and 23rd St.
It was in the belfry of this place that the nude bodies of Blanch
LaMont and Minnie Williams were found - These girls were both
members of the congregation, They had been keeping company with
Theodore Durant who by engagement met them in the church
and murdered them hiding their bodies Durant was tried,
for this crime convicted and Hung.

California State Library

The cursed Emanuel Baptist Church on Bartlett Street between 22nd and 23rd Streets, where proto serial killer Theodore Durrant brutally murdered Blanche Lamont and Minnie Williams in 1895. Above: a handwritten note included with the image by the California State Library details the crimes.

often-contradictory testimony didn't convince the jury—the only audience he really needed to sway. The jury found him guilty in just 22 minutes on November 1, 1895.

Durrant's final public appearance came in San Quentin's death chamber on January 7, 1896.

"I am an innocent man," Durrant protested from the gallows at 10:34 a.m. "I bear no animosity toward those who have persecuted me, not even the press of San Francisco, which hounded me to the grave," he added during a four-minute speech that was described as "poorly constructed" by the press he excoriated. A few minutes later, Durrant was dead.

"After the drop, Durrant did not struggle," the *Deseret News* reported. "In fifteen minutes, he was cut down; the neck was broken by the fall."

After the murders, Mission residents called for the cursed church to be burned to the ground, but again it endured. Even the earthquake of 1906 and the fires that followed failed to take down the building. The church was finally dismantled plank by plank in 1915. City College's Mission Center stands on this site today.

## THE SUGAR KING

Blackmail had been a major part of the *Chron*'s business model since the de Young brothers founded it in 1865. Charles and Michael slung mud at the city's well-to-do on the paper's editorial pages but weren't above taking bribes to squelch a story. And besides, they needed the extra cash to fend off the libel suits that were a regular cost of doing business. But not everyone decided to pay off the de Youngs or take them to court. After Charles de Young was shot to death in the paper's newsroom in 1880, his brother Michael, now going by the tonier M.H. de Young, took over the paper without changing its business model. It was only a matter of time before history repeated itself.

In 1881, de Young set his sights on the "Sugar King," Claus Spreckels, a hard man from Hanover, Germany, who built a trans-Pacific empire with his Hawaiian cane fields and San Franciscan refineries. The Spreckels clan weathered the initial series of *Chron* exposés that alleged the use of slave labor at the family's Hawaiian plantations. However, when the paper ran a story in November 1884 that accused Spreckels of swindling shareholders in his Hawaiian Commercial and Sugar Company just days before a major board meeting, Spreckels's son Adolph went ballistic—literally.

On November 19, 1884, Adolph Spreckels followed de Young into the *Chron*'s business office and fired his pistol at the newspaperman. Fortunately for de Young, a stack of children's picture books that he was carrying slowed down the first bullet, keeping it from hitting the subclavian artery "by about a sixteenth of an inch," according to the *Chron*. When de Young couldn't find cover behind his desk, he turned and lunged at Spreckels, but slipped and "fell forward in a half-stooping posture." Spreckels shot de Young again, hitting him in the upper left shoulder.

At nearly the same moment that Spreckels delivered his second shot, George W. Emerson, a clerk at the *Chron*, pulled a revolver out of a counter drawer and shot Spreckels, hitting him just above the elbow. Spreckels was wounded but still deadly when cashier J.P. Chesley ran from behind his desk and "thrust his hand over the hammer" of Spreckels's revolver. A split-second later, business manager J.C. Elliot and a clerk named J.M. Reuck tackled the heir-turned-assassin. "Spreckels struggled desperately to get his pistol hand free," the *Chron* reported, "but the odds were against him."

De Young survived but was in a weakened condition. Spreckels was free on bail soon after he was arrested, when it was determined that de Young's wounds weren't fatal.

"Should there be any appearance of de Young getting worse, Spreckels will be immediately re-arrested and held in confinement until after all danger of de Young's life has passed," a *Deseret News* story, delivered "per Western Union Telegraph Line," assured its readers.

"This is the second time that the hand of an assassin has been raised to silence this journal," an uncredited *Chron* editorial following the shooting declared. "Respect for the honored dead—sympathy with him who may yet escape from the shot of the assassin—forbids us at this time to say more."

A piece in the *Brooklyn Daily Eagle* was decidedly more snarky. "The fact that editors, as a rule, are not shot but generally die in their beds like other men, is evidence that there has been a marked peculiarity in the editorial methods adopted by the de Young brothers," an unnamed editor quipped.

Spreckels never saw the inside of a cell again, as he was acquitted on July 1, 1885, after a lengthy trial that the *Chron*, of course, called a "judicial farce." Relatives and employees of Spreckels greeted the not guilty verdict by howling and stamping their feet in the courtroom, and even a *New York Times* correspondent implied that things weren't quite on the up-and-up.

"The result of the protracted trial was a genuine surprise to the community," the *Times* reported. "The comment heard on all sides tonight is, 'Well, money can do anything in this city.'"

Ambrose Bierce held more sympathy for the jurors, however. "Hatred of de Young is the first and best test of a gentleman," wrote the author and satirist.

Despite the lack of consequences, no one in the Spreckels clan ever shot at de Young again, but the feud continued in newsprint. Claus Spreckels bought the *San Francisco Call* in 1895, and the competing paper's front pages exposed de Young's crooked dealings in a way that the *Chron* never would. Both houses eventually laundered their violent legacies by establishing museums: de Young established what's now the M.H. de Young Memorial Museum in Golden Gate Park in 1895, and Adolph Spreckels's wife, Alma, gifted the Legion of Honor Museum near the Golden Gate Bridge to the city of San Francisco in 1915.

Michael de Young died in 1925. His only son, Charles de Young, named after his slain brother, died in a fishing accident in 1913 when he was just 32, leaving de Young's four daughters to carry on the family dynasty, if not its name. One of his daughters, Constance Marie de

Young (1885–1968), married Joseph Tobin, an heir to the Hibernia banking fortune. Patricia Hearst, granddaughter of de Young's wealthiest rival, *Examiner* publisher William Randolph Hearst, held up a branch of the Hibernia Bank on April 15, 1974, and carried on the violent newspaper feuds of the previous century without even knowing it.

## CHAPTER 4

# GANGS OF THE BARBARY COAST

### LITTLE DICK

Crime was on the rise in San Francisco in the 1870s as new disruptive railroad routes allowed cheap goods from other parts of the country to flood the city. Local factories closed, forcing the children who used to labor in them to form hoodlum gangs. When the kids weren't passing their now idle time by beating on Chinese people, they robbed the Barbary Coast blind.

"There is one evil which I mention with regret," San Francisco police chief Patrick Crowley wrote in his 1872 annual report. "It is the disposition on the part of many young men and lads to commit acts of violence and mischief."

Journalists started using the word "hoodlum" to describe the violent youths who plagued San Francisco as early as a *Cincinnati Commercial* article in 1871. In 1875, Samuel Williams wrote in *Scribner's Monthly* that the "Hoodlum is a distinctive San Francisco product," and "He drinks, gambles, steals, runs after lewd women, and sets buildings on fire."

However, not all of the hoodlums were male.

"The memberships of many of the early hoodlum gangs included girls, and several were captained by maladjusted representatives of the so-called gentler sex," Herbert Asbury wrote in *The Barbary Coast*, his 1933 tome on crime in early San Francisco.

"These girls were almost more ferocious than their male companions," Asbury continued, "and their fertile minds devised most of the unpleasant methods of torture which the hoodlums employed upon their victims."

Mary Avery was just 13 years old when she led a gang that included boys as old as 16. Known as "Little Dick," Avery became notorious after a night in the San Francisco city prison on March 28, 1877. She smuggled cigarettes and a knife into the holding tank within her "petticoat of double-thickness" that the *Chronicle* speculated she used "as a means of concealing her plunder" from shoplifting. Guards confiscated the smokes and the blade, but Little Dick took things to a new level when she propositioned a boy in the cell next to hers using "the unintelligible slang used by criminals, and in which they were adept." Guards confined Avery to a dark solitary cell and described her antics as "one of the worst cases of juvenile depravity that they had ever witnessed."

Despite her "corpulent and careless-looking" mother's pleas, the judge committed Avery to serve at least some time. But Little Dick was out by November 1877 when she masterminded the burglary of Feigenbaum & Co. at 122 Sansome Street on a Sunday afternoon. She and her crew broke in by lifting up a grating in the back of the store and made off with three large music boxes, 19 steam engines(!), and some toys. Three days later, the gang got their hands on something way deadlier than toys and music boxes: they pilfered 112 revolvers from a shop at 515 Market Street. It took three trips to clear all the guns out of the store.

With a veritable arsenal out on the streets, cops scoured Tar Flat, a section of South of Market that reeked from toxic sludge produced by the company that became PG&E. One of the kids, Bennie Schmidt, was caught trying to sell 11 revolvers. More arrests followed, until police busted Little Dick after finding six pistols in her house. Avery was sent to the Industrial School, a grim workhouse for juvenile offenders (near what's now City College) where kids were abused far more than they were reformed. Two years later, Little Dick was boozing it up on a rooftop on Jesse Street with several young boys who were "screaming and swearing at the top of their voices." The boys split when the cops climbed onto the roof, but Little Dick and another girl were taken back to the city prison.

"The round oaths which fell in a continuous stream from their lips were shocking in the extreme," the *Chronicle* reported on May 22, 1879. The tender-eared city prison guards once again shut Little Dick into a dark cell of her very own.

## "BUTT" RILEY, KING OF THE HOODLUMS

James "Butt" Riley claimed he had "the hardest head in all Christendom," and proved it by battering down doors and people with his impervious dome.

Born in New York in 1848, Riley sailed from the East Coast to San Francisco in 1868 where he quickly established himself as the King of the Hoodlums. Although he wasn't part of any gang, "there wasn't a band of rowdies in the city that wouldn't flock to his support when he called upon it," Asbury wrote in *The Barbary Coast*.

Riley was also reportedly so handsome that he sold nude photographs of himself to the city's prostitutes. "The greatest pride of scores of San Francisco's most popular and prosperous courtesans was the signed photograph of the King of Hoodlums which hung above their beds," Asbury wrote. Riley even roamed the red light district with a black satchel filled with images of himself in the buff, selling them to ladies of the evening for 50 cents a pop. And just because this all sounds like so much bull, Asbury added a footnote claiming, "At least a dozen old-time San Franciscans, whose names cannot be published for obvious reasons, told the present author that they remembered having seen Riley's photographs in the houses of prostitution."

When he wasn't selling nudes to hookers, Riley often led raids on Chinatown whorehouses, a seemingly popular pastime for white boy lowlifes in the 1870s. During these sieges, Riley entertained his men by showing them how far he could head-butt Chinese immigrants, reportedly sending a 160-pound man flying 10 feet back.

Riley's career as the head hoodlum in San Francisco was a comparatively short one, however. In September 1871, Riley was ramming his noggin into the stomach of John Jordan, a 22-year-old

The Jon B. Lovelace Collection of California Photographs in Carol M. Highsmith's America Project, Library of Congress, Prints and Photographs Division

**Beating on Chinese immigrants was a favorite activity of San Francisco's hoodlums and other lofan (white) lowlifes in the 19th Century. The racist violence is depicted here in Anton Refregier's warts and all "History of San Francisco" mural at Rincon Annex Post Office located near the Embarcadero at 101 Spear Street, San Francisco, California.**

carriage painter. As Riley backed up to deliver another blow, Jordan pulled out an "English self-cocking pistol" and shot Riley in the gut. At the county hospital, when physicians mistook Riley for a dead man, he shocked a coroner by waking up with a rant. "I ain't going to die," Riley proclaimed. "There's a chance for me yet. I know lots of men who lived with bullets in their belly."

While Riley survived, he was left diminished by the injury—and by years of crashing his skull through doors. Once a king, Riley was reduced to toiling in the lower levels of thuggery. In 1872, he was sentenced to 16 years in San Quentin for robbery and burglary. During his trial, witnesses recalled Riley repeatedly head-butting a man who wouldn't shake hands with him "until his wish was complied with," according to a January 17, 1872, *Daily Alta California* article.

"Men and women in the neighborhood where he lived, on Sixth Street, were afraid of him, and dared not protest against his low actions and conduct," the *Daily Alta California* reported.

Judge Davis Louderback waxed almost lyrically while sentencing Riley. "You are a bold and bad man," the judge scolded. "You respect neither the laws of God nor man."

On February 28, 1876, Riley risked his life to help fight a deadly fire that broke out in San Quentin. Riley's hoodlum friends and a San Francisco attorney lobbied the governor to pardon him, and the State Prison Committee recommended commutation in March 1876. Riley was released from prison on November 5, 1880, having served half of his original sentence.

## LITTLE PETE

The first Chinese immigrants arrived in the city that would become San Francisco in 1848. They were often stoned by white schoolchildren and beaten by hoodlums, and they soon formed deadly gangs of their own, often called tongs. The first known tong war in Chinatown didn't happen until spring 1875. With Chinese women being a rarity in California, it was fought over Kum Lo, a prostitute better known as the Golden Peach. Low Sing, a member of the powerful Suey Sing tong, loved her so much that he planned to buy her freedom. Ming Long of the Kwong Duck tong wanted the Golden Peach for himself, so he whacked Sing with a hatchet and left him to die at the corner of Waverly Place and Ross Alley.

The Suey Sing wanted retribution for their fallen comrade, so they posted a challenge on the corner of Grant Avenue and Clay Street. The Kwong Ducks accepted it an hour later. Men from both factions spent the next day sharpening their axes and curved snickersnee blades, and 25 Suey Sing men met 25 of Kwong Duck's best fighters just before midnight at the scene of the crime.

"Hatchets waved and knives flashed and half a hundred men met in the middle of the street," Eng Ying Gong and Bruce Grant wrote in *Tong War!*, a pulpy 1930 history of Chinatown gangs. "Skulls were split and abdomens ripped."

As the men fought with more brutality than focus, neither side gained much of an advantage until the Suey Sing made one big charge that forced the Kwong Duck hatchet men to flee. The police arrived a few seconds later, sending the Suey Sing men on a retreat of their own despite their bloody victory. In all, three Kwong Duck men and one Suey Sing combatant died from their wounds, with several more suffering from cuts and stab wounds.

Watching the brawl from the window of his parents' Waverly Place apartment was 11-year-old Fung Jing Toy. In the days that followed, the young immigrant from China's Guangdong (then Canton) province replayed the melee in his mind. He imagined how a different thrust here or parry there could have changed its outcome. By the 1890s, his mind for strategy transformed him into "Little Pete," the king of Chinatown. The problem for Little Pete, however, was that Chinatown preferred to be ruled by committee.

During Little Pete's decade-long criminal reign over Chinatown, the *San Francisco Call* reported that he "instigated Chinese murders, imported women, ran gambling games, swindled people at the races

"LITTLE PETE" IN THE BOSOM OF HIS FAMILY


Courtesy of UC Berkeley, Bancroft Library

Chinatown boss Fung Jing Toy aka Little Pete with his family in 1897.

and bribed juries in a way that white men would never undertake." That closing bit of racism is especially rich when you consider that the son of the *Call*'s owner shot the publisher of the *Chronicle* only a few years before this was written.

Little Pete learned English by studying at the Methodist Chinese mission, which gave him "a peculiar faculty for making friends among white people," according to the *Call*. It also allowed him to rise from translator to boss of the Sam Yup Company, one of the Six Companies or associations that ran Chinatown. He became the protégé of prominent criminal lawyer Thomas Riordan and forged an alliance with blind political boss Christopher Buckley, whom Little Pete referred to as "the Blind White Devil."

With these associations extending his power beyond the confines of Chinatown, Little Pete was able to engage in human trafficking, enslaving Chinese women to work in his brothels, while legitimate merchants were barred from bringing in their families because of the

Chinese Exclusion Act. He also used the city's white police force to shut down his rivals' casinos, opium dens, and brothels. When they reopened, Little Pete's Sam Yup men were in charge.

His rough handling of Chinatown's other powerbrokers earned Little Pete so much enmity from the rival See Yups and other groups that he walked the streets wearing a coat of chainmail armor with a steel dome inside his hat. He also never left his apartment above his shoe factory without a trio of white bodyguards in addition to his army of Chinese immigrant boo how doy, or "highbinders" as the New York press called tong foot soldiers.

Little Pete finally went too far when he gave fake police badges to some of his racetrack thugs so they could bust up the See Yup headquarters while posing as detectives. Even though Little Pete's Irish goons were trounced by a See Yup badass called "Hot Stuff," the damage was done. Little Pete had to die, so the See Yups placed a bounty of $3,000 on his head.

Drawn by the prospect of earning the equivalent of at least $77,000 in today's money (online inflation calculators only go back to 1914), aspiring assassins Lem Jung and Chew Tin Gop staked out Little Pete and waited for their chance.

They got it on January 23, 1897, at 9 p.m. when Little Pete went from his spacious apartment to the barbershop at 817 Washington Street—right across the street from the location of the Golden Dragon Massacre 80 years later.

Little Pete only had one of his bodyguards with him, whom he sent down the street to get a newspaper so he could see the racing forms. Murphy, the bodyguard, advised against this, but Little Pete insisted.

"That's all right," Little Pete said. "I'll take care of myself."

While Murphy ran down a newsboy on Washington Street, Jung and Gop burst into the barbershop. As the barber washed Little Pete's long hair, Jung said, "I am going to give you a birthday celebration!"

"Before anybody could comprehend what the visitors meant one of them drew a revolver and fired four times with great rapidity," the

*Call* reported. "One shot penetrated the right eye and one entered the brain just above it."

The barber fainted. Knowing that Little Pete wore body armor, Jung lunged at him and jammed his .45 automatic down the gang boss's shirt and pulled the trigger. The bullet entered Little Pete's left breast and tore through his heart, lungs, and right kidney.

The impact of the blast caused the barbershop's lights to flicker out, and the glare of the muzzle flash at close range blinded Jung further. Gop lead his partner to Ross Alley where they tossed their pistols, presaging a scene out of *The Godfather*. Aided by grateful See Yups, Jung and Gop fled to Oregon and then back to China where they reportedly lived the rest of their lives as very wealthy men.

Tensions between the See Yups and Sam Yups remained so high following the murder of Little Pete that police flooded Chinatown in advance of the Lunar New Year celebration a week later. With cops crowding every street corner, several street vendors and furniture repairmen were arrested for obstructing the sidewalks. The chief of police even banned the use and sale of fireworks, making it a rare Lunar New Year festival unaccompanied by the pop-pop-pop of strings of firecrackers.

## BUTCHERED BY RUSSIAN NIHILISTS

Luther Weber let himself into his parents' modest grocery store on L Street in Sacramento at 10 a.m. on Sunday, December 30, 1894. As he made his way to the storeroom, he was startled to find a pool of drying blood on the floor. Seeing that the blood was dripping down from his parents' upstairs apartment, he rushed up the back staircase. There was more blood on the walls and floor of his parents' living quarters. Luther pushed his way through the kitchen door and found his father, F.H.L. Weber, with a gaping wound in his head "from which the brains had oozed until they formed a ghastly pile beside the lifeless body," according to a "Special Dispatch" to the *San Francisco Chronicle*.

His mother was slumped over only a few feet away.

"Her skull had been split wide open to the upper part of the nose and her brains were splattered all over the floor and walls for a distance of many feet," the *Chronicle* read, sparing none of the gruesome details.

Luther ran out of his parents' store screaming for police. The cops came, but so did a thousand onlookers who had to be kept from tromping through the crime scene in search of ghastly souvenirs. Police determined that at least two men had murdered the Webers. The killers had ransacked the apartment, leaving bloody bare footprints and finger marks throughout the bedroom and living room. They made off with two men's suits, two watches, $200, a revolver, and some underwear. Investigators found the Webers' axe covered in blood and matted hair in the backyard along with a metal bar that the killers had used to break into the house. Police also found some blood-soaked clothes that the killers had likely discarded, redressing in Mr. Weber's wardrobe.

F.H.L. Weber survived crossing the plains in 1858. He and his wife had run their store close to the state capitol for 30 years. They were well liked. Police told the *Chronicle* that if the killers were caught that night, "they would be immediately hung." State agencies offered a $1,500 reward for the arrest of "these fiends" as the *Sacramento Daily-Union* called them.

The next night, New Year's Eve, San Francisco police had rounded up more drunks on the Barbary Coast than they had space for in the county jail. They stuffed 10 of them into a tight holding cell in the California Street station. After the drunks were kicked loose a day later, a trustee cleaning out the cell found a lady's gold pocket watch behind the toilet. The watch bore an inscription that read, "To M. Weber, from Mother." Luther Weber took a train from Sacramento to San Francisco and identified the watch as a gift to his mother from his grandmother. The cops had had the killers, held them for a night, but let them go.

The Webers' murderers went free for six months until a private detective agency seeking the reward broke the case. Questioning San Franciscan pawnbrokers and Russian immigrants led the gumshoes to Ivan Kovalev, alias John Koboloff, who had drunkenly boasted about hacking up the Webers. A search of Kovalev's room on Howard Street near Fourth Street turned up a pair of suspenders that belonged to F.H.L. Weber. Kovalev was arrested in June 1895 and turned over to Sacramento authorities by the end of that month.

Kovalev had been a prisoner in a czarist dungeon on Sakhalin, a Russian island off the coast of Siberia and north of Japan. In August 1893, he and nine other prisoners escaped across the Pacific in a small boat "where their sufferings from exposure, thirst and hunger were about to drive them insane," according to Thomas Duke's *Celebrated Criminal Cases of America* (1910). The men were found and taken aboard an American sailing vessel to San Francisco where they claimed they were political prisoners fleeing persecution by the czar. This may have been true for some of the men, but it wasn't the case with Kovalev, who had massacred a Russian family before his island exile.

By the time he was arrested in San Francisco, Kovalev had murdered his accomplice in the Weber murders after a botched robbery of another merchant in San Jose on March 31, 1895. Kovalev's partner, Mathien Stcherbakov, was stabbed by the merchant during the attempted holdup. Fearing that the wounded Stcherbakov would talk, Kovalev stabbed him through the heart and buried him in a shallow grave in the South Bay.

Kovalev was sentenced to death and hung in Folsom on February 21, 1896. In the hours before his execution, Kovalev refused "a tempting breakfast" and a glass of whiskey. He also wouldn't meet with a priest. Kovalev didn't believe in God or an afterlife. An autopsy on Kovalev found that his brain "was in a normal condition, weighing slightly more than average."

## THE GAS PIPE THUGS

While the great earthquake on April 18, 1906, and the fires that followed left San Francisco in ruins, commerce had already returned to downtown by late summer. Unfortunately for the merchants setting up shop along a rebuilt Market Street, they were soon terrorized by one of the city's most brutal gangs.

German immigrant Johannes Pfitzner was waiting on a customer in his small shoe store at 964 McAllister Street late in the afternoon on August 20, 1906. As Pfitzner knelt down to help the man try on a pair of size 8 shoes, the man picked up a window weight and bashed in Pfitzner's head with it. The killer took $200 in cash and a gold watch worth $130 and left the store as if nothing had happened. Pfitzner died later that evening at the Central Emergency Hospital.

A little less than a month later on September 14, 1906, 15-year-old Thelma Anderton took her younger brother Robert out shopping for a new suit. No one came to meet them when they entered a clothing store at 1386 Market Street. After 10 minutes of unfettered browsing, they made their way to the backroom to see if anyone was there. They found proprietor William Friede lying in a pool of his own blood, his skull pulverized so thoroughly that you could see the brain through the fractures.

"We gazed at the awful sight for I don't know how long," Thelma Anderton told the *San Francisco Chronicle*. "The sight of the blood and the man lying in it nearly made me faint."

Friede had been beaten with an unfound blunt instrument, and the cash register drawer had been yanked off its chain and cleaned out of every coin. A tape measure found on the floor indicated he had been killed while helping someone try on merchandise, just as in the Pfitzner murder. The position of Friede's body also showed that more than one man had carried out the crime. A day later, Friede's watch was found on Market Street at Dolores near a 14-inch piece of gas pipe covered in blood and wrapped in paper.

On October 3, 1906, the killers stormed the Japanese-run Kimmon Ginko bank at 1588 O'Farrell Street. They beat bank teller A. Sasaki to the ground with a piece of gas pipe wrapped in paper before caving in the head of vice president S. Murakata. The *San Francisco Call* ran a diagram showing the thugs' path of destruction and the location of the blows on the bankers' heads. The *Oakland Tribune*'s report of the crime was peppered with racial slurs describing the victims. Sasaki survived his injuries but couldn't remember much about his attackers. Murakata died later at the hospital. The thugs, as they were now called by the press, made off with $2,800.

The killers next moved on the Steiner Street jewelry store of Harry Behrend on November 3, 1906. While one man stood lookout, two others worked over the jeweler with their signature gas pipe. Behrend struggled against his attackers, causing one of them to slam his pipe down on his accomplice's hand, nearly severing off a finger. Two of the robbers fled as Behrend, still covered in his own blood, grabbed onto the man with the gas pipe and held him until two cops rushed over from the bar across the street.

The man that Behrend had captured was Louis V. Dabner of Petaluma. His roommate, John Siemsen, matched Behrend's description of his other attacker. Siemsen, a Hawaiian who posed as the heir of a vast island fortune, was soon turned in by his father-in-law. Siemsen had married Hulda Von Hofen the day before the botched jewelry store heist in a ceremony that the bride later claimed was "forced upon her by the point of a revolver." However, the Oakland minister who performed the wedding contradicted her, telling the *Call* that he'd never seen a more elated bride.

Police soon got a confession from Dabner detailing the gas pipe murders and their spending spree at the Macey's Jewelry Company on Fillmore Street after knocking over the Japanese bank. Dabner also confessed to other robberies, including one that had the wrong man sentenced to 50 years in prison for it. Dabner and Siemsen were hung in the San Quentin prison yard on July 31, 1908, in front of 200 spectators. The third man in the Behrend robbery, Harry Kearney of Sacramento, served a sentence in Washington for another robbery.

## CHAPTER 5

# OFFICIAL MISCONDUCT

### FORESHOCK AND AFTERSHOCK

Police Sergeant Jesse Cook was standing on Market Street near the old Washington Street produce market when a massive foreshock hit at 5:12 a.m. on April 18, 1906.

"There was a deep rumble, deep and terrible, and then I could see it actually coming up Washington Street," Cook said. "The whole street was undulating. It was as if the waves of the ocean were coming towards me, billowing as they came."

Cook was thrown down hard to the cobblestoned street, but he survived. All around him, streetcar tracks twisted and snapped apart. Chimneys and building facades made from bricks and sandy mortar crumbled with that initial jolt, crushing people and workhorses below. The roof of the Denver House Hotel on Third Street crashed through two floors, killing two people and injuring 18 others. The Brunswick Hotel on Sixth caved in on its 300 rooms.

The shaking stopped after a little more than 20 seconds. While the foreshock devastated what are now South of Market and the

Embarcadero, the western neighborhoods built on bedrock, instead of shipwrecks and muck, were mostly spared. People thought the earthquake was over, but it hadn't even started.

After a 20-second respite, another quake hit the city, far worse than the first. City Hall, in the triangle formed by Market, Larkin, and McAllister Streets, was damaged by the first shock but was utterly destroyed by the second. The homeless, who then as now slept at Civic Center, were buried underneath mounds of mortar dust and the remains of Grecian columns. The hospital in the basement of City Hall was rendered useless. The next closest hospital, City Emergency, became a mass of busted roof beams and chunks of plaster.

Mission Street sunk five feet into the ground. A new apartment building on Valencia and 19th plummeted until its second floor was at ground level. A fireman sticking his head out of a window at a station on Third and Mission was killed by a falling piece of decorative molding. Just as the city needed him most, Fire Chief Dennis Sullivan was fatally injured when the roof of the California Theater and Hotel crashed through the station. He died five days later.

The Great 1906 San Francisco Earthquake had gone on for nearly 60 seconds, ending at 5:14 a.m. It registered a magnitude of 8.3 on the Richter scale, making it 30 times more powerful than the Loma Prieta Earthquake that struck the Bay Area in 1989. In the moments before that first shock, Sergeant Cook had looked forward to the end of his shift. Now his shift would go on for days.

After the earthquake, fires raged through San Francisco, eventually burning through 4.7 square miles of the city's most densely populated real estate. With water mains and pipes sheared or broken by the shaking, firefighters could only get a trickle of water to flow out of fire hydrants if anything at all. Army troops under the command of Brigadier General Frederick Funston used dynamite to combat the flames, but this often exacerbated the situation, creating a firestorm that lasted half the week. What had been left of the Barbary Coast, Chinatown, and the wharf after the quake was obliterated by the inferno.

Library of Congress

**Standing in the ruins from the 1906 Earthquake, San Franciscans on Sacramento Street watch as their city is engulfed by flames.**

Mayor Eugene "Handsome Gene" Schmitz, a former fiddle player, was a better bagman for political boss Abe Ruef than he was a public servant, but the disaster compelled him to perform his elected duties. With City Hall gone, Schmitz coordinated evacuations, firefighting, temporary hospitals, and food distribution from the Hall of Justice. When reports started coming in of mass lootings and even corpse mutilations, Schmitz deputized 60 volunteer police officers and declared that all looters were to be shot. Unfortunately, trigger-happy troops and volunteers gunned down some solid citizens in the days that followed.

Joseph Meyers, superintendent of the city's Children's Playgrounds, surveyed a refugee camp at Colombia Square on Eighth and Harrison Streets on April 19, 1906. As flames advanced towards the square, Meyers got into a shoving match with a National Guardsman named Bush. During the scuffle, another National Guardsman named Jacob Steinman shot Meyers dead. Steinman claimed that he thought Meyers was going to pull a gun on him. Some witnesses later testified that Meyers was drunk. Another witness said that Steinman and all the soldiers in the square were drunk, and still other witnesses swore that just about everybody in the square was sloshed after a nearby brewery had been looted. Despite the judge in the case advising the jurors that Mayor Schmitz's declaration of martial law was void and illegal, the jury returned a not guilty verdict for Steinman after 15 minutes of deliberation.

And there were two incidents of deadly force being used on San Francisco citizens on April 20, 1906. National Guardsman Lawrence Bechtel charged Philippine–American War veteran Frank Riordan with his bayonet during a brawl on Octavia Street. Riordan grabbed onto Bechtel's rifle, so Bechtel shot him dead. That same day, retired National Guard captain Ernest Denicke put on his old uniform and gunned down an unidentified man on East and Battery Streets that he suspected of stealing chickens. After the John Doe was weighted down and tossed into the Bay, it came to light that he may have gotten the chickens through a food distribution program. "At the time I was under the impression that martial law prevailed, and I had in mind the order to kill all persons caught stealing," Denicke said in his defense. The charges were dismissed in both cases.

On April 22, millionaire merchant Herbert Tilden took a break to visit his family in San Mateo after days of using his large car to transport injured people to shelter. When he returned, volunteer police at 24th and Guerrero waved Tilden through their makeshift checkpoint after seeing the large Red Cross flag on his car. Tilden drove for two blocks and came to another security checkpoint and thought that the Red Cross flag gave him a free pass. The "citizen police" at 22nd Street were vigilantes not even deputized by Schmitz. They opened fire on Tilden, and he died behind the wheel. Three of the wannabe cops were charged with murder, but as with Steinman, the jury returned a quick not guilty verdict.

But the actions of a few gun-crazy deputies didn't stop papers around the country from lauding Mayor Schmitz with gripping accounts of him leading efforts to quell the fires before they ravaged the wood-framed homes of the Western Addition and Richmond

Districts. With the catastrophe bringing his protégé to national prominence, boss Ruef thought the time was right to put Schmitz in the governor's mansion while taking a U.S. Senate seat for himself. Schmitz's "America's Mayor" moment was shorter lived than Rudy Giuliani's, however. Schmitz and Ruef were indicted just two months later on corruption charges for holding up the liquor licenses for several "French restaurants" (read: brothels) until their proprietors kicked back hefty retainer fees to Ruef.

With the city still in ruins, Schmitz was tried in a synagogue and convicted of extortion and removed from the mayor's office on June 7, 1906. Schmitz beat his conviction on appeal and was elected to the Board of Supervisors in 1921 where he served until 1925. Ruef was sentenced to 14 years in San Quentin. He was the only one to serve time for the scandal. After his release, Ruef ran a small real estate office on the fourth floor of 916 Kearney Street until he died on February 29, 1936.

## THE DISAPPEARING POLICE CHIEF

William J. Biggy was maybe the only honest man in a thoroughly corrupt city when he was appointed chief of police in September 1907. Mayor Schmitz had been found guilty of extortion only three months earlier. Biggy's predecessor, Jeremiah Dinan, was forced to resign while facing perjury charges. Political boss Abe Ruef, the head crook who'd installed all these other crooks in office, was on trial in a massive corruption case in which every member of the Board of Supervisors confessed to receiving bribes from Ruef and his bagmen. Biggy himself rose to prominence when he was appointed to guard Ruef at the St. Francis Hotel because nobody who worked in the jails could be trusted with the job.

But Biggy couldn't remain above the fray for long. On November 13, 1908, Ruef bagman Morris Haas, who was on trial for extortion (what else?), smuggled a pistol into the courtroom and shot Assistant District Attorney Francis J. Heney. While Heney survived, Haas somehow didn't. Haas was found dead in his cell the next day with a pistol ball lodged in his brain. A small one-shot Derringer was found in his shoe. Papers called it a suicide, but, like everything else in San Francisco in 1908, it was suspicious as hell.

Following the shooting and "suicide," Biggy was hammered in the pages of the *San Francisco Call*. Charges of "gross incompetency and inefficiency" were filed against him. The embattled police chief countered by filing charges against the officers who allowed a gun to get into Haas's cell, but trying to redirect the blame couldn't free Biggy from a crisscrossing web of corruption.

In the early evening on November 30, 1908, Biggy boarded the SFPD launch for a clandestine meeting in Belvedere with Police Commissioner Hugo Keil to discuss stepping down. Keil advised Biggy against doing "anything hastily" and the two agreed to meet again in Keil's office the next morning. Biggy then boarded the boat for the trip back to San Francisco, but when it docked in the city, Biggy was no longer aboard. The police chief had disappeared.

The only other person on the launch with Biggy was its pilot, Captain William Murphy. Fighting back sobs, Murphy said that he last saw his chief when the boat had passed Alcatraz. The two men talked about how cold it was, and then Biggy returned to the boat's cabin and was never seen alive again. Biggy's body was found two weeks later "floating with an ebb tide in the channel midway between Yerba Buena Island and the Lombard Street wharf," according to the *Call*.

The *Call* spared no details, reporting that the features of the late chief "had been destroyed beyond the possibility of recognition" and the head was "reduced to a skeleton." By the time William Biggy's body was brought back to the Hunter's Point shipyard, "hundreds of morbidly curious idlers had gathered at the wharf and were packed far into East Street into a solid mass."

The body was identified through clothing and personal effects. City officials were quick to rule Biggy's death an accident, but questions about the drowning remained. Before his disappearance,

*The Washington Times*, Library of Congress

**The mysterious death of Chief of Police William J. Biggy, whose decomposed body was found in the bay, rocked a city already mired in scandal.**

Biggy had told several police officials that he believed he was being followed and that his life was in danger.

"He knew that they would go to any length to get rid of him," acting police chief A.D. Cutler testified during the coroner's inquest. When pressed for further details, however, Cutler refused to elaborate. If Biggy had met with foul play instead of just falling off the boat, the people investigating the crime were probably the ones who'd done it. Two years after Biggy's death, Captain Murphy, the boat pilot, was committed to a mental institution. "I don't know what happened. I don't know what happened," he muttered repeatedly.

## THE BUNCO MEN

The con artists of the 40 Thieves gang thought that they had a good thing going with the San Francisco cops who were supposed to be investigating them. Starting around 1910, the con men or bunco men (named for a crooked card game called bunco or bunko) had free rein to run their scams, bilking Italians and other unfortunate immigrants out of thousands using what were basically low-tech versions of the Nigerian prince email scam. The bunco men paid off the cops, and the cops promised to keep the bunco men out of jail.

This arrangement seemed to work so well that the 40 Thieves still honored it even when their boss, Mike Gallo, was sentenced to five years in San Quentin in 1913. To smooth things over, the corrupt detectives agreed to give Gallo's wife $30 a month while he was in prison. Gallo agreed to "stay mum" in the hopes that the rest of his gang would remain free.

When con men Maurice di Martini, Frank Du Bois, and Frank Corrogan (alias Carlo Cardano) were also found guilty and sent to the big house, it was clear that "the bunco men themselves were being buncoed by the police," according to a May 17, 1913, story in the *Pittsburgh Press*. Realizing that they'd been double-crossed, the bunco men started talking to anyone who would listen.

With San Francisco district attorney Charles M. Fickert listening "in amazement," Martini, Du Bois, and Corrogan confessed to cash handoffs between police and crooks at "a popular grill" at 544 Broadway in North Beach, an area still referred to as the Barbary Coast in an April 23, 1913, *Chron* article. Money also changed hands at "the hotel of Lello Pellegrini" at 15 Pinckney Place, now the Basque Hotel at 15 Romolo Place, which boasts on its website of once housing speakeasies and brothels.

Chief of Police D.A. White and Captain of Detectives John Mooney, who also sat in on the bunco men's depositions, "listened with mingled emotions," according to the *Chron*, "as the names of police officers came in rapid succession." It didn't help the chief's reputation that this level of collusion had gone on for years without him learning about it.

A few days later, Mike Gallo made a 40-page confession taken over several hours. At first, Gallo only had to pay $20 to Detective Frank Esola of the bunco squad, but as Gallo and his gang "had a chance to do two or three tricks a week," they had to give Esola and his partners 15 or even 25 percent of their hauls. The *Chron* ran a detailed ledger on April 26, 1913, listing victims, "bunko men," the amount of money taken, and the amount paid to police. When Du Bois fleeced Louis Dodere out of $7,700, he kicked back $1,115 to police. When Di Martini took someone named Massie for a grand, the cops got $250. In total, the *Chron* and other news sources estimated that the

40 Thieves raked in $300,000 during their protracted crime wave, which would total $7 million today.

In all, four detectives and four patrolmen were suspended from the force and later indicted on criminal charges. Five of the officers pleaded guilty and were sentenced to nine months in the county jail in June 1913. Frank Esola, a fifteen-year veteran of the force, was found guilty of selling protection and sentenced to five years in Folsom. Esola requested that he not be sent to San Quentin because he was once a guard there.

## PREPAREDNESS DAY

Dynamite was popular with both sides of the Pacific Gas and Electric labor disputes that started in 1913. Striking workers used it to blow up power transformers on the Bay Area's hinterlands. Private dicks hired by a power company more concerned with union busting than seeking justice used well-planted sticks of TNT to frame the labor leaders. Framing was the go-to strategy employed by Pinkerton detective Martin Swanson, but it didn't really get results. A trio of union men in Berkeley sent to San Quentin for plotting to sabotage power lines were all pardoned by the governor after union officials recorded an ex-Pinkerton agent bragging about the frame-up.

In January 1914, San Francisco union organizer and militant socialist Thomas Mooney and two other electrical workers were arrested in Contra Costa County after a team of PG&E detectives found explosive devices and several pricey firearms on board a leaky skiff the workers used to travel around the Delta. Mooney was charged with plotting to blow up a pair of giant steel towers at the Carquinez Straits. Unfortunately for Swanson and PG&E's other hired guns, a local deputy sheriff had searched Mooney's boat a short time earlier and found it empty. Mooney's first two trials ended with hung juries. He was acquitted after the third when the jury couldn't figure out how struggling strikers could afford the expensive guns preferred by corporate security agents.

The bloody site of the Preparedness Day bombing on Steuart and Market Streets, San Francisco, on July 22, 1916.

Swanson was let go by the Pinkertons but was soon hired on as PG&E's head detective with an office at the company's San Francisco HQ at 444 Sutter Street. Humiliated in court, "Swanson tracked Mooney as intently as Javert followed Jean Valjean," according to Fremont Older, the rabble-rousing editor of the *San Francisco Bulletin*. Swanson's attempt to pin the June 10 dynamiting of two electrical towers on San Bruno Mountain in Daly City on Mooney also came up empty. While railroad company spies reported that Mooney had left a union meeting that night, he had just called a recess and quickly returned to the hall to address some 200 Wobblies.

With Mooney being well alibied for that night, Swanson offered a $5,000 reward to anyone who could implicate the labor leader in the bombing, but no one came forward despite that reward being worth $117,000 in today's money. Mooney was able to enjoy an anarchist picnic in Colma on the 4th of July as if the biggest power company in Northern California wasn't out to get him. But having failed twice now to bust Mooney, Swanson couldn't resist the opportunity to use the high body count from a grisly bombing to realize his obsession.

The Preparedness Day Parade of July 22, 1916, was a jingoistic spectacle sponsored by the city's Chamber of Commerce and other business interests to gin up enthusiasm for the U.S.'s entry into World War I. The parade began near the Embarcadero at 1:30 p.m. Leading the way and waving a flag was popular Mayor "Sunny Jim" Rolph, the man credited with ridding the city of its Barbary Coast wickedness even though he owned a cathouse at 21st and Sanchez called the Pleasure Palace. Behind Sunny Jim were over 51,000 marchers with 52 bands, mostly playing "The Star-Spangled Banner" interspersed with the works of John Philip Sousa.

The bomb went off near the Ferry Exchange Saloon on Market and Steuart Streets at 2:02 p.m. just as a battalion of aging Civil War veterans wearing their Union blue uniforms marched past. "The massed crowd around the corner was mowed down as if the bomb had been a machine gun," the *Chronicle* reported. The blast shattered plate-glass windows, and shards of glass rained down on the heads of hundreds of parade watchers. A mother holding up her daughter to see the parade was cut down by the shrapnel while her child wasn't hurt at all.

Police Lieutenant Charles Birdsall was standing on the corner of Steuart and Market at the time of the explosion. "There was a sudden roar, and I was knocked to the ground," he said. "The body of a young girl crashed into me with full force. Then a silence as heavy as the pall of smoke that hung over the scene prevailed. I arose, looked down at the girl and found one of her legs was hanging by a thread. All around the bodies of the men and women almost stripped of their clothes, lay in horrible grotesque heaps."

In all, the bombing killed 10 people and hospitalized 40 more. Jonah Owen Lamb, writing on the tragedy for the *Examiner* in 2015, noted that "no other single act of violence" in San Francisco history "would match it in sheer body count"—not the Zebra Murders or the Golden Dragon Massacre in the 1970s, nor the mass shooting in the high-rise at 101 California Street in 1993.

Suspects were many. Mexican patriots angry over the U.S. Army invasion of Mexico in March and German espionage agents trying to keep America out of the war were possible culprits. Witnesses described the man they saw leave a suspicious suitcase next to the brick wall of the Ferry Exchange Saloon as "a Mexican" and "dark complexioned." The explosive itself was the nasty type of shrapnel bomb, similar to ones used by the Germans on the European front. None of these leads were investigated, however, after District Attorney Charles Fickert—who owed his political career to the largess of PG&E—put Martin Swanson in charge of the bombing investigation.

As with the San Bruno bombing, Mooney had an alibi during the tragedy. He was seen by several people watching the parade from his roof when the bomb went off. He was even photographed with a clock visible in the background, but it hardly mattered. After illegal searches and warrantless arrests, Mooney and his compatriot Charles Billings—who had served time for being caught with dynamite in Sacramento—were charged with the slaughter. Billings was sentenced to life and Mooney received the death penalty.

Swanson had finally won, it seemed, but questions surrounding his investigation—or lack thereof—led President Woodrow Wilson to ask California's governor to commute Mooney's sentence to life in 1917.

In 1920, Draper Hand of the San Francisco Police Department admitted that he helped Swanson and Fickert to frame Mooney. John McDonald, one of Fickert's star witnesses, confessed that police had forced him to commit perjury during the trial. Despite the revelations, Mooney and Billings rotted in prison for nearly 20 more years. One of the governors who refused to pardon them was Sunny

Courtesy of UC Berkeley, Bancroft Library

Tom Mooney, the anarchist labor leader framed for the Preparedness Day Bombing, yucks it up behind the bars of San Quentin on May 19, 1933.

Jim Rolph, who either couldn't be convinced of their innocence or didn't want to fess up to how much corruption had been going on under his nose when he was mayor of San Francisco. Finally, liberal governor Culbert Olson pardoned Mooney and commuted Billings's sentence to time served in 1939.

Swanson died before he could see the undoing of his well-orchestrated miscarriage of justice. Mooney lived to stick it to the city by marching in a union parade up Market Street, but he died at St. Luke's Hospital in 1942. PG&E caught little or no blowback for its role in framing Mooney and allowing the real bomber to go unpunished. But now when the company blows up a swath of San Bruno or sparks the fires that have now become a constant in Northern California, there just aren't enough anarchists around to blame anymore.

## THE KKK TOOK SFPD AWAY

A mob of about 30 hooded Klansmen stormed through the backdoor of the farmhouse of a suspected moonshiner named Fidel Elduayen in the Los Angeles suburb of Inglewood on April 23, 1922.

"Where's the still?" the masked men demanded, pushing revolvers into the faces of Elduayen; his wife, Angela; and his brother, Mattius. Before anyone could answer, the Klansmen grabbed the Elduayen brothers, tied them up, and ransacked the house. They overturned mattresses and roused the Elduayens' teenaged daughters out of bed.

"The two girls were in their nightgowns," Fidel Elduayen recalled. "The masked men yelled at them to dress at once. The girls closed the door, but the men threw it open again. They made the girls take off their nightclothes and dress in front of them with the door open."

The Klansmen dragged Fidel and Mathias into the yard. Angela cried to be taken with them, but the raiders slammed her against the door and ordered her to stay in the house. As Fidel was dragged outside, he saw "probably 100 masked men" amassed on his farm.

The hooded men shoved Fidel and Mathias into a black sedan with some unmasked men who drove them to the Inglewood police station and demanded that the Elduayens be jailed for bootlegging. The police refused but didn't bother to free the Elduayens either. The abductors then drove the brothers to the Redondo police station with the exact same results. The hoodless Klansmen continued to question the Elduayens about their still and threatened to tie the brothers to railroad tracks or hang them from tree limbs if they didn't talk. The Elduayens kept mum. Eventually, the Klansmen freed Fidel and Mattius about five miles from their farm.

While more than 100 Klansmen still swarmed the Elduayens' property, some Japanese neighbors got nervous and called Medford Mosher, the city's constable. Mosher wasn't in, so Deputy Marshal Frank Woerner took the call. Woerner showed up at the farm and got into a shootout with several men in hoods. When the smoke cleared and the hoods were removed, Woerner realized he had killed his boss, Constable Mosher, and wounded Mosher's son, Walter, and another deputy. For whatever reason, none of Woerner's coworkers had thought to let him in on their Klan raid.

William S. Coburn, the grand goblin of the Pacific domain of the KKK, denied approving the raid but applauded the raiders' efforts to "turn the offending Mexican over to the police authorities." The Elduayens were Basques from Spain. Not buying the grand goblin's denial, Los Angeles district attorney Thomas Woolwine obtained a warrant and led a raid on Coburn's downtown L.A. office on April 27, 1922. Along with all the sheets and hoods and other Klan regalia, Woolwine also discovered the KKK's membership records for its entire western region. City governments throughout California were soon embroiled in scandal when prominent citizens were exposed as cross-burning bigots. San Francisco was not spared.

Nine San Franciscan policemen, two city firemen, and several Muni streetcar conductors were revealed to be dues-paying members of the Klan. While city leaders in Fresno and Sacramento moved quickly to dismiss KKK members from their city's police departments, San Francisco police chief Daniel O'Brien delayed taking any action against his officers until he could find out "what kind of an organization the KKK is."

It appears that O'Brien never solved the riddle of the Klan, and nothing happened to the sheet-wearers on the force. The leader of the San Francisco KKK, a dentist with an office on Geary Street next door to what used to be Lefty O'Doul's bar and hofbrau, was later arrested for selling oil stocks without a permit. Back in Los Angeles, the 37 Klansmen who had taken part in the Inglewood raid were indicted but found not guilty. Many of the jurors from that trial made public statements calling their decision "a patriotic verdict."

CHAPTER 6

# POPULAR ATTRACTIONS

## THE LOST PRIEST IN THE CITY OF SOULS

By 1880, San Francisco's 70 square blocks of cemeteries had become so dilapidated that they posed a threat to public health. Tombstones and statues were falling over. Once ornate mausoleums were stripped of bronze doors, and San Franciscans carted away whole skeletons and used them as Halloween decorations. The growing population of the living was also hungry for the land that the dead occupied. Under pressure from a growing anti-cemetery movement, the city migrated graveyards and at least some of the departed south to the town of Lawndale, which was later incorporated as the necropolis now called Colma.

Around 1921, Father Patrick Heslin of County Longford, Ireland, had transferred from the Catholic parish in Turlock to the Holy Angels Church in Colma. There, he ministered to a modest congregation of living people and a burgeoning population of dead ones entombed in nearby Holy Cross Cemetery, the largest graveyard in a city of them. Heslin was reportedly dissatisfied with his new assignment, which was likely heavy on funerals.

On Tuesday, August 2, 1921, a man clad in goggles and a heavy overcoat came knocking on Father Heslin's door. Heslin's housekeeper, Marie Wendel, later told the press that the mysterious man "appeared to be excited." The man claimed he was on "a death call" and needed the priest to administer last rites to a dying man. Heslin gathered his sacraments and got into the man's car. Wendel and a neighbor watched the car as it headed towards the coast before it disappeared in the fog. Heslin was never seen alive again.

The next day, Archbishop Edward J. Hanna received a partially typewritten ransom note at St. Mary's Cathedral in San Francisco. The abductor wrote that Heslin was "fastened with chains" in a heavily booby-trapped bootleg cellar where a candle burned in a cradle filled with "all chemicals necessary to generate enough poison gas to kill a dozen men." The cellar door was also supposedly rigged with matches set to ignite a gas can if anyone but the kidnapper tried to enter.

"I had charge of a machine gun in the Argonne, and poured thousands of bullets into struggling men," the kidnapper boasted. The missive closed with a badly scrawled run-on sentence: "HAD TO Hitt [sic] Him four times and he is unconscious from pressure on Brain so better hurry and no fooling."

Experts agreed that the letter writer was not only demented but "a fanatic who harbors animosity toward the Roman Catholic Church," according to the *Chronicle*. Police also believed that Heslin had already met with foul play despite the kidnapper's all-caps demand for "SIXTY-FIVE HUNDRED DOLLARS IN FIVES, TENS, AND TWENTIES, FIFTIES AND HUNDREDS."

Still hopeful of rescuing the priest, San Mateo County sheriff Michael Sheehan organized a posse to comb through all the cow paths, smugglers' shacks, and mazes of scrub oak that dotted Pacifica's Mori Point at the time. However, even with hundreds of Catholic men supplied by a massive Knights of Columbus convention in San

Francisco that week, the posse found few "clews" (as the *Chronicle* spelled it back then). Father Heslin remained missing.

In desperation, the Archdiocese of San Francisco offered a $5,000 reward on Monday, August 8, 1921, for the return of Father Heslin, dead or alive. Two days later, William A. Hightower came forward, claiming that a pair of prostitutes had told him where Heslin was buried. Hightower led San Francisco police chief Daniel O'Brien and several detectives to a spot in the sands of Salada Beach (now Sharp Park Beach in Pacifica), where he said he'd uncovered a priest's prayer scarf before he stopped digging. As Hightower assisted police with digging, an officer asked him to slow down for fear that he might strike the dead priest in the face with his shovel.

"Don't worry," Hightower replied. "I'm digging near the feet."

Police knew they had their man, and soon unearthed Father Heslin. The priest had taken two bullets—one in the heart, and another through the skull. Hightower was arrested and taken to jail in Redwood City. During a search of Hightower's apartment, detectives found the rented Corona typewriter used to type the ransom note, as well as an "infernal machine" constructed from metal pipes and shotgun shells.

"Authorities who examined the contrivance say it is diabolical in its ingenuity and one of the most deadly things ever conceived," according to the *Chronicle*. Police believed that Hightower planned to place this old-school IED on Pedro Mountain Road in Pacifica to cover his escape after collecting the ransom.

Hightower was born in Waco, Texas, in 1878. As an adult, he migrated westward, working for a time as a railroad camp cook near Salt Lake City. In 1910, he moved to Bakersfield to find work in oil fields. Instead, he opened a bakery there and became known for his pastries. He also invented a machine gun that he tried to sell to the army during World War I, but the rejection of it "affected his mind," according to the *Los Angeles Times*.

An early polygraph machine was used in interrogating Hightower, but he was really undone by a mountain of evidence and witnesses who contradicted him. Despite public calls for the death penalty, he was sentenced to life instead. The jury, it seems, believed that he was non compos mentis.

"When I get to thinking, it seems like my head begins to expand and it keeps on growing until I feel every minute like there is going to be a big explosion," Hightower said as he awaited trial. "I wonder if I am going crazy."

Hightower never gave a reason for murdering the Irish priest, but he did reveal that he was raised by an Irish family. "They used to whip me hard," he recalled. "Harder than any boy I have ever known was whipped, but I guess they were the best friends I ever had. The only real friends, I sometimes think."

"SOUL SEARCHER" GRILLS MURDER SUSPECT

This composed photo of principals and device accurately pictures the midnight prison scene at Redwood City, Cal., when William A. Hightower, suspect in the Father Heslin murder case, was grilled by a "mechanical detective" in an effort to adjust circumstantial evidence to the remarkable outward calm of the man.

The mechanism, called the Sphygmo-mano-meter, registers the affect of emotional stress on a man's breath-

The photo shows Hightower in the center, at the le[ft] Dr. J. A. Larsen, former instructor of psychology [at] Harvard and perfector of the machine, and at the rig[ht] Philips Edson, Larson's assistant.

Inset are two series of records made by the devi[ce] the upper three showing normal respiration, hea[rt] pressure and pulse; the lower revealing evidence of a[gi]tation when the prisoner was asked significant questio[ns]

Library of Congress

William A. Hightower is interrogated in the Father Heslin murder case using the Sphygmo-mano-meter, an early lie detector referred to in this August 29, 1921, *Arizona Republic* caption as a "mechanical detective."

After nearly 44 years of baking pastries in San Quentin, Hightower was released on parole in 1965 and died soon after. Father Heslin can still be found in Colma, buried in the priest plot at Holy Cross Cemetery.

## A FIT OF JAZZMANIA

Dorothy Ellingson was off to an early start. By the time she was 12, she was already knocking back gin and running with jazz musicians at the New Shanghai Café in Prohibition-era Chinatown. After four years of this, her mother, Anna Ellingson, finally put her foot down. On January 13, 1925, Anna tried to keep her daughter from "running wild at jazz parties." It didn't work. Dorothy got her brother's army pistol, shot her mother in the back of the head, and pilfered $45 from her mom's purse on her way out the door. She spent the rest of the night partying at a friend's apartment while her mother's corpse grew cold in the family's Richmond District flat.

When Ellingson was arrested two days later, newspapers as far away from the murder scene as New York and Miami carried the story of the "16-year-old Swedish girl" who "killed her mother in a fit of jazzmania." Matricide moved newsprint, and reporters dubbed Ellingson the "Moth Girl," "Jazz Girl Murderer," or (my personal favorite) "Jazz Baby Mother Slayer." Jazzmania somehow never made it into the *Diagnostic and Statistical Manual of Mental Disorders*, although it was floated as a legit defense at the time.

In the wake of the murder, prohibition officials promised raids on San Francisco's "jazzland." Described as "the wickedest spot in America," this "kindergarten of vice" was just off Bartlett Street in the Mission. Police also combed through Ellingson's diary and charged some of her boyfriends in the jazz scene with contributing to the delinquency of a minor. Keith Lord, a banjo picker with the Frisco Five, told police, "She said she was 19." Some things never change.

Ellingson's trial began in March 1925. After collapsing in the courtroom several times and threatening to choke her own attorney, she was

Library of Congress

Dorothy Ellingson, who murdered her mother in what the press dubbed "a fit of jazzmania." From the *Indianapolis Times*, January 20, 1925.

sent to Napa State Hospital for treatment in April before returning to San Francisco later that summer to resume the trial. Despite Ellingson's courtroom histrionics, Dr. Jau Don Ball, "chief defense alienist," testified Ellingson was "slightly abnormal, but completely sane." On August 22, 1925, Ellingson was found guilty of manslaughter and sentenced to 10 years in San Quentin, which held women prisoners until 1932.

Brother's Hate of Girl Slayer
Is Overcome by Ties of Blood

Ellingson was released on parole in February 1932 after serving six years and six months. "I deeply regret that I never did appreciate my parents," she said upon her release. A year later, she attempted suicide after being accused of stealing jewelry and a black velvet dress from her roommate. All charges from this incident were dismissed. Ellingson got married two years later and became a mother herself, having two children. She died on September 16, 1967.

## THE PHANTOM OF THE CURRAN

Many phantoms have haunted the stage of the Curran Theater since it opened on Geary Street in 1922. The venerable venue hosted Andrew Lloyd Weber's *The Phantom of the Opera* for half of the 1990s; Stephen King and John Mellencamp's *Ghost Brothers of Darkland County* scared up a much shorter run there in 2014; and *Harry Potter and the Cursed Child* cast its spell on audiences during the 2019 Christmas season (with its December 2020 return postponed due to Covid-19). However, the Curran's longest-running spirit won't be seen in the stage lights but has been startling theatergoers in its ornate lobby since a ticket taker met his tragic end there in 1933.

Massive crowds were still lining up to see the hit production of *Show Boat* at the Curran at 7:30 p.m. on November 28, 1933. During a break in the line, a young hatless man in a brown suede jacket stepped up and shoved his revolver through the ticket window. A shot was fired and hit theater treasurer Hewlett G. Tarr right in the chest.

"What was that noise?" Tarr asked as he staggered forward. He looked down and saw the blood leaking onto his coat and collapsed down a short flight of stairs.

"Tarr never knew he was hit," Lee Parvin, stage manager of *Show Boat*, told the *Examiner*.

Doctors worked on him as police tried to quell the panic, but Tarr died five minutes later. Only minutes after that, Tarr's 23-year-old fiancée, Dorothy Reade of Sutter Street, arrived at the theater and wept over his body. The couple had spent five years saving up their ticket-taker wages for a wedding that was planned for the following Thanksgiving weekend.

"The worst part of it is that he needn't have been there at all," Reade told the *Examiner*. Tarr had come back early from dinner so he could finish up work and meet Reade a little earlier than usual that night. "He had just gone into the box office when that man shot him," she said.

After shooting Tarr, the killer sprinted past horrified onlookers in front of the Curran and escaped in a cab. Minutes later, he held up the Koffee Kup Restaurant on Mason Street for $100 and had the unwitting cabbie drop him off at the ferry building. Inside the auditorium, the show went on while Tarr's body was still in the room where he had fallen. Paying customers weren't denied seeing what George C. Warren of the *Chronicle* had hailed earlier as "a luxurious production" featuring Hattie McDaniel six years before her Oscar-winning performance in *Gone with the Wind* (1939).

Over two weeks went by, and "The Hatless Slayer"—as the *Examiner* dubbed him for having the temerity to not wear a hat in

1933—was still at large despite being suspected of several downtown stickups. He was finally apprehended after a shootout with police on December 18, 1933. The killer had just made off with $1,950 from robbing a Bank of America branch at Geary and Jones Streets. He tried to get away in a cab as he had so many times before. As the taxi was climbing the hill on Jones Street, Inspector Phil Lindecker swung his patrol car in front of the cab while Inspector Peter Hughes charged the car on foot. The killer fired on Hughes through the cab's rear window. A bullet tore through the inspector's leg.

"He got me, Phil!" Hughes cried before peppering the back of the cab with a volley of shotgun shells as "scores of pedestrians" scurried for safety and cabbie Anthony LaRocca leapt from his hack. After pumping the cab with 21 shots, Inspector Lindecker reached into the car and slapped the cuffs on the suspect, who survived by cowering on the floor of the sedan. The bandit was Eddie Anderson, a 25-year-old electrician. At the beginning of the interrogation, Anderson admitted he'd committed half a dozen holdups but wouldn't cop to murdering Tarr.

"It means the rope," he said. However, after hours of Miranda-free grilling, Anderson broke down sobbing and confessed to killing Tarr.

"I did it, but I didn't mean to kill him," Anderson said. "I put my gun up against the box office wicket. It went off—accidentally."

Anderson was drawn to crime "because of his desire to impress women with money and importance" but women "expressed little interest in his fate," according to the *Examiner*.

"I liked him alright, but he wasn't any great spender," said Lorne Fancher of O'Farrell Street, the bandit's supposed sweetheart. Fancher was hauled in for questioning along with 22-year-old Rae Birch, the other woman Anderson had eyes for.

"My wages were small," Anderson explained to police. "I made $14 a week and that's not enough to entertain girlfriends with."

A strange aside: Manuel Voyages was in his Jones Street apartment above the bank branch that Anderson had just robbed, visiting with some relatives. When they discussed the day's shootout, he ran to the bathroom and shot himself through the head. Voyages had recently lost his grocery business, making him another casualty of the Great Depression which had then lurched into its fourth year.

With the notorious lynching of a pair of murder suspects in San Jose only weeks earlier, Anderson was convicted in the speediest murder trial in California history. He "went jauntily" to the San Quentin gallows and was hung at 10:04 a.m. on February 15, 1935.

Although Tarr's mother and fiancée expressed relief that Anderson was brought to justice, Tarr himself evidently felt no sense of closure. For decades now, patrons of the Curran have reported seeing the spectral image of a handsome young man in the oversized mirror near the theater's entrance. He is described as "wearing 1930s clothes," possibly all dressed up for a wedding that will never happen.

## DEATH CHAIN AT THE ZOO

When banker and philanthropist Herbert Fleishhacker came upon 30 acres near the southwestern coast of San Francisco, he thought he'd found the perfect place for his zoo. However, after recent tiger maulings and dead baby gorillas, you have to wonder if the San Francisco Zoo isn't built on an ancient burial ground. The tragedies there are nothing new. The place was snake-bitten from the start.

To expand his zoo from a couple of sad grizzly bears in cages into a world-class menagerie, Fleishhacker hired George Bistany, a big game hunter and animal expert he'd met while on a world cruise in 1929. Born in Egypt, Bistany carved a harrowing career out of capturing animals for zoos and "escaping death in a score of tight situations in the jungles and mountains of four continents," according to the *Fresno Bee*. He also believed that there was a psychic bond between humans and apes.

"Monkeys have a well-developed communication system," he said. "In the tailless varieties, it is both spoken and telepathic."

"What is more, I can understand them and talk with many," Bistany added.

The proof of Bistany's far-out ideas came when one of his orangutans saved his life. Bistany had leapt into a cage to separate a pair of brawling apes. An orangutan named Michael bit Bistany savagely on his arms and legs in the melee. Just when it looked like Bistany was done for, another 200-pound orangutan named Ginger gave Michael a drubbing, allowing Bistany to escape with his life.

The first in the San Francisco Zoo's enduring myriad of tragedies struck in December 1935 when a visitor gave Ginger a piece of poisoned candy, causing the beloved ape to die an agonizing death. Compounding the sorrow, Bistany's assistant zookeeper, Jack Bamberger, dropped dead from shock two days later. After the two deaths, Bistany himself collapsed at his desk from soaring blood pressure brought on by the stress. He was treated and released by University of California, San Francisco, but died on January 1, 1936. Bistany was just 45.

The death toll continued to climb when Mickey Borneo, another of Bistany's prized orangutans, sat in his cage and moped until he succumbed to insurmountable grief and died. The poisoner who started what the *San Jose News* called the "death chain" was never caught, but Bistany had harsh words for him before his own death.

"The killer of Ginger is a murderer just as if he had killed a human being," Bistany told the *Santa Rosa Republican*. "If I could get my hands on him, I'd throw him in the cage with the lions."

Four higher primates dead in the space of four weeks, and that wasn't the end of it. In 1936, Wally the elephant impaled zookeeper Ed Brown on one of his tusks and hurled the dead man to the ground. Four years later, in 1940, Big Bill the polar bear killed his mate in front of horrified onlookers. And more recently in 2007, there was Tatiana the tiger's deadly Christmas Day rampage, and Kabibe the baby gorilla was crushed by a door in 2014. The place is either cursed or maybe just having zoos is a bad idea. If only the apes could tell us.

CHAPTER 7

# THE STATE-SANCTIONED LYNCH MOB

## NOSTALGIA FOR VIGILANCE

The vigilantes of San Francisco were real, but their reputation only grew more mythic as decades passed since those days in 1856 when bodies of the accused dangled from the roof of Fort Gunnybags on Sacramento Street. To journalist Herbert Asbury, writing in his book *The Barbary Coast* from the comparative safety of 1933, the vigilante revival of 1856 marked "the second cleansing" that had "San Francisco basking in the glow of municipal righteousness."

To someone who was in San Francisco at the time, however, the vigilantes' glowing reputation was more fabricated than deserved. West Point graduate William Tecumseh Sherman put his military career on pause to run a bank in Gold Rush–era San Francisco and later wrote about the Second Vigilance Committee in his memoirs.

"As they controlled the press, they wrote their own history, and the world generally gives them the credit of having purged San Francisco of rowdies and roughs," he wrote, "but their success has given great stimulus to a dangerous principle, that would at any time justify the mob in seizing all the power of government; and who is to say that the Vigilance Committee may not be composed of the worst, instead of the best, elements of a community?"

And the really savvy grifters found a way to save themselves, as Sherman observed that "the same set of bailiffs, constables, and rowdies that had infested the City Hall were found in the employment of the 'Vigilantes.'" Of course, Sherman had reason to be a bit bitter. He had been recruited by California governor J. Neely Johnson to put down San Francisco's vigilante insurrection, but Sherman resigned almost as soon as he was appointed when he couldn't get guns to arm his militia. He later sacked the South during the Civil War, presumably to work off the frustration.

"I can handle a hundred thousand men in battle and take the City of the Sun, but am afraid to manage a lot in the swamp of San Francisco," he wrote in 1864 after the burning of Atlanta.

By 1933, cosmopolitan San Francisco had done much to distance itself from its swampy past—at least outwardly—but 50 miles away in San Jose, things hadn't changed all that much since its old courthouse was built in 1868. The one-time capital of California was little more than a small downtown surrounded by fruit orchards and toxic quicksilver mines where livelihoods were earned the same way they had been during the Gold Rush. With the Silicon Valley tech boom decades away, the San Jose of the Great Depression was still the kind of place where the idea of good men rising up to mete out frontier justice at the end of a rope retained its grim appeal.

## HUMAN DEVILS

Harold Thurmond was a little slow and highly suggestible after a childhood head injury. He worked at his dad's gas station in downtown San Jose where he couldn't get into too much trouble, or so thought his pious family. They didn't figure on John M. Holmes, a salesman for local oil companies who exuded a wicked charisma that helped him move oilcans. Holmes met Thurmond on a sales call

John C. Gordon

Hart's department store in downtown San Jose, a few years before the kidnapping of its young and beloved heir, Brooke Hart.

in 1933, and the two soon teamed up to hijack the intended payroll deposits of Holmes's former employers. They made off with $1,400 from that caper, but Holmes believed he could convince his high school sweetheart to dump her husband and run away with him if he only had a lot more cash.

Obsessed with the 1932 kidnapping of the 22-month-old son of hero aviator and future Nazi sympathizer Charles Lindbergh, Holmes hatched a plot to snatch college-aged retail heir Brooke Hart and ransom him back to his family for $40,000. Even with their meticulous planning, however, the aspiring kidnappers didn't bother to secure a hideout to stash Hart while they haggled over the ransom, so they went and bought three 22-pound concrete blocks and 70 feet of wire clothesline instead.

At 6 p.m. on November 9, 1933, Brooke Hart got into his brand-new Studebaker President roadster to leave L. Hart and Son, the popular department store in downtown San Jose owned by his father, Alex Hart. As the younger Hart started to drive off the parking lot, Holmes stepped onto the car's running board. He opened the passenger-side door, slid onto the seat, and jammed a pistol into Hart's ribs. Holmes forced Hart to drive to Evans Road in nearby

Milpitas where they met Thurmond and switched to Holmes's black Chevy, ditching the Studebaker. After nightfall, they drove Brooke onto the eastern span of the San Mateo-Hayward Bridge, which linked the sides of the Bay five years before construction of the Bay or Golden Gate Bridge had even begun.

They stopped the car when they got out over the water, then yanked Hart out and bashed his skull in with one of the concrete blocks. "They were pretty good blows and [Hart] didn't give us much trouble after that," Thurmond recalled. The kidnappers then tied up Hart with the clothesline, weighed him down with the blocks, and shoved him into the Bay. Fearing that he might have survived, they fired a few shots into the water after him just to make sure, but Hart still lived.

Vinton Ridley and Cal Cooley ran a woodcutting business out of Oakland. They were scrounging for driftwood in the mudflats near the bridge's eastern span when they heard muffled cries for help coming from the Bay at 7:35 that night.

"Hold on," they shouted. "We are coming!" Their feet sunk deep into the muck of the putrid morass with each step as they struggled towards the source of the cries. When they felt they were getting close, the man screamed, "Help! Help! My God! I can't hold on much longer!" And then silence. Not knowing where to go, Ridley and Cooley turned back. They reported the cries to the Hayward police, who didn't do all that much with the information.

Holmes and Thurmond's first attempts at ransom notes were so full of secret codes and talk of masked men that FBI agents dismissed them as fakes. The kidnappers' zeal for disposing of anything that linked them to Brooke Hart also left them with nothing to prove that they'd ever had him in the first place. Not one to act on impulse, Alex Hart wanted proof of life before he forked over a $40,000 ransom. Making things even more like something out of a Three Stooges short, Holmes and Thurmond demanded that Alex drive down to Los Angeles by himself to deliver the payoff, unaware that the elder Hart didn't know how to drive.

At 7 p.m. on November 15, 1933, a desperate Thurmond called Alex Hart. The negotiations over how the ransom would be delivered dragged on so long that police were able to trace the call to the Plaza Garage on Market Street, just one block from the San Jose police station. Officers descended on the garage and caught Thurmond just as he was hanging up the phone. He confessed and Holmes was arrested later that night.

Holmes dreamed of masterminding the perfect crime but had to settle for committing what the *San Francisco Chronicle* called "the most stupid crime in California history." But the stupidity of Holmes and Thurmond's criminal enterprise didn't dampen the rage felt by the people of San Jose. L. Hart & Son was where everyone in the mostly rural community bought their shirts, socks, and Christmas presents. Alex Hart was as beloved a South Bay business figure as Steve Jobs would be some 80 years later, and Brooke, with his blond curls and athletic build, had been even more well liked than his father. Huge crowds of angry locals gathered at the jail as soon as word of the arrests got out, and the local news media only made things worse.

The *Chronicle* soon reported "lynch talk" coming out of San Jose and stoked its fires with an editorial calling for hanging the killers "without the law's needless delays, at the earliest date." The *San Jose Evening News* went even further with an op-ed titled "HUMAN DEVILS" that read, "If mob violence could ever be justified it would be in a case like this and we believe the general public would agree with us."

One person who definitely agreed was Governor "Sunny Jim" Rolph, the former 10-term mayor of San Francisco who'd led the Preparedness Day Parade past that ticking time bomb back in 1916. With tensions mounting in San Jose, Rolph refused Santa Clara County sheriff William Emig's request to send in the National Guard if a lynch mob stormed the jail to get the confessed murderers. In a possible fit of nostalgia for the vigilance committees of his city's past, Rolph even let it be known that he would pardon the lynchers.

California governor "Sunny Jim" Rolph's endorsement of mob violence is savaged in Edmund Duffy's Pulitzer Prize-winning editorial cartoon.

"I am not going to call out the Guard to protect the kidnappers who willfully killed a fine boy," Rolph told reporters. "Let the law take its course."

On Sunday, November 26, 1933, a pair of duck hunters found Hart's half-decayed body near the Alameda shore. Any hope that Brooke Hart was still alive was lost. The angry mob swelled outside the Santa Clara County jail again once the news of the grisly find hit the papers. With no backup coming from the governor, Sheriff Emig and 35 officers barricaded themselves in the stone fortress of a jailhouse with a stockpile of tear gas grenades. Emig was confident he could hold off any mob even though he had ordered his deputies not to use anything stronger than tear gas. Like those vigilance committees of the Gold Rush days, this mob was made up of solid citizens. They were members of the Elks Club and Chamber of Commerce;

they owned businesses; they were Brooke Hart's fraternity brothers from the University of Santa Clara; and they voted. You couldn't just shoot these people. Non-lethal force would have to do.

After nightfall, someone fired two gunshots and the riot started like it was a horse race at Bay Meadows. Bricks and stones gathered from a nearby post office construction site were hurled at the jail's edifice. The guards launched their first barrage of tear gas canisters into the crowd, which had grown to as many as 3,000 angry people.

The gas drove the mob back, but they just bided their time before mounting another assault. After the noxious fumes cleared, a gang of men charged the jailhouse gates with a 20-foot-long steel pipe they had confiscated from the post office site. The jail's doors shook but held. The deputies shot off another round of tear gas, and the mob fell back again. Rioters even turned a firehose onto the walkway in front of the jail to dispel the gas more quickly. With the next attack, the mob deployed two steel rods as battering rams. The jail's doors caved in. Sheriff Emig was knocked out by the mob and other officers were sent to the hospital. The vigilantes seized Holmes and Thurmond and dragged them into St. James Park across the street.

Thurmond was the first to hang. As the crowd hoisted him in the air, somebody pulled off his pants and exposed the confessed kidnapper's naked manhood to most of San Jose. Someone tried to light Thurmond's pubic hair on fire while he slowly strangled to death and the crowd chanted, "Brook-ie Hart! Brook-ie Hart!"

Holmes was a powerfully built man. He fought against the crowd, but too many people wanted him dead. They stripped him naked save for a shoe on one foot and a sock on the other. Booze-swilling teens beat him with clubs, and women lit matches and put them out on his skin. After a ten-minute search, the amateur executioners finally found an elm tree with load-bearing branches near the odd statue of martyred President McKinley standing over a cannon, which still marks the spot in the park today.

The rope was placed around Holmes's neck and he was pulled aloft by a team of Brooke Hart's frat brothers from Santa Clara

University. Among them was former child star Jackie Coogan who costarred with Chaplin in *The Kid* (1921) and later played the kooky Uncle Fester in the 1960s sitcom version of *The Addams Family*. Dangling above Coogan and his fraternity mates, Holmes pulled himself up hand over hand and started to slip the rope off his neck. The crowd lowered him, broke his arms, and pulled him up again. As Holmes neared death, he rained piss down on the mob as if to give one final fuck you to the people of San Jose. The sound of laughter echoed through the park as women held up their babies to see the dying, urinating man that an entire city had all conspired to kill.

With wisps of tear gas still wafting through the air, the headlights of cars and photographers' flashbulbs cast an eerie glow on the bodies as they hung in the park. After Thurmond was cut down hours later, crowds again swarmed the park to break twigs off the hanging trees to save as souvenirs. When Governor Rolph was informed of the lynching, he said, "This is the best lesson that California has ever given the country. We showed the country that the state is not going to tolerate kidnapping."

**MOB HANGS TWO CONFESSING**

Jack Holmes, 29, above, left, and Thomas Harold Thurmond, 23, right, had been in San Jose, Calif. jail less than a week as confessed kidnapers and killers of Brooke Hart, son of a wealthy San Jose merchant, when they were taken out and hanged last night after the body of their victim was taken from the bay into which he was thrown.

From Library of Congress, Newspaper Navigator Dataset: Extracted Visual Content from Chronicling America

Jack Holmes and Thomas H. Thurmond, the confessed murderers of Brooke Hart and the victims themselves of vigilante violence, in a November 27, 1933, item in the the *Times-News* (Hendersonville, NC).

A week later, another mob used a pipe as a battering ram to overcome a National Guard tank attachment; they stormed the jail in St. Joseph, Missouri, to kill Lloyd Warner, a 19-year-old Black man accused of rape. Holmes and Thurmond had been white, but Black Americans bore the brunt of lynching's new legitimacy. And the public clung to the idea that the lynching had dissuaded would-be kidnappers when the opposite appeared to be true. There were 10 major kidnappings in 1933. The next year, there were 18, with steady increases each year after until there were 37 U.S. kidnappings in 1938. If anything, the publicity out of San Jose served as an advertisement for the crime as well as a primer on mistakes to avoid.

And just as ominous if not as far-reaching, several eyewitnesses who observed Holmes and Thurmond during various stages of the kidnapping claimed they had seen them with other men. With the suspects dead in the park, it could never be determined if they'd had coconspirators. If they did, those accomplices got away with it.

Governor Rolph faced harsh criticism from the ACLU, NAACP, church groups, and even former president Herbert Hoover for his praise of the lynch mob, but he died from a series of strokes on June 2, 1934, before his reelection bid that year could become a referendum on California's return to vigilantism. Teenaged Anthony Capaldi boasted openly of his role in finding the hanging ropes and became the only person prosecuted for the hangings. His case was dismissed, and he went on to become a prominent South Bay real estate developer.

## THE LAST LYNCHING

The hanging of Holmes and Thurmond is often labeled as California's "last lynching," but that dubious honor—at least officially—goes to the town of Yreka near the Oregon state border. Nearly two years after the San Jose lynching, a mob of 20 or more masked vigilantes pushed their way into the Siskiyou County jail on August 3, 1935. They quickly overpowered Deputy Sheriff Martin Lange, the lone guard on duty that night. The raiders wanted the keys to the cells, but Lange wouldn't talk so a few of the vigilantes bound his wrists and drove him nine miles into the country where they turned him loose.

"I didn't have any shoes," Lange recalled.

Back at the jail, the rest of the mob ransacked the place until they found the keys. Once they could get into the cells, they seized Clyde L. Johnson and dragged him from the jail. Johnson, a bank robber from Reno, was suspected of killing F.R. Daw, chief of police of Dunsmuir, California, where most of the mob had come from via a long motorcade that started sometime after 1 a.m.

Restaurant owner Fleming Martin was on the street when the mob emerged from the jail with their quarry. "Johnson was kicking and pulling but never said a word—no, not a word," Martin told the Associated Press. "They all swore and cussed and once in a while would sock him, but they didn't do anything real bad."

One of the vigilantes held a gun on Martin until they all got back in their cars and took off. After the mob drove into the darkness, Martin went home, got his car, picked up his brother, and drove in the direction of the lynchers. The brothers soon found Johnson hanging six or eight feet off the ground from the limb of a large pine tree.

"It was an awful sight," Martin said.

County coroner Selix Kuntz (no, really) arrived on the scene two hours later and a deputy cut Johnson down from the tree. Martin had called county sheriff Chandler about the lynching, but Chandler stayed home, claiming that he was sick in bed. Instead of praising the lynch mob as his predecessor Sunny Jim had done, Governor Frank Merriam called the hanging "a blot upon the fair name of California." A year earlier, Senator Edward Costigan of Colorado had introduced a bill to make lynching a federal crime but it died in a filibuster.

While the Yreka incident marked California's last lynching, a pair of political assassinations and a bad jury verdict would bring the spirit of the vigilantes back to the city in 1979 in an echo of San Francisco's past, if not quite a full repeat.

## CHAPTER 8

# CHICAGO TO THE BAY

### ISLAND OF INCORRIGIBLES

As the Great Depression dragged millions into grinding poverty, Midwest outlaw John Dillinger became America's homicidal Robin Hood. Although he robbed from the rich far more than he gave to the poor, it helped his public image that he stuck it to the bankers who foreclosed on everyone's farms and the sheriffs who served the eviction notices.

Dillinger and his gang robbed a bank in Chicago and shot two policemen on December 30, 1933. They lammed it to faraway Tucson, Arizona, where Dillinger was nabbed and packed back off to Indiana, the state of his birth where his crime spree had begun. Indiana State Police captain Matt Leach urged local law enforcement officials to hold America's public enemy number one in the higher security state prison in nearby Michigan City, Indiana. His advice went unheeded, and Dillinger was detained in the Lake County jail in Crown Point, Indiana, instead.

FBI

View of the interior of the Alcatraz Island prison in 1986, looking south from the third level guard station with cell block B on the left and cell block C on the right.

"John Dillinger may be able to fight his way out of some prisons, but he won't break out of the Lake County jail," Sheriff Lillian Holley wrote in the *Times* of Munster, Indiana, on January 31, 1934. Holley had been appointed sheriff after her husband was killed by a demented farmer during a fierce gun battle in which 10 other men were wounded. As one of the few women in law enforcement at the time, much was made in the press about her tidying the cell that would soon house the bank robber with a reputation as an escape artist.

"We will take all the necessary precautions to guard against any attempts to deliver Dillinger, but I don't expect any," Holley said. "I think a lot of these stories about Dillinger are somewhat exaggerated."

Dillinger escaped barely a month later on March 3, 1934. According to the legend depicted in the Hollywood film *Dillinger* (1945) starring Lawrence Tierney, the master criminal bluffed his way out with a fake gun carved from wood. Other accounts say he got his hands

FBI

John Dillinger's notorious prison escapes influenced a desperate U.S. Justice Department to convert an aging Civil War fortress on Alcatraz Island in the San Francisco Bay to America's own Devil's Island.

on a real gun somehow. But back in Washington, D.C., the details hardly mattered to U.S. Attorney General Homer Stille Cummings, a liberal New Dealer who wasn't above unleashing expanding federal powers on an unprecedented crime wave that bordered on open rebellion. Something had to be done to prevent anything like this "Dillinger fiasco" from ever happening again, and Cummings already had big plans for Alcatraz Island, a stark rock protruding from the cold waters of San Francisco Bay.

When he mapped the Bay in 1775, Spanish explorer Lieutenant Juan Manuel de Ayala named the island Isla de los Alcatraces (Island of the Pelicans) after the seabirds that shat upon it. After California was annexed by the United States in 1848, the island served as the site of a Civil War fortress and an internment camp for Native Americans before becoming a military prison. To house America's most dangerous criminals in the 1930s, the aging military lockup was converted into the federal government's own bastille, fortified with machine gun nests and tear gas chutes. And if that wasn't enough to keep the public enemies in, Cummings figured the harsh riptides around the island would do the rest.

On August 2, 1934, Robert Bradford Moxon became the first prisoner transferred to what the *Chronicle* called "Uncle Sam's new penitentiary for incorrigibles." Hardly a John Dillinger or "Machine Gun" Kelly, this parole violator and passer of bad checks had Alcatraz's rows of foreboding cells nearly all to himself. At least he was familiar with the place though. Moxon had served as a guard there when he was in the army.

Dillinger died on July 22, 1934, in a bloody shootout with FBI agents at the Biograph Theater in Chicago before he could stress test the Rock, but America had another even more notorious public enemy that she could make an example of. At midnight on August 19, 1934, 53 desperate criminals were rousted from their cells in the federal penitentiary in Atlanta, Georgia, and packed onto a heavily guarded "ghost train" headed west. Among them was "Scarface" Al Capone.

Standing at just an average five-foot-nine, Capone was a towering figure in every other sense. His explosive rages became his business model as he monetized extreme violence to dominate Chicago's vast illicit liquor market during America's disastrous flirtation with alcohol prohibition in the 1920s. As an American forerunner of Mexico's El Chapo, orders from Capone once filled Chicago's streets with tommy gun fire. Yet at the time of his midnight rail trip, he was serving an 11-year sentence for the effete crime of income tax evasion, a legal and historical irony that once haunted the midnight tweet storms of the 45th president of the United States. Capone's red-eye special arrived in the North Bay enclave of Tiburon near Marin, California, via a track that had not been used in 26 years. The cars were then loaded onto a barge and towed across the bay to Alcatraz by a tugboat shadowed by a well-armed Coast Guard cutter.

FBI

Mug shot of "Scarface" Al Capone in Alcatraz prison circa 1934.

"But I'm a model prisoner," Capone protested about his unwanted change of venue. The statement turned out to be true, but it wasn't going to win him any friends where he was going.

## THREE DAYS OF MADNESS

Jack Allen became the first prisoner to die on Alcatraz on January 17, 1936. The counterfeiter who had transferred from Leavenworth complained of stomach pains the day before, but the hospital intern just gave him two aspirins and told him to come back in the morning. Allen moaned in his cell throughout the night, so the guards stuck him in an isolation cell on D block to shut him up. The next morning, Allen was found with a swollen stomach and a sky-high fever, so the guards moved him to the hospital. He was diagnosed with a gastric ulcer that was followed by full-on pneumonia. Doctors operated but it was way too late.

Even though Alcatraz's austere regime forbade prisoners from conversing, news of the negligence that led to Allen's death traveled through the cell blocks. Alcatraz's lack of radios and movies, which were permitted in other federal prisons, already had inmates planning a strike as best they could. The callous treatment of Allen pushed them over the edge.

The cons walked off the job in the laundry room on January 20, 1936. The strike soon spread to the carpentry, blacksmith, and tailor shops. In the kitchen, convict Henry Young dumped 400 pounds of vegetables on the floor before joining the walkout. More of a work stoppage than a riot, guards were able to march the strikers into their cells, but this didn't stop the acts of civil disobedience. The prisoners turned on their faucets and flooded their cells and chanted so loudly that boats passing by Alcatraz could hear the unrest. After expletive-filled chants, the prisoners settled into a chilling call and response.

"Who killed Jack Allen?"

"The doctor killed Jack Allen!"

Warden James A. Johnston broke the strike quickly by sending its organizers to "the dungeon"—a lower level of solitary confinement more horrible than even the dreaded D block—and threatening the rest with starvation rations of bread and water. However, Norman

T. "The Fox" Whittaker—a coconspirator in the Lindbergh kidnapping hoax—and others carried on the fight from the prison's lower depths with a hunger strike. The guards force-fed them through tubes over what the *Examiner* called "three days of madness."

Strikers looking for solidarity from Alcatraz's most notorious inmate found themselves more than disappointed. Capone stayed at his job in the laundry room through the strike, never veering from his plan to get time off for good behavior. As Capone kept pressing clothes, the strikers gave him a mountain of shit.

"So Capone is yellow after all," they chided. "What happened to the big shot gang leader?"

"Those guys are crazy," Capone observed, according to an exposé in the *Examiner*. "They can't get anything out of it."

"I've got to protect my own skin if I'm going to get out of here alive," he added.

Capone's newfound compliance with authority enraged John Paul Chase, a strikingly handsome Sausalito bootlegger who robbed banks with Dillinger and "Pretty Boy" Floyd. After they were both locked in their cells, Chase continued to curse out the fallen Chicago crime boss, calling him "a scab" and "a yellow rat."

"If I ever get out of here, I'll fix him," Capone said.

When Capone was released from Alcatraz in 1939, his brain was ravaged by late-stage syphilis. He died on January 25, 1947. John Paul Chase remained in Alcatraz until 1954 when he was

FBI

John Paul Chase, the strikingly handsome bank robber who called Capone a scab during the 1936 Alcatraz strike.

transferred to Leavenworth. He was paroled in 1966 and moved into a small room in a residential hotel in Palo Alto. He worked as a custodian at St. Joseph's Seminary in Mountain View until his death from cancer on October 5, 1973.

## NORTH BEACH

After Capone was transferred to Alcatraz, some of his gang followed the big boss out to San Francisco. One of them was a near Capone clone named Nick De John. He was as big as his former boss but not nearly as memorable. Capone's big-lipped grin filled the frame with an ominous sense of mirth, while De John bore a doughy expression punctuated by cold, dead eyes.

De John was raised in the family business in Chicago's Northside by his uncle, Vincenzo Benevento, a Mafia don with an organized crime lineage going back to the original Black Hand. During prohibition in the 1920s, De John provided muscle for his uncle and rose through the ranks of Capone's organization. After Capone was transferred to Alcatraz in 1934, Don Benevento and his protégé moved in on Big Al's illegal lottery, known then as the numbers rackets. Over the course of the ensuing conflict, several wise guys in Benevento's crew met grisly ends, and the old don himself was mowed down in a hail of bullets in 1945. A year later, De John turned up in the Bay Area with $250,000 in mob collection money.

De John bought a spread in Santa Rosa, but he couldn't resist the nightlife of San Francisco's North Beach, the city's Italian neighborhood where he would most likely be recognized by the wrong people. He bought a home in the Mission District and sunk $90,000 into a North Beach nightclub. On May 7, 1947, he went to the city to check in with his real estate agent. Two days later, an irate resident reported that a flashy purple Chrysler was hogging up all the parking in front of his Laguna Street flat. A pair of officers were dispatched to check that the car wasn't stolen. When they popped open the land yacht's cavernous trunk, the lucky cops were confronted by the sight of De John's bare ass. His body had been crammed face-down into the trunk with his well-tailored slacks pulled down around his knees.

The gangster had been strangled with a garrote. "From ear to ear was a deep red mark where his slayer had tightened the wire or thin cord around his neck," the *Chronicle* reported. His roll of cash, diamond-studded wristwatch, and 7-carat diamond ring were all gone, leaving just 77 cents in his pockets.

In the nights that followed, squads of police inspectors tore through North Beach and Tenderloin nightspots looking for leads but turning up nothing. Mayor Roger Lapham went into full damage-control mode. For over a decade, civic leaders had crafted an image of San Francisco as a city free of the organized crime that was baked into New York and Chicago. "We do not propose to have this city made the victim of such criminal mobs as have operated in some other cities," the mayor said in a statement. Lapham had already faced a recall attempt over raising streetcar fares from 7 cents to a dime. He didn't want to be the mayor holding the bag when it was revealed that the city was just as mobbed up as anywhere else.

The police investigation stalled but became an obsession for homicide inspector Frank Ahern. In November 1948, Ahern announced that he and Chief of Inspectors James English had retraced De John's steps on the day of his murder. During a news conference, the detectives detailed how the gangster had dinner at the Poodle Dog on Polk Street and then settled down for a game of pinochle with the men who would kill him at La Rocca's Corner, a triangular dive bar at the severe corner of Columbus Avenue and Taylor Street in North Beach. At some point during the card game, the garrote was slipped around De John's neck and pulled tight until he drew his last breath.

In February 1949, a trio of local goons—Leonard Calamia, Sebastiano Nani, and Micheli Abati—were brought to trial for murdering De John. They all had ties to a North Beach outfit called Sunland Oil and Cheese Company that moved more narcotics than aged pecorino. De John was muscling in on their business, and they weren't having it. District Attorney Edmund G. "Pat" Brown's case looked like a strong one. His star witness, Anita Rocchia Venza, claimed she had overheard the defendants plot the mob execution in a basement apartment owned by Papa La Rocca, but she didn't hold up under cross-examination. When defense attorney James C. Purcell asked Venza if she'd forged her neighbor's signature and cashed a stolen pension check to buy a rabbit, she answered, "Absolutely not."

"What did you buy?" Purcell asked.

"A turkey," Venza replied. "I don't eat rabbit."

That exchange along with evidence that Venza was an abortionist had Brown feeling that his case was slipping away in a city that was far more Catholic and conservative than the San Francisco of today. While the jury deliberated, Brown asked that they be dismissed before they could render a verdict. Inspector Ahern stormed out of the courtroom in anger. He never forgave Brown, although the extraordinary move preserved the chance that the defendants could be tried again if new evidence ever surfaced. At the time of the dismissal, a majority of the jurors leaned towards acquittal.

While the De John murder remained unsolved, Ahern and Brown didn't suffer career setbacks from their failed effort. Ahern became San Francisco's chief of police in 1956, and Brown was elected California's 32nd governor in 1959. His son, Edmund G. "Jerry" Brown Jr., carried on the family dynasty by becoming governor in 1975 and again in 2007.

In North Beach, the cartoon image of Al Capone chomping on a cigar and holding a tommy gun still looms over Columbus Street on the sign of Big Al's, the one-time home of "Tosha, the Glo Girl, in her dynamic topless bathing suit." When bare breasts seemed a little tame, the club went totally nude before becoming a porn shop and then a cigar store. The joint appears to be vacant today, but the sign remains to stake San Francisco's claim to America's most notorious criminal.

Bob Calhoun

Capone still looms over the remnants of the old Barbary Coast on the Big Al's sign on Broadway at Columbus Avenue in the heart of North Beach.

## A WEALTHY AND PROMINENT SPORTSMAN

While North Beach is where you'd expect mafiosos to get whacked, Chicago-style gangland violence came to suburban San Mateo on the morning of February 5, 1952, when Tom Keen started his brand-new Cadillac. Once the engine turned over, the car blew up before Keen could even back out of his garage. The blast sheared off his legs and blew his upper body through the front seat of the car, wedging his torso into the backseat upholstery. The explosion was so powerful it hurled the Cadillac's big-block V8 engine through the wall of the garage, which was fortunately separated from the five-bedroom Spanish-style home. In the main house, Keen's wife, Emma, was spared from the impact—at least physically.

The *Chicago Tribune* reported that "the front end of the auto was shredded." First responders on the scene were sickened by the magnitude of the carnage. The direction of the blast indicated that three or four sticks of dynamite had been placed under the steering column and wired to a spark plug.

"It looks like one of those gangland killings you read about," San Mateo County assistant district attorney Fred Wykoff told the *Tribune*.

Described in the *San Mateo Times* as a "wealthy and prominent sportsman," Keen had owned dog-racing tracks in Belmont and near Geneva Avenue in Daly City until California banned the spectacle in the 1930s. At the time of his murder, he owned the International Totalizer Company in Belmont, which manufactured electronic tote or score boards that Keen leased to racetracks for a portion of the betting proceeds. Keen had recently made trips to Florida and Arizona to install his equipment before being blown to bits in his garage.

While the *San Mateo Times* painted a picture of Keen as a pillar of Peninsula society who rubbed elbows with local police chiefs and mayors, the *Chicago Tribune* dished the dirt on his mobbed-up past. Keen got his start in dog racing in the 1920s by running tracks in Florida for Capone. By the end of the decade, Keen had made his way to Chicago where he fell in with Edward "Easy Eddie" O'Hare, a St. Louis lawyer who ran the Sportsman's Park racetrack in Cicero, Illinois, a Chicago suburb controlled entirely by the Capone mob. O'Hare soon turned on Capone and helped federal prosecutors convict the gangster for income tax evasion in 1931.

With Capone in prison and O'Hare responsible, Keen hightailed it to the Bay Area in 1932. Ironically, he found himself closer to his old boss two years later when Capone was shipped to Alcatraz in 1934, but it's not known if the two were ever in contact during the four and a half years Big Al was on the Rock. News reports of the time maintained that Keen had severed ties with Capone years earlier. As for O'Hare, he was gunned down while driving from his Cicero racetrack on November 8, 1939, a week before Capone's release from prison.

According to a February 8, 1952, UPI story, Keen had taken out a $66,000 loan with "unusually strong terms" to finance a new totalizer system for dog tracks. San Mateo police chief Martin McDonnell announced that a "special crime council" would investigate the bombing, but it uncovered nothing but rumors and false leads. The murder of Tom Keen is currently open with the cold case unit of the San Mateo Police Department.

## CHAPTER 9

# NO PARTS LYING TOGETHER IN ONE PLACE

### SPECTER OF THE ROSE

The four boys ran down Market Street past a row of grand movie palaces on Sunday, September 8, 1946. *Two Guys from Milwaukee*, a since-forgotten Warner Bros. comedy romp, was playing at the Warfield while Cary Grant and Ingrid Bergman were foiling a Nazi plot in Alfred Hitchcock's *Notorious* at the RKO Golden Gate on Taylor Street. The marquee of the Esquire boasted a "DOUBLE SHOCKER" with showings of *Devil Bat's Daughter* and *House of Horrors* running from 9 a.m. through 1 a.m. the next morning. When the kids got to the Paramount, they caught a whiff of something even more ghastly than the zero-budget horrors at the Esquire. They followed their noses to the alleyway at the side of the theater at Jones Street where they found a pair of large cardboard egg crates. The boys kicked at the crates until they broke open, and rancid human remains spilled onto the ground.

When police inspected the boxes, they found a man's dismembered limbs and torso, all neatly packed and wrapped in a spangled cotton commonly used at the time to ship orchids and gardenias. Some internal organs were stuffed into a three-gallon milk can. The janitor of the Paramount had hauled the can of guts into the theater thinking it was dumped by a nearby restaurant. The head, the hands, and the upper arms—all the parts that could help identify the remains—had been removed with the skill of a trained butcher, or maybe even a surgeon. Fifty cops made a room-by-room search of the 13-block area around the theater for the head and hands, but came up empty.

Due to the body parts being wrapped in a cotton material favored by florists, detectives theorized that the deceased might be Ramon B. Lopez, described by the *Examiner* as "a wealthy carnation grower." Lopez grew his flowers at his San Leandro nursery and sold them from a stall at the San Francisco Flower Market on Fifth Street. He had been missing since he made the rounds in North Beach on Wednesday, September 4. Lopez's wife, Mrs. Guiden-Garcia Lopez, was able to identify her husband's detached limbs and torso based on "a mole, round and smaller than a dime" and "an ingrown nail on the big toe of the right foot," according to the *Chron*.

Al Nalbandian, who ran the flower stand at Union Square on Geary and Stockton Streets until his death in 2017, used to see Lopez almost every day. "People called him Spanny because he was Spanish and spoke with a thick accent," Nalbandian recalled. "Nobody called him by his real name."

"He was a character in the best sense of the word," Nalbandian added, "but he never went down on his price. I'll tell you that."

Lopez was rumored to have $2,000 on him at the time of his disappearance, but police ruled out robbery as a motive for a crime this grisly.

"I can't recall a murder with money as the motive, that employed such terrible mutilation," an unnamed official told the *Chron*. "This was motivated by some deep revenge."

Homicide inspector Al Corrasa told the *Examiner* that the manner of dissection suggested a sex abnormality. Police found 14 pairs of nylons in a room that Lopez kept at the Mint Hotel on Fifth Street not far from the flower market.

"He was quite a ladies' man," Nalbandian said.

Police arrested Benito Cisheros, a former employee of Lopez's, but kicked him loose after determining he wasn't a suspect. They were also after a 40-year-old man with a blue pickup truck. Officer Walter Harrington had seen the man put the boxes in the alleyway but didn't question him or even take down his license plate number. Harrington said it looked like "a normal delivery procedure," so he "didn't think anything about it."

Frustrated with the police investigation, Lopez's brother, Mateo Lopez, and son, Anselmo, showed up in San Francisco ready to take the law into their own hands.

"If police find the man who did this to my brother, just let them run him over to me for justice," Mateo Lopez, a one-armed former bar owner and fight manager, told the *Daily Review* on September 11, 1946. "I'll make sure he doesn't die too soon as I cut him up like they did to my brother."

The official investigation went nowhere, and the family wasn't telling if they turned up any leads. The case went cold. Eighteen years later, a man found Lopez's skull on the beach at Hunter's Point. The case remains unsolved.

The movie that was playing at the Paramount the night pieces of Lopez were found in the alley was *Specter of the Rose*, a surreal noir where strange ballet promoters engage in extended discussions about murder, insanity, and vampires. The first person you see in the film's opening shot is wearing a carnation pinned to his lapel.

## THE CORPSE MUTILATORS OF MENLO PARK

Today, Menlo Park is known as the home of Facebook and tech workers who can't quite afford Atherton, but in 1944 this tree-lined suburbia was the site of one of the most bizarre crimes in Bay Area history.

Dolores Sifuentes of Redwood City was just 21 years old when she died from tuberculosis at the Canyon Sanatorium on Thursday, April 6, 1944. She was buried in Holy Cross Cemetery in Menlo Park on the following Saturday. Strangely, this was only the beginning of her ordeal.

Sifuentes's deathbed wish was for some of her high school English compositions to be buried with her. In her parents' crushing grief, they forgot to inter the notebooks in their daughter's coffin. Later that week, Sifuentes's mother was visited by her dead daughter in a dream where Dolores called for the notebooks from beyond the grave. Jesse Sifuentes and Augustine Ochoa, Dolores's father and uncle, respectively, returned to the cemetery with the papers on the night of Thursday, April 13. As they started to dig a small hole over Dolores's grave for the writings, the two men were shocked to find a pair of pallbearer's gloves under only a few layers of dirt. They dug a little further and unearthed Dolores's pale outstretched hand.

After the Menlo Park police and San Mateo County sheriffs arrived on the scene, the officers summoned Walter Perry, 32, the 175-pound gravedigger who had buried Dolores only days before. In what the *San Mateo Times* described as "an eerie night scene of rain and black clouds," Perry unearthed Dolores's naked corpse "on top of the redwood lining box that formed the sepulcher for her coffin." The blue-and-white silk dress that she had been buried in "was found mud-stained and bedraggled beside the box," according to the *Santa Cruz Sentinel*.

The police questioned Perry who broke down and confessed to dragging Dolores from her casket and "ripping off her silken shroud." Perry also admitted to slashing at the body with a pocketknife. The *San Mateo Times* reported grimly that "authorities were making a search for a part of the body which had been severed."

"[Perry] was frequently in tears apparently from emotional instability rather than remorse for his act," the *Times* continued.

Law enforcement officials called the crime abnormal and the press speculated that Perry was maddened by necrophilia or even lycanthropy, which the *San Mateo Times* dubbed "a variation of the 'werewolf' mania." The *Times* reminded its readers that Perry violated Dolores's grave on the day of the full moon and that "moon phases have been declared by scientists to be associated with this type of crime."

Two days later, the *San Mateo Times* reported that Perry had violated several graves in Holy Cross Cemetery, stealing rings and other pieces of jewelry from the dead. Cole M. Madison, 18, a discharged sailor from Mountain View, had helped Perry carry out his desecration spree. Both men were brought to trial in October 1944 after a lengthy stay in a state psychiatric hospital. According to the *San Mateo Times*, "alienists" declared "the ghouls" had "mentalities of children."

Dolores Sifuentes's body was reburied on April 14, 1944. "The same casket was used again and a fresh burial dress was placed upon the body," reported the *San Mateo Times*. "There were no services other than prayers at the graveside."

## THE BLACK DAHLIA LIES IN OAKLAND

Phoebe M. Short, 46, arrived at the San Francisco airport on January 18, 1947. She had flown to California from her home in Medford, Massachusetts, that Sunday afternoon to see two of her five daughters. One, Virginia West, who lived in Berkeley, was there to greet her. The other, Elizabeth Short, was dead in Los Angeles.

Elizabeth Short was known as Betty to her friends and family. With her blue-green eyes and raven hair, she was maybe the prettiest girl in Medford. She had moved to California when she was still a teenager with hopes of making it in the movies. She didn't, but she achieved the notoriety in death that had eluded her in life. Elizabeth was found in a vacant lot at Norton Avenue and 39th Street in southwest Los Angeles on the morning of January 15, 1947. She had been cut in half at the waist and drained of blood at some other location. The two sections of her body appeared to be arranged

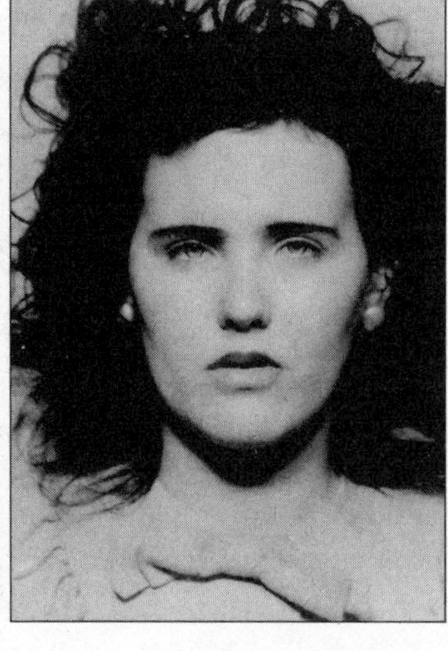

FBI

The mugshots and fingerprint of Elizabeth Short, better known as the Black Dahlia.

in the weeds with artistic intent. Her bottom half was posed with legs spread wide open. Her top half was laid with her arms above her head forming a U shape.

Her face was a massive bruise from where she had been pummeled to death with a blunt object, and her mouth had been cut at the corners to form a gruesome grimace. She also had rope marks on her legs and arms indicating that she had been tortured for several hours, and police found brush bristles on the body from where the killer had scrubbed her clean. She was just 22 years old.

The gruesome murder fueled several weeks of front-page headlines in L.A.'s four major news dailies at the time. Reporters referred to Short as the "Black Dahlia," a nickname bestowed upon her either by sensationalist headline writers or a Long Beach soda jerk, depending on which urban legend is actually true. Either way, the name came from *The Blue Dahlia*, a 1946 noir starring Veronica Lake that now seems inadequate when measured against the crime to which it's forever linked.

Phoebe Short learned about her daughter's death from Wain Sutton, a rewrite man for the *LA Examiner*. Sutton first told the mother that her daughter had won a contest and they were checking with her for background info. After squeezing Elizabeth's life story out of the mom for a while, *Examiner* city editor Jimmy Richardson told Sutton to give Phoebe the bad news. The treatment of the Shorts by the press only got worse with news reports that blamed the victim. Elizabeth was labeled a prostitute and an actress in stag flicks, even though she wasn't. She was a young girl who fell on hard times and wasn't above dating a guy to get a meal out of him. That was all, but reporters and their sources were still overcome with the need to embellish.

"We just can't understand the things they say about her in the papers," Phoebe told the *Oakland Tribune* on the day she flew into San Francisco. "She was never like that. We can't believe it."

Phoebe Short was flown down to Los Angeles for the inquest on the *LA Examiner*'s dime as an exclusive. She refused to ID her daughter's body for two days, telling the coroner that she wanted to remember Elizabeth as she was. Phoebe appeared at the inquest on January 22, 1947. The *Los Angeles Times* described her testimony as being "without a trace of emotion."

Elizabeth's body arrived in Oakland a day later; at the same time, police in Los Angeles were conducting house-to-house searches to find the murder site. They never did.

**Elizabeth Short, aka the Black Dahlia, was born in Massachusetts, murdered in L.A., and is buried in the hills of Oakland at Mountain View Cemetery.**

For reasons lost to history, Elizabeth's remains didn't make it back to Massachusetts, and she was buried in the slope of a hill in Oakland's Mountain View Cemetery on January 25, 1947. Her funeral was a lonely one attended by her mother, sister, brother-in-law, and a pair of men in trench coats who could have been cops or reporters. A funeral notice in the *Oakland Tribune* that described Elizabeth as "a beloved daughter" and "loving sister" was the only chance the Shorts had to tell their own story. Phoebe Short moved to Oakland for a time to be near both of her daughters, but moved back east in the 1970s where she lived into her early 90s. The murder of the Black Dahlia is still unsolved.

## THE MONKEY WRENCH MURDER

William Sanford was a 20-year-old Mission District orphan with a mass of wavy black hair piled atop his long face. He was a genius, to hear him tell it, but all he'd managed to accomplish was detailed on his rap sheet. He was busted for petty theft in 1944 and again in 1946. He drew a suspended sentence the first time and got three months the second. His crimes were strictly small time, but he still made an impression on probation officers. They urged psychiatric treatment, noting his "future conduct was unpredictable." Their recommendations went unheeded, but Sanford did read a lot of Freud on his own and diagnosed himself as "a schizoid."

Sanford was busted for armed robbery in 1947 and sentenced to a prison for "tough kids" in Lancaster, California. He was transferred to a California Youth Authority forestry camp in Ben Lomond, near Santa Cruz. After escaping the camp on June 14, 1948, he made his way back to the Mission, where he rented a room in a Capp Street flophouse. Somewhere along the way, he became obsessed with 19-year-old Rita Gerstmann, described by the *Examiner* as "an attractive brown-haired girl" who lived with her mom and stepdad on San Jose Avenue. Sanford claimed Rita was his longtime girlfriend. She denied that she ever went steady with the weird kid she'd known since childhood. Her mother worried about Sanford being "too possessive." He visited Rita when he was on the lam in late June. Rita asked him to stay away.

After Rita broke off the romance that had existed only in Sanford's mind, he returned to his room on Capp Street. He brooded for a spell, before deciding he had to kill Rita and needed to buy a gun to do it. He went upstairs and asked to borrow a monkey wrench from his landlady, Felipa Griffith, a 55-year-old widow who had also lost her son in World War II. Griffith handed Sanford the wrench, and he beat her over the head with it.

"I hit her on the head once and she staggered and let out a feeble scream," he recalled. She fell into a closet and made some gurgling sounds. With blood spurting all around, he threw some clothes over her head and slammed the wrench into her several more times until she died.

With all the other boarders away for the day, he ransacked the flat and came up with just $1.50 plus some watches and other jewelry. Sanford missed $75 that Griffith had pinned inside of her dress—more than enough to buy a pistol from a pawnshop back then. On his way out, he tore out the page with his name on it from his landlady's receipt book and stuffed it in his pocket to cover his tracks.

Griffith's body was found by her daughter on June 29, 1948. Inspectors Frank Ahern and Ralph McDonald noticed the missing page from the receipt book when they searched the house. After questioning the daughter and some of the tenants, they found out that Griffith spoke little English and relied on a roomer who was on vacation in Oregon to write her receipts for her. When police finally got ahold of him, he said that he had made out a receipt for a Bill Sanford. Police linked Sanford to his escape from Ben Lomond and scoured every boarding house in the Mission District looking for him. They also staked out his brother's house on 30th Street in the Excelsior where they caught him crawling in through a back window on July 1.

Once in custody, Sanford gave lengthy interviews to the press. Carolyn Anspacher of the *Chronicle* described him as having "the easy calm of a host at a cocktail party," as he justified committing a murder as brutal as it was pointless.

"This is a pretty grim world, and the old lady had less than most people to live for," he explained. "I like to think I inflicted on her the minimum of pain, and for this reason I don't think there was anything sadistic involved in the murder.

"I used her as a means of getting back at society—because society had not provided me with love," he continued, as if to foreshadow the future tweet storms of angry incels.

Of Rita, he said that what he really wanted in a girlfriend was "a kind of human dog" that he could "cuff around and abuse" but "would remain loyal until the end." He then talked about his love of Shakespeare, and how he'd written three books in prison but had only finished one. "It wasn't very good but it kept me busy," he said.

Sanford was sentenced to die in San Quentin's gas chamber on November 19, 1948. After the judge read the sentence, Sanford nudged his attorney and said, "Please thank the judge for carrying out my wishes."

## THE TORTURE KIT SADIST

On Saturday, July 20, 1957, James Lonergan, a 26-year-old teacher, was out on a date with an unidentified 19-year-old student nurse. The ride started to get bumpy, so Lonergan pulled over by Golden Gate Park. As he was checking for a leak in his gas tank, a man stepped up behind him and pressed a 10-inch knife into his back.

"I want no trouble, only your wallet," the man said. Lonergan handed over his wallet and wristwatch, hoping that would be the end of the ordeal. It was just the beginning.

The man got into the car and made Lonergan drive to an isolated spot inside the park. Lonergan was then bound and gagged with medical tape and cord the man had with him in a cardboard-boxed torture kit. The man made the nurse get into the back seat and tied her arms behind her and shackled her legs with a pair of handcuffs attached to each other with an overly long length of chain. The nurse struggled. The attacker punched her in the face and beat her with a belt.

"Scream!" the attacker commanded. "Yell that it hurts! I want to hear you scream with pain!"

The attacker then burned the nurse with a cigarette, cut off some of her hair, and raped her. After he was done, he sat in the car silently for nearly 30 minutes before announcing he was going to give the couple "an injection." They felt a slight twinge of pain before the attacker gathered his tools and walked into the darkness of the park, torture kit in hand.

Lonergan managed to slide out of the front seat and inch his way like a worm to Lincoln Way where people heard his screams. The nurse was found naked, bruised, and sobbing in the back seat of the car.

The rapist wore horn-rimmed glasses and had nylon pantyhose pulled over his scalp. The victims described him as swarthy and bucktoothed. The press dubbed the suspect "The Torture-Kit Sadist," and some reporters called him "The Fang" because of his exaggerated overbite.

Four days after the rape, police had John Alvin Rexinger, 23, in custody. Rexinger was a convicted forger who was living on Franklin Street while he served out his parole. He had been busted for statutory rape when he was 18. Detectives hauled Rexinger to the female victim's hospital room where she positively IDed him.

"That's him! That's him!" she cried.

The police thought they had their man. Rexinger had the right glasses, but he didn't have the buckteeth. He wasn't the Torture-Kit Sadist. His alibi, however, was thin and weird. He claimed he had been at home making audio recordings of his poetry for his parole officer. Even worse for Rexinger, his poetic imagery—conjuring "the frosty crunch of young bones under steel" and "bars and young flesh over iron chains"—only made him look guilty as hell. Inspector

Frank Gibeau of the SFPD told the press that the audio "clearly indicates [Rexinger] is a sexual psychopath and sadist."

With his priors, and with shopkeepers identifying him as the man who had bought cord and tape from them, Rexinger feared he was being marked as fodder for the hungry maw of San Quentin's gas chamber.

After eight days in the stir, Rexinger had his reprieve when police arrested a 21-year-old heroin addict named Melvin N. Bakkerud for burglarizing a pharmacy. When police searched Bakkerud's apartment, they found the torture kit and John Lonergan's wristwatch. Rexinger said he felt "as though a steamroller had been lifted off [his] chest" when he was told of the arrest, but he was still held in custody due to parole violations. By the time he was freed, he had lost both his girlfriend and his job.

Bakkerud told police that he got the idea for his brutal crimes from a detective magazine. A few months later, Bakkerud himself was featured in a strange photo spread for the cover story of the November 1957 issue of *Inside Detective*, starting the cycle all over again.

## CHAPTER 10

# URBAN RENEWAL

### THE CURSE OF FOX PLAZA

The Fox Plaza building looms over Civic Center. Its expanse funnels the bracing winds that chill Market Street most afternoons. In the apartments above its labeled 13th floor, curtains in various stages of closure give the structure a war-torn look, and the rows of rectangles that line its facade make it resemble an old air filter yanked from a mid-1990s Toyota. While it's easy to dismiss its sins as merely aesthetic, the 29-story mixed-use building has a history of residents leaping to their deaths from its concrete balconies.

"That's at least three suicides from Fox Plaza since we moved here just about a year and a half ago," Dieter Bohn, executive editor of *The Verge*, tweeted on November 6, 2013. Marcus Wohlsen, a reporter for the Associated Press from 2006 to 2012, concurred. "AP bureau was there years ago. Bodies a regular feature then too," he replied.

The ugliness of Fox Plaza stands on the site of the 4,651-seat Fox Theater, a rococo extravagance that was once the largest movie palace west of Chicago. According to urban legend, Church of Satan founder Anton LaVey played the organ at the Fox during its final show on Saturday, February 17, 1963, three years before he declared Anno Satanas—the first year of the reign of Satan—in 1966. As LaVey struck the last chord that would ever echo through the Fox's gold-leafed auditorium, he reportedly cursed whatever building would replace his beloved cinema. A gold wrecking ball wrapped in tassels from the Fox's oversized stage curtain slammed into the theater's west wall just 11 days later, shattering the wall-length mirror in the third-floor ladies' lounge, bringing more than just seven years of bad luck.

The curse appeared to take effect before the new Fox Plaza building was even completed. A crane collapsed and hurtled through the metal skeleton of the upper floors on July 20, 1965. One man had his legs crushed under the crane's five-ton mast, and four others were injured. Fox Plaza opened without incident on May 2, 1966, a day after LaVey's reign of Satan had begun. The suicides in the high-rise

Bob Calhoun

**According to urban legend, Church of Satan founder Anton LaVey put a curse on the Fox Plaza building when they tore down the ornate Fox Theater for it. The building has been plagued by suicides and other freak accidents ever since it opened.**

started the following year when 49-year-old William B. Dederer shot himself in his girlfriend's 26th-floor apartment in March 1967.

The tragedies continued in the next decade when a man jumped 22 stories to his death on September 4, 1971. A 45-year-old cabbie shot himself in the face with a skeet gun in his apartment and crawled off his 14th-story balcony on February 15, 1972. Other accidental deaths and suicides have been regularly reported ever since. And not all of the tragedies connected to Fox Plaza were self-inflicted. A fire truck responding to a small wastebasket fire in the building jumped the curb on Market and Taylor Streets on December 5, 1975, killing three people at a crowded Muni stop. A sniper rained down bullets on the plaza itself in 1979.

While decades of death falls from Fox Plaza may strengthen the rumor of LaVey's curse, the Fox was a troubled enterprise even back in its theatrical glory days. Less than a month after William Fox opened his "theater of dreams" in June 1929, the movie studio magnate was severely injured in a car accident that killed his chauffeur. Fox was kept alive by a blood transfusion from J. Carrol Naish, a character actor who later played a murderous hunchback in *House of Frankenstein* (1944). The theater hit hard times after the stock market crash of 1929, closing for six months in 1932. After reopening, the Fox was the scene of several holdups, a suicide, and an accident where two ushers stepped into an empty elevator shaft and fell to their deaths.

The cause of the building's history of suicides may have more to do with unfettered balcony access than the supernatural, and death curses seem out of place with the gothic hedonism LaVey espoused. It's also unclear if LaVey really played the organ during the Fox Theater's farewell, although he was a more than capable organist. According to a 2000 *Chronicle* obituary, Everett Nourse was the organist for the Fox, "where he delighted audiences until the theater closed down in 1963." But even if LaVey didn't possess the power to conjure a half century of tragedy, the destruction of the Fox Theater brought one era of San Francisco to a close. The construction of Fox Plaza in its place marked the beginning of a colder, more violent time.

Jay Blakesberg

Anton LaVey, founder of the Church of Satan. According to urban legend, he put a curse on Fox Plaza after they tore down his favorite movie palace to build it.

## THE MAYOR OF FILLMORE STREET

Orlando Martinez and his girlfriend had just gotten off work at 2:45 a.m. on August 2, 1966, when they noticed a car with its lights on parked on Fifth and Bluxome Streets near the San Francisco train yards. Ortiz went to check it out and found the six-foot-tall, 250-pound body of Charles Sullivan dead on the ground next to his rental car. "There are no sidewalks in this area as it is an industrial district, and deceased was lying where a sidewalk would be if there was one," according to the coroner's report. There are sidewalks there now, along with sleek apartment buildings and an exclusive tennis club, but in 1966 it was a road lined with dirt and gravel.

Sullivan was lying on his back and dressed in a dark suit with a white dress shirt. He was a Black man from the Fillmore District and wouldn't be caught dead going out in a T-shirt and jeans back then—not even to hand off a bag of cash after midnight. Lying next to Sullivan's right hand was a five-shot Smith & Wesson revolver with one spent cartridge and three live ones. Sullivan had been shot in the chest at close range. The bullet ripped through his heart and lungs and broke a couple of ribs along the way. Sullivan "came to his death at the hands of party or parties unknown"—that was the verdict in the coroner's report. The party or parties are still unknown, not that anybody lost any sleep trying to find them.

The death of Charles Sullivan should've been called the end of an era, but it didn't help that the era in question had been marked for demolition long before he took that bullet to the chest. Hailed by Warren Hinckle in the *Chronicle* as "the richest Negro west of the Mississippi," Sullivan had built a business empire of bars, liquor stores, juke boxes, and cigarette machines. Flush with cash, he branched out into concert promotions. In 1952, he started booking a former whites-only skating rink on Fillmore Street and Geary Boulevard called the Ambassador Dance Hall, soon renamed the Fillmore Auditorium. The name change made the place into a monument to the Black neighborhood that was already being bulldozed over and under for something called "urban renewal," only nobody was sure what was being renewed.

That neighborhood in San Francisco west of Market Street and southwest of Nob Hill has been named several times over, and each name stuck around depending on who you talked to. It was called the Western Addition when its first Victorians were built there in the 1870s. It became Nihonmachi, Japantown, or J-Town, when Japanese immigrants and their children moved there after the 1906 earthquake. It stayed that way until World War II when President Roosevelt signed Executive Order 9066 in 1942 and all Japanese Americans were imprisoned in internment camps. At the same time, San Francisco's shipyards needed workers for the war effort, and Black Americans ditching the racism of Texas and Alabama found work and a different kind of racism in San Francisco. With white landlords unwilling to rent to them in the rest of the city, Black workers filled Japantown's empty Victorians. They transformed the neighborhood into the Fillmore.

Former mayor Willie Brown called the neighborhood "the closest thing to Harlem outside of New York," and for a brief era from the

1940s into the '60s it was the Harlem of the West. There were 29 jazz clubs on the eight blocks of Fillmore Street between California and Eddy Streets, with even more nightspots just off that main drag. Dizzy Gillespie, Charlie Parker, and Miles Davis laid down the cool jazz and bebop at Jimbo's Bop City where musicians got in for free but everyone else had to shell out a buck. Louis Armstrong blew horn at the Texas Playhouse, which was usually so packed that the crowd spilled out onto the street. And then there was the Primalon Ballroom, Jack's Tavern, Minnie's Can-Do, the Blue Mirror, and on and on and on.

"You could walk down Fillmore Street and see all kinds of clubs lined up one behind the other, and the musicians could gig all the time," Sugar Pie DeSanto is quoted as saying in the book *Harlem of the West: The San Francisco Fillmore Jazz Era* (2006). "I mean, just music out of doors, windows, people's houses."

Although Charles Sullivan was a little late to the Fillmore's music scene, his success was so great that he became known as the "Mayor of Fillmore Street." Sullivan's background was anything but glamorous, however. In 1911, Bell Mary Williams scrawled her X on a contract that gave "complete control and possession" of her two-year-old son Charles to Robert Sullivan, a Black farmer in Monroe County, Alabama. Baby Charles became an indentured slave, and like the enslaved people of the Antebellum South, he took his master's surname. The contract that Charles's mother signed stated that her boy was "to learn the art, trade, occupation, and mysteries of farming" and be treated "humanely." These were terms that Robert Sullivan chose not to honor.

"The old man drank a lot and when he drank, he beat people. Mostly he beat me," Charles recalled to Warren Hinckle in the *Chronicle*. "The old man sent his kids to school but he wouldn't let me go. I had to stay on the farm and work."

Charles Sullivan became a runaway slave decades after the end of the Civil War when he fled Alabama for Los Angeles in 1928. He studied to be a machinist and got to be a pretty good one, but racism kept him from getting hired when he moved to San Francisco in 1934. "I couldn't get into the machinists union," he told Hinkcle. "They would not take any Blacks." Like many African Americans who moved to San Francisco a few years later during the Second Great Migration and World War II, the city's less overt racism forced Sullivan to become entrepreneurial. He saved his income from driving a suburban socialite to ritzy cocktail parties and bought a hamburger stand in San Mateo in 1940. He opened another restaurant that year and then opened a bar called Sullivan's in 1942. People drank a lot during the war, and they drank even more after it, so he kept on buying bars, and then he diversified into juke boxes, cigarette machines, and liquor stores. His liquor store on Post Street in San Francisco delivered, and it raked in $400,000 a year—nearly $6 million in today's dollars.

After taking over the lease of the Fillmore Auditorium in the mid-1950s, the capital from his other enterprises enabled him to bring in big acts that his competition could not afford. "He did all the bookings for big names—entertainers like James Brown and Gladys Knight," Sugar Pie DeSanto recalled. "He was into the big productions. If you wanted to get a big gig, you better call Charles or you wouldn't get one."

And Sullivan's piece of the music business grew beyond the confines of the Fillmore and its namesake auditorium. He booked Ray Charles and James Brown at the 12,000-seat Cow Palace, paving the way for the arena rock shows there that dominated the 1970s and '80s. He put together packaged tours for top African American acts that spanned the West Coast from Seattle to Los Angeles. "He was the man. He was the circuit," Oakland record producer and talent agent Jim Moore said. "You never worried about getting paid. Sometimes he'd pay guys ahead of time."

Thanks to his success, Sullivan and his wife, Fannie, lived in a two-story home on Grove Street decorated in a modern Japanese style as if in an homage to the displaced Issei and Nisei residents of the Fillmore. In a magnanimous but strange gesture, Sullivan brought his former master, Robert Sullivan, out to San Francisco along with Robert's 11 adult children and gave them all jobs in his bars and liquor stores. "I always wanted a family—anybody I could say was a family—but all the time I knew I had none," Charles explained. In 1963, social workers mistook Robert for Charles's father and the city sued Charles for $75 a month for elder support and $1,344 in back payments after Robert went on welfare. "That man was my master, not my father," Charles said. The city attorney dropped the suit.

Although Sullivan was at his zenith, the Fillmore's jazz and blues era had been on borrowed time since it began. Starting in 1942—the first year that Black people moved into Western Addition en masse—the Hearst *Examiner* began running regular editorials that labeled the former Japantown or "Little Tokio" [sic] as "a slum menace" and "San Francisco's shame." The war delayed the inevitable push for urban renewal, but the San Francisco Redevelopment Agency was created in 1948 with a mandate to tear down Western Addition's old wooden buildings. Like the Japanese residents before them, the neighborhood's Black residents were given no guarantee that they could move back into their homes once they were moved out. On July 15, 1953, the Victorian at 1717 Eddy Street was the first to be torn down, with many more to follow. And more homes and minority-owned businesses were razed for the conversion of two-lane Geary Street into a sunken six-lane thoroughfare so that the mostly white residents of the new suburban developments in the Richmond District could get to their jobs in downtown financial and insurance firms more quickly.

"When redevelopment began, the vibrant community I knew, my friends, my whole world started to change," Japantown community activist Steve Nakajo recalled. "I used to look down the street and see nothing but Victorians. And then, at one point, you'd leave in the morning and there would be a bulldozer parked in front of some buildings, and by the time you came back from school, the houses weren't there anymore."

By January 1966, the neighborhood looked like it had been leveled by Allied bombing raids, so Sullivan was happy to sell his lease of the Fillmore Auditorium to Bill Graham, who was packing hippie kids in there on off-nights for psychedelic rock shows featuring Jefferson Airplane and the Grateful Dead. While Sullivan had given up running the Fillmore Auditorium, he was still in the music business when he was found dead in the dirt on Fifth and Bluxome Streets on August 2, 1966. He had just promoted a James Brown concert in Los Angeles the day before, and Fannie said that he had a valise containing $6,000 to $7,000 in receipts from the show with him when he was killed. The valise was found empty in the trunk of his car, but it looked like it had been rifled through. Police told the *Chronicle* that Sullivan may have shot himself, but the coroner's report did not confirm this theory.

While the murder of semi-employed gardener August Norry on San Bruno Mountain in Daly City in 1959 generated weeks of headlines until it was solved, the mysterious death of one of the city's most successful Black businessmen was a one-and-done affair for the *Chronicle* and *Examiner*. They reported Sullivan's death the day it happened and never mentioned it again, except in Bill Graham career retrospectives. As for police records, they have been "purged or destroyed in conformance with the SFPD Record Destruction Schedule." The scope of the San Francisco Police Department's investigation into the likely murder of Charles Sullivan will forever remain unknown.

## FREE HUEY

West Oakland was being squeezed by urban renewal just like the Fillmore District across the Bay. In the 1940s and '50s, Seventh Street was jumping with blues clubs and pool halls. But in 1960, 12 city blocks of Victorian homes and nightclubs were leveled for a massive postal facility while the new Nimitz Freeway cut the neighborhood off from the city's downtown. West Oakland's remaining

Black residents were blamed for the resulting urban blight despite having nothing to do with the decisions that made it that way.

As a response to the resulting displacement in West Oakland and the increased police presence that went along with it, Merritt College students Huey P. Newton and Bobby Seale founded the Black Panther Party for Self-Defense on October 15, 1966. Whenever Black people were pulled over by Oakland's mostly white cops, the Panthers were there with their rifles in plain sight, using the Second Amendment to prevent police brutality. While California's conservatives were traditionally big supporters of the constitutional right to bear arms, the Panthers had even Governor Ronald Reagan embracing gun control through the Mulford Act, a state bill that banned the open carry of firearms.

In May 1967, Newton masterminded the storming of the State Assembly in Sacramento by Panthers armed with shotguns and rifles to protest the bill. Reagan was holding a press conference on the capitol steps when the Panthers approached. The reporters ran to the Panthers while Reagan ducked for cover. The protest for African Americans' right to bear arms scared the bejesus out of suburban whites, but transformed the Black Panthers from a hyperlocal organization into a national, and later international, movement.

On October 28, 1967, Newton and Panthers fundraiser Gene McKinney went out on an early morning food run. At 4:51 a.m., Officer John Frey spotted them in a beige VW Bug driving down Seventh Street past the rows of unfinished columns topped with tangles of rebar that would later become the West Oakland BART tracks. After finding out that the VW was a known Panther vehicle, Frey pulled over Newton and McKinney on the corner of Seventh and Willow using unpaid parking tickets as an excuse.

Officer Herbert C. Heanes rolled up on the scene shortly after Frey had radioed for backup. The officers told Newton to get out of the Bug. Newton emerged carrying the dog-eared law book he read from to school cops and authority figures. The cops marched Newton to the back of Heanes's patrol car. Newton and Frey scuffled on the trunk of Heanes's car. A gun went off. Heanes was hit in the right forearm. Heanes fired back, hitting Newton in the gut. As the smoke cleared, Newton fled the scene with McKinney. Heanes was shot three times and survived. Frey was shot five times and died. Frey, 23, had been on the force for a little over a year and had a three-year-old daughter.

A bloody Newton staggered into the emergency room at Kaiser Hospital in Oakland at 5:30 a.m. that Saturday morning.

"Are you a Kaiser?" emergency room nurse Corrine Leonard said, asking for Newton's proof of insurance.

"Yes, yes," Newton replied, stomping his feet. "Get a doctor. Can't you see I'm bleeding?"

"I see this, but you're not in any acute distress," Leonard said as Newton continued to bleed. Newton took off his coat and shirt and threw it on the desk to show her his wound.

"Can't you see all this blood?" he said.

"Well, you'll have to sign our admission sheet before you can be seen by a doctor," Leonard replied.

Newton refused, called Leonard a "white bitch," and said, "I'm going to die anyway, and you're going to watch me die!"

Just as Newton was finally allowed to get onto a gurney to be wheeled out of the waiting room to see a doctor, Oakland police showed up and handcuffed him to it. Leonard had called the police before she called for a doctor.

"No one acutely injured can talk like that," Leonard said. When a doctor examined Newton 25 minutes later, it was found that a bullet had pierced his small intestine in four places. He was transferred to Oakland's Highland Hospital and then to jail.

Newton claimed he blacked out from the gut shot and didn't remember what happened. He later speculated that the cops had shot each other since all of the bullets recovered from Frey, Heanes, and Newton came from police-issued revolvers.

Henry Grier had been driving his AC Transit bus past Seventh and Willow just as shots were fired. He told police he saw a "very short . . . sort of pee-wee type fellow" pull a gun out of his shirt. Frey grabbed the pee-wee by the arm and the gun went off. Grier later identified the five-foot-ten, 165-pound Newton as the shooter. He was the only witness who placed a gun in Newton's hand. Because of the size discrepancy, his testimony did not hold up in court.

Incarcerated, Huey Newton became a living martyr. His arrest inspired "Free Huey" buttons, banners, and funk jams. The image of him sitting in a wicker chair—a rifle in one hand and a spear in the other—became the Panthers' most powerful recruitment tool. A Free Huey rally on Newton's 26th birthday on February 17, 1968, drew 6,000 people to the Oakland Arena where Black Power firebrand H. Rap Brown proclaimed, "The only thing that is going to free Huey Newton is gun powder."

Newton's liberation was more mundane, however. In September 1968, he was convicted of voluntary manslaughter, a compromise verdict that was reversed on appeal in May 1970. After two trials resulted in hung juries, Alameda County district attorney Lowell Jensen gave up on the Sisyphean task of trying Newton, and the charges were dismissed. Huey was finally free, but he made for a better symbol than a leader.

After three years in jail, Newton had become a Jekyll and Hyde figure. He could still be the thoughtful revolutionary who authored books and met with Chinese communist leader Chou En-lai a year before Nixon did. But then there was the megalomaniac who freebased cocaine in a penthouse apartment high above the people he once sought to liberate. At a time when the FBI's counterintelligence operation, or COINTELPRO, worked to sow dissent among the party's ranks, Newton purged Panther members and split the party into two hostile factions. As the 1970s went on, Newton's Panthers became more of an organized crime outfit than a band of activists. He ran extortion rackets, sold drugs, pistol-whipped a tailor, shot a prostitute, and reportedly attacked his old friend and Panthers cofounder Bobby Seale with a bullwhip over a movie deal.

Blair Stapp (photographer)

Huey P. Newton, co-founder and minister of defense for the Black Panther Party, holds a rifle in one hand and a spear in the other in the famous photo that became a widely-circulated poster in the 1960s and '70s.

Years after the Panthers disbanded, Newton was shot three times in the head in a drug dispute on August 22, 1989. His bloody body was found near a bus stop on the 1400 block of Ninth Street, in the same part of West Oakland where the Black Panthers were born and just blocks away from where Officer Frey was shot in 1967. The neighborhood hasn't changed all that much since 1989—or 1967—but gentrification is just around the corner.

## CHAPTER 11

# WHEN THE GARDEN FLOWERS, BABY, ARE DEAD

### THE HAND IS MAN'S HISTORY

Paul McCartney visited the Haight in May 1967 to spin a copy of the unreleased *Sgt. Pepper's Lonely Hearts Club Band* album for the members of Jefferson Airplane. The Summer of Love hadn't quite begun, and the mood was still optimistic. Months later, George Harrison and his wife, Pattie Boyd, walked along Haight Street to Hippie Hill in Golden Gate Park on August 7, 1967. Asked what he thought of the scene, the quiet Beatle said, "If it's all like this, then it's really too much." And it was. The Summer of Love was giving way to fall—the dying season.

Just four days earlier on Thursday, August 3, 1967, most of the body of John Kent Carter, 25, had been found in his Parnassus Heights apartment. Carter was an out-of-work flutist who went by the name of Shob and dealt acid on the side. He was stabbed in the chest and his arm was chopped off just above the elbow. A trail of blood showed where Shob had been dragged from the living room to the bedroom of what the *Chronicle* called "the brightly decorated pad" covered in "the

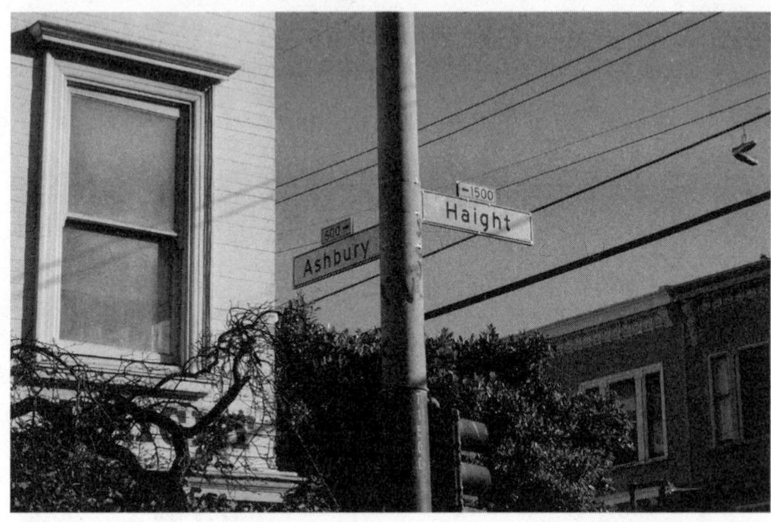


Bob Calhoun

The now iconic sign at the corner of Haight and Ashbury Streets, the epicenter of the Summer of Love in 1967. The spirit of those years is now kept alive by gift shops selling Beatles merchandise and clusters of crusty-punk squatters on the sidewalks.

colorful swirls and sun-bursts of psychedelic art." Carter's battered VW van, a handgun, $3,000 that he and his girlfriend had been saving for a trip to Europe, and his arm had all gone missing.

Two days later, patrolman Charles Baker arrested Eric Dahlstrom at 11 p.m. on a Saturday night for speeding through sleepy Sebastopol in Carter's stolen van. In the van, police found Carter's loaded 9 mm P38 semiautomatic, $2,657.53 in cash, a whole mess of pills, and the arm.

"He had this arm rolled up in leather chamois-like material," Baker, now retired and still living in Sebastopol, said. "There were several shammies it was rolled up in. I'd unroll one and find another shammy. I went through that about three times, and out popped the arm."

"It was sort of a shock, you know, to see that kind of thing," Baker added.

Dahlstrom, looking dirty and harried in newspaper photographs, was a 26-year-old daredevil motorcycle racer from Sebastopol. He had taken the top prize in the Cotati Motorcycle Grand Prix in May 1967, but things were already going wrong for him. Dahlstrom told reporters that he had been on an 18-month (!) LSD binge when he killed Carter over some bad acid.

"He was convulsing as he went down," Dahlstrom told Mary Carter of the *Examiner* during a jailhouse interview. "That's why I stabbed him some more—maybe a little too much. I hadn't had life in my hands before like that."

Dahlstrom couldn't explain why he chopped off Carter's arm with a butcher's knife, however. "The hand is a man's history," Dahlstrom said. "I'm a Cancer. I'm not a hard person normally."

The same day that Carter's body was found, William E. Thomas took a ride up to Sausalito with between $35,000 and $55,000 in cash to buy the makings of a massive batch of LSD. Thomas, a 26-year-old African American man from the Mission, was better known around the scene as Superspade, a modified racial slur that he reclaimed by wearing an oversized button that read "Superspade, faster than a speeding mind." Thomas reportedly had plans to buy into a restaurant in Marin and hoped this drug deal would be his last. It was, but not in the way that he had planned. His body was found wrapped in a sleeping bag and dangling off a 300-foot cliff near Point Reyes on Sunday, August 6, 1967. He had been shot through the back of his head and stabbed in the heart. Only $15 remained of the wad he'd brought with him to make his score.

"Superspade was the first guy I saw who had a real bona fide Afro," attorney Patrick Hallinan recalled. "He was just a very pleasant guy. There was nothing aggressive or nasty about him at all."

Hallinan, a liberal rabble-rousing attorney from a family of them, was Thomas's lawyer after the dealer had been rounded up in a pot raid with a Hillsborough debutante and some other Peninsula rich kids in December 1966. The bust and Thomas's "super-smart" fashion sense made him a local celebrity with regular mentions in Herb Caen's *Chronicle* column, and a prominent but posthumous role in *You Are What You Eat* (1968), an incoherent half-documentary, half–music video with appearances by Tiny Tim and Timothy Leary.

Even though police had Dahlstrom in custody for the Carter murder, rumors flew around the Haight that the Mafia, or "the Eastern crime syndicate," was moving in. The ensuing panic even had hippies buying guns, but police were dismissive of this angle. Instead homicide detectives searched for the two men in a tan car whom Thomas was last seen with, "a bearded New York Negro hippie known only as 'Joe'" and "the Sausalito hoodlum," but neither lead panned out.

One person not mentioned in connection to the Thomas murder who was in the Haight during the Summer of Love and definitely capable of this kind of mayhem was Charles Manson. According to Karina Longworth's epic "Charles Manson's Hollywood" series in her *You Must Remember This* podcast, Manson's followers claim credit for as many as 35 murders. While it's safe to call bullshit on most of this, the Thomas murder bears similarities to the attempted murder of Bernard "Lotsapoppa" Crowe and the torture and killing of Gary Hinman. These precursors to the more infamous 1969 Tate–LaBianca murders were both botched shakedowns of drug dealers by Manson that ended in extreme violence.

When he was still living on Cole Street in the Haight, Manson often took long drives in his VW bus up to Mendocino on a route that went past the craggy cliff where Thomas was dumped. "There is nothing like the drive up Highway One along the north coast of California," Manson told Nuel Emmons in *Manson in His Own Words* (1986). But Manson's recollections of San Francisco show he hadn't yet embraced violence. Nearly driving into a knifing on Lyon Street and later seeing a beat cop flee from a shooting in the Haight unnerved him.

"Fuck, if everything was getting so bad that even the cops didn't want to hang around long enough to do their jobs, Haight-Ashbury was no place for me and my girls," he explained. He soon hightailed it to Topanga Canyon in Los Angeles County, and the rest is history.

With the vibrations "at an evil confluence" in October 1967, a group of the original hippies staged a mock funeral procession for the "Death of the Hippie." They carried a large coffin down Haight Street before burning it in Golden Gate Park. It was reported that the coffin was filled with hair shorn from several beards and two kilograms of weed. The Summer of Love was over, and the murder of the man who called himself Superspade went unsolved.

"Who would've done that? That's beyond me," Hallinan mused. "I think you still have a mystery on your hands."

Mug shot in the public domain; source: Wikipedia

left: Charles Manson, a little less than a year after he felt the Haight-Ashbury was getting too violent and fled San Francisco for Los Angeles.

below: The flat near the corner of Cole and Haight Streets where Charles Manson became just another hippie guru in a neighborhood crawling with them during the Summer of Love.

Bob Calhoun

## STOP! STOP! I'M ALREADY DEAD

Housekeeper Winnifred Chapman showed up a little late for her Saturday shift at 10050 Cielo Drive on August 9, 1969. What she found at the estate just north of Beverly Hills sent her running to the house next door.

"There's bodies and blood all over the place!" Chapman screamed. The neighbor called the police. After half a dozen police cars arrived on the scene, Chapman was taken to UCLA Medical Center to be treated for shock.

Actress Sharon Tate, whom the massacre would be forever named for, was found dead near her former lover and hair salon entrepreneur Jay Sebring. Tate was eight months pregnant. Somebody had stabbed her 16 times anyway. Her husband, film director and future fugitive from a rape conviction, Roman Polanski, was in London at the time of the killings.

On the well-trimmed front lawn, the bloody body of 25-year-old San Franciscan coffee heiress Abigail Folger was slumped under a fir tree just yards away from the corpse of her boyfriend, Wojciech "Voitek" Frykowski. Folger and Frykowski had nearly 80 knife wounds between them.

Abigail Folger, known as Gibby to her friends, was the great-granddaughter of J.A. Folger, who had arrived in San Francisco in 1850 to pan for gold but made his fortune in coffee instead. He founded the Folgers Coffee Company in 1860, and the name is still synonymous with the red cans of stale java that your grandmother probably buys in bulk at FoodMaxx. Abigail's father, Peter Folger, sold the company to Procter & Gamble in 1963 but still ran it from the building at 101 Howard Street that his father, James Folger Jr., had built in 1904. The Folger Coffee Company Building survived major earthquakes in 1906 and 1989 because the building's supports had been driven 40 feet into the SOMA muck with a steam-powered pile driver. The University of San Francisco purchased the building for $37 million in 2011.

Abigail attended her debutante cotillion at the Sheraton Palace Hotel on December 27, 1961. The *Chronicle* described it as a "fantasy-like blaze of pinks and reds." Folger soon left these rich-girl trappings behind but hung onto the trust fund. Inheriting a sense of noblesse oblige, she volunteered at the Haight Street Free Clinic with her mother, Ines Mejia Folger, who helped raise money for the clinic. Abigail then moved to New York where she worked at the Gotham Book Mart and met Frykowski, a Polish expat who coasted on his charms and his friendship with Polanski.

By 1969, Abigail was splitting her time between the Folger mansion in Woodside and Los Angeles, but things were a bit more hectic for her down south. Folger volunteered for Tom Bradley's campaign to become the first African American mayor of Los Angeles. Bradley's opponent, Sam Yorty, embarked on what Harold Meyerson of *LA Weekly* described as "the most vile and demagogic campaign in the history of modern L.A." Yorty paid young Black men to drive around L.A.'s whiter suburbs in a Cadillac convertible plastered with Black Panthers and Bradley for Mayor stickers. The idea that Bradley, a former police chief, was connected to Black Power radicals was absurd, but it didn't matter. Yorty still won.

Folger also volunteered in some of L.A.'s poorest neighborhoods for the county welfare department, but the work left her spent. "A lot of social workers go home at night, take a bath, and wash their day off," she said. "I can't. The suffering gets under your skin."

Folger and Frykowski moved into 10050 Cielo Drive in April 1969 to keep Sharon Tate company while Polanski was in London putting together movie deals and cheating on his wife. Tate got along fine with Folger, but Frykowski drove her nuts. He even ran over Tate's Yorkshire terrier in July.

"I should have thrown him out when he ran over Sharon's dog," Polanski said when he returned to the house after the murders.

A month after Frykowski squashed the pooch, Charles Manson, a failed folk singer and inept pimp who smelled like hot garbage, sent Tex Watson, Susan Atkins, Linda Kasabian, and Patricia Krenwinkel to the house on Cielo Drive with orders to slaughter everyone there. If Manson had gone on the raid himself, he may have recognized Folger from his days as a frequent patient at the Haight Street Free Clinic.

"I never questioned what Charlie said, I just did it," Susan Atkins recalled.

During the night of carnage, Folger overpowered Krenwinkel and made it outside where Krenwinkel and Watson stabbed her 28 times. At least seven of these wounds were classified as fatal.

"Stop! Stop!" Folger begged after several blows. "I'm already dead."

Although Folger was often described in the press as "being in the wrong place at the wrong time," other news sources speculated that a séance she had attended with Mia Farrow, star of Polanski's Satan worship blockbuster *Rosemary's Baby* (1968), could have brought on the ritualistic slayings. Revelations of Frykowski's drug dealing, the traces of MDA found in his and Folger's systems, and dirty movies Polanski had made with Tate also inspired new rounds of victim blaming by the media. Manson and his followers were arrested for the crimes four months later; the mélange of motives for the slaughter on Cielo Drive would only ever make sense to them. Manson chose the site to send a message to the home's previous occupant, record producer Terry Melcher, for not giving him a record deal.

Abigail Folger's funeral was held at Our Lady of the Wayside Catholic church in Portola Valley on August 13, 1969. She is interred in the main mausoleum at Holy Cross Cemetery in Colma.

## ALTAMONT

A melee broke out on December 6, 1969, in front of the hastily constructed stage at the Altamont Speedway as the Rolling Stones played "Sympathy for the Devil." Several Hells Angels jumped into the crowd. Sawed-off pool cues came down on skulls, and boots broke bones. Somewhere in all the dust and tangled humanity was the glint of a gun followed by the flash of a blade. Mick Jagger, in an orange and black satin blouse, resembled a frightened harlequin as he struggled to calm a crowd of 300,000 people, many of them hard-tripping on acid, mescaline, and Lord knows what else.

"Everybody be cool now," he said after getting Keith Richards to stop riffing on a slightly out-of-tune guitar. "People! Who's fighting and what for?" he pleaded.

Unknown to the Stones at the time, Meredith Hunter, an 18-year-old African American from Berkeley, was stabbed and beaten to death right in front of the stage during that break in the music.

Albert and David Maysles's acclaimed documentary *Gimme Shelter* (1970) appears to show the violence of the Altamont concert unflinchingly. In the film, Jagger and Charlie Watts stare sadly at a Moviola showing footage of Hunter jerking a revolver from his green suit right before a Hells Angel stabs him in the neck. Even with the knifing, however, veteran *Chronicle* rock critic Joel Selvin doesn't think *Gimme Shelter* goes far enough.

"The story is much more grim, much more sordid, much more violent," Selvin said during a phone interview. "The movie is tampered the most, I suspect, by the fact that the Rolling Stones themselves were partners in the movie," Selvin explained. "I'm sure the filmmakers felt those eyes over their shoulders."

Over 20 years spent researching the Altamont fiasco for his book, *Altamont: The Rolling Stones, the Hells Angels, and the Inside Story of Rock's Darkest Day* (2016), brought Selvin to some harsh conclusions. "The blame is much more directly on the Rolling Stones and the decisions they made than the movie would allow," Selvin said.

The Stones' free concert in the San Francisco Bay Area, then touted as "Woodstock West," was originally planned for Golden Gate Park. After that fell through, it was booked at Sears Point Raceway (now the Sonoma Raceway). The deal got held up when Filmways, the Sonoma-based movie company that owned the speedway, found out that the free show at its track was going to provide the third act of a concert movie the Stones were making. Filmways attempted to negotiate exclusive distribution rights for the movie or $100,000 to walk away from it. Filmways executives "did not believe the Stones when they said, 'This movie's profits are going to charity,'" according to Selvin. "The Stones utterly refused to negotiate with them."

With barely 24 hours before showtime and VW vanloads of hippies streaming into Northern California from as far away as New York, the concert was moved to the Altamont Raceway in between the cow towns of Tracy and Livermore. Maximizing the potential for future chaos, the Hells Angels were promised $500 worth of beer to work security, and $500 bought a lot of Hamm's in 1969.

With the concert held in Altamont, no particular Hells Angels chapter held jurisdiction over it, so the place became what Selvin described as "a complete mob scene of Hells Angels from all over the area." Many of the bikers causing problems in front of the stage were prospects from the newly formed San Jose chapter. But violence was contagious at Altamont that day, and Hells Angels weren't the only ones causing it.

"People were shoving and pushing a lot," Karen Blackstock recalled. Blackstock lived in Berkeley at the time and got to Altamont early that day. She had dropped acid with Micky Dolenz of the Monkees at Monterey Pop in 1967, and was expecting this same kind of "fabulous" concert. She found a "nightmare of horribleness" instead.

"The fact that they had it way over in the East Bay, there was a whole rougher crowd of people that came to that than if it had been over in San Francisco," she said.

Mick Jagger was punched right after he got off the helicopter. Marty Balin of Jefferson Airplane was knocked out onstage during his band's set. Rex Jackson, the Grateful Dead's road crew chief, was assaulted moments later. Denise Jewkes of the band Ace of Cups—the one all-woman band to emerge from the Haight Street scene in the 1960s—was hit in the head with a full bottle of beer and needed cranial surgery, without anesthesia since she was pregnant at the time.

"If Jesus had been there, he would have been crucified," a "forlorn" Mick Jagger later told the Associated Press.

Meredith Hunter wasn't the only one to die at Altamont that day. Mark Feiger and Richard Savlov, two 22-year-olds from Berkeley, were crushed to death in their sleeping bags when a Plymouth plowed into their campfire. Another young man drowned in an irrigation ditch.

While Altamont is often talked about as "the end of the '60s," Selvin is quick to point out that "it did take place in December 1969."

"I don't think Altamont was the end of anything," he mused. "I don't think it was the end of the counterculture. It wasn't even the end of free concerts in meadows."

## CHAPTER 12

# ZODIAC ADJACENT

### THE FIRST

David Faraday and Betty Lou Jensen went to different Vallejo high schools. They'd only known each other for two weeks when they went on their first date on Friday, December 20, 1968. Wearing a purple dress with a Christmas bell brooch pinned to its white collar, Betty took David home to meet her folks at 8 p.m. The pair then stopped by a friend's house and went to a holiday concert at Betty's school, Hogan High. After the concert, David drove his two-tone Rambler station wagon to a secluded spot near a pumping station on Lake Herman Road, a rural shortcut between suburban Vallejo and Benicia that was known as a local lovers' lane. They were both supposed to be home by 11 p.m. They never made it.

Stella Medeiros left her ranch on Lake Herman Road at 11:10 p.m. to pick up her 13-year-old son at a movie theater in Benicia. Four or five minutes later, her headlights shone on two bodies lying in the dirt outside of Faraday's Rambler. Medeiros floored it to

Benicia where she flashed her lights and honked her horn at the first police car she saw.

Benicia police detective and future chief Pierre Bidou had pulled into the police department parking lot after confiscating a pound and a half of weed when he heard the call reporting a possible shooting on Lake Herman Road. Bidou had just driven along there but hadn't seen anything. When he returned to the spot, he found Faraday lying outside of the passenger door of the station wagon.

"It appeared that he had a gunshot wound above the left ear," Bidou recalled in the 2007 documentary *This Is the Zodiac Speaking*. Faraday was still breathing—"You could actually see his breath," Bidou said—but Faraday died before he got to Vallejo General Hospital.

Betty's lifeless body was sprawled 28 feet from the rear of the Rambler. Her face and head were covered with blood. She had been shot five times in the back "in close pattern on the right side," and twice from the front. One bullet passed straight through her body and was discovered when the coroner removed her clothes. Small caliber Winchester Super-X shell casings littered the ground around the car and victims. One round had been shot through the rear of the station wagon. Investigators speculated that the killer may have fired it as a warning shot to get David and Betty out of the car before murdering them.

"I don't think that that was ever decided," Bidou said.

Benicia police were the first on the scene, but the murder site was in the Solano County Sheriff Department's jurisdiction. Deputy Russell T. Butterbach arrived at the scene as a patrolman. He was promoted to investigator the next morning and assigned to assist Detective Sergeant Les Lunblad with the double homicide case.

"We never had too many murders," Butterbach said. "We solved them all, but there was just a few."

"It wasn't handled as you would handle it today," Bidou said.

Lunblad and Butterbach followed what few leads they had, as if this was a normal case when it was anything but. Ricky, Betty's jealous ex-boyfriend, was the main suspect but he had been home watching a Bob Hope movie with several members of his extended family on the night of the double homicide. A pair of creepy yokels with guns spotted by the pump station around the time of the killings explained they were hunting racoons. People did that back then. Their guns did not match the murder weapon. A pair of white men in a blue sedan had chased a teen couple in a sports car down Lake Herman Road about 90 minutes before the shooting. Investigators could never ID the blue sedan or a white Impala seen by the racoon hunters earlier that night.

The sheriff's investigators questioned Betty's and David's friends and classmates. Sharon Henslin Stutsman had been best friends with Betty since the fourth grade and the two shared a locker at Hogan High. She described being questioned by the police as "the most terrifying thing I have ever been through."

"There were no serial killers back then," Stutsman said. "All the detectives thought it had to be because of drugs; they refused to hear anything else."

But David and Betty were hardly part of the 1960s counterculture. David was an Eagle Scout and a member of his high school wrestling team. Betty was an honor student and a grand royal guide of the Pythian Sunshine Girls, a junior order of the Pythian Sisters service club that has been around since 1888.

David's funeral was held just two days before Christmas. His fellow Eagle Scouts, dressed in dark uniforms with white sashes, served as the pallbearers. They looked so very young as they loaded his casket onto the hearse while even more uniformed scouts gave a solemn salute. Services were held for Betty later that same day.

After working 20-hour shifts over the holidays, Lundblad realized that Betty and David were slaughtered by "a murderous maniac who was not acquainted with either of the victims." This theory was confirmed when another teenaged couple was shot in the parking lot of Blue Rock Springs Park on the outskirts of Vallejo on July

5, 1969. The killer called the Vallejo Police Department 45 minutes after the attack. "I also killed those kids last year," he said in a monotone, according to dispatcher Nancy Slover who took the call.

Letters containing details of the murders that only the killer could know arrived at the *Chronicle*, *Examiner*, and the *Vallejo Times-Herald* by the end of July. Each letter contained a piece of a cipher that the killer demanded each paper print on its front page or else he would go on a "kill rampage." The *Chronicle* ran the cipher but held it back to page four. The *Examiner* didn't run it all, but the correspondence continued.

"This is Zodiac speaking," the killer wrote at the beginning of a letter to the *Examiner* received on August 4, 1969. Detectives and reporters had no idea who he was, but now they knew what to call him.

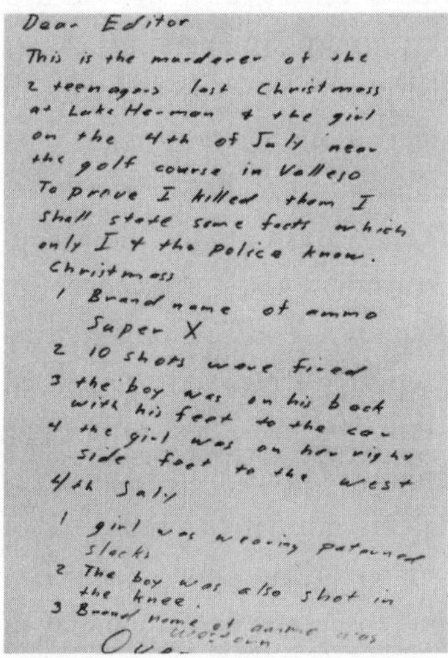

Dear Editor

This is the murderer of the 2 teenagers last Christmass at Lake Herman & the girl on the 4th of July near the golf course in Vallejo To prove I killed them I shall state some facts which only I & the police know.

Christmass

1 Brand name of ammo Super X

2 10 shots were fired

3 the boy was on his back with his feet to the car

4 the girl was on her right side feet to the west

4th July

1 girl was wearing patterned slacks

2 The boy was also shot in the knee.

3 Brand name of ammo was Western

Over

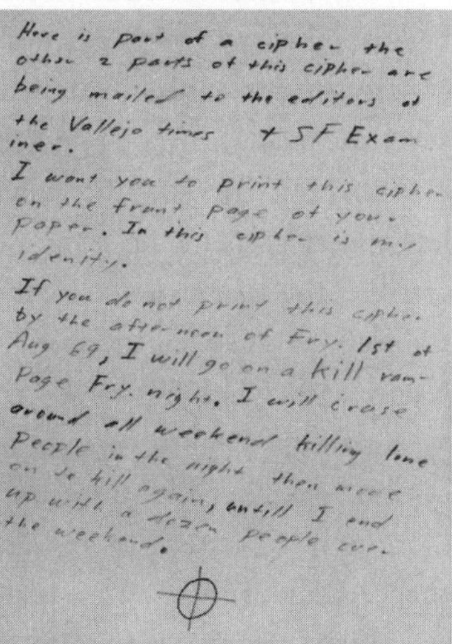

Here is part of a cipher the other 2 parts of this cipher are being mailed to the editors of the Vallejo times & SF Examiner.

I want you to print this cipher on the front page of your paper. In this cipher is my identity.

If you do not print this cipher by the afternoon of Fry. 1st of Aug 69, I will go on a kill ram-Page Fry. night. I will cruse around all weekend killing lone people in the night then move on to kill again, untill I end up with a dozen people over the weekend.

The Zodiac's July 31, 1969, letter to the *San Francisco Chronicle* where he takes credit for gunning down teenagers David Faraday and Betty Lou Jensen five days before Christmas in 1968. He signs it with his crosshairs symbol but has yet to take the name Zodiac.

## SATAN SAVES ZODIAC

Robert Salem designed fashionable lamps in his converted firehouse at 745 Stevenson Street near San Francisco's Civic Center. His hurricane-style light fixtures were sold in specialty shops throughout the world, and a few of his designs were even displayed in museums as high art. Salem had friends who worked at the nearby Franciscan Hotel, and he told them they could stop by his place anytime. The hotel workers grew worried when they hadn't seen the middle-aged artist in several days, so they went to Salem's live-work space on Sunday, April 19, 1970, to make sure he was okay. They noticed a rank odor coming from his apartment, so they broke down the door. Trails of dried blood were throughout what the *Chronicle* described as "an expensively-decorated hippie-style pad" with tatami mats on the floors and tree branches climbing up the walls.

They found Salem's mutilated body on one of mats. He had been stabbed several times with a very sharp knife, and his throat cut from ear to ear in a botched attempt at decapitation. Unable to sever the head from the body, the killer cut off Salem's ear and took it with him. Investigators never found the ear. Before the killer left the apartment, he took a shower to wash off the blood and cranked the heater up to 90°F to exacerbate the putrescence. On the wall, he scrawled the words "Satan saves Zodiac" in his victim's blood with what *Chronicle* crime reporter Paul Avery described as "a strange symbol resembling a crucified man" next to it. (The symbol was later identified as an ankh.) Homicide inspector Gus Coreris was hesitant to say that Salem's murder was the work of the "Zodiac Killer," who had been terrorizing the greater Bay Area since gunning down Betty Lou Jensen and David Faraday in Benicia on December 20, 1968.

"Probably the person we are after wanted us to think it was the Zodiac," Inspector Coreris said with a bit of caution.

It had been nearly six months since the Zodiac's last known murder. On October 11, 1969, the killer hailed Paul Stein's cab on

The San Francisco Police sketch of the Zodiac Killer, an image that has haunted Northern California for over 50 years.

the corner of Mason and Geary Streets. He rode it to Washington and Cherry Streets in Presidio Heights, where he shot Stein in the back of the head with a 9 mm automatic. Two days later, the Zodiac sent a bloody swatch of Stein's shirt to the *San Francisco Chronicle* to needle reporters and police. Zodiac was the grandfather of all trolls.

On April 20, 1970, the same day that the *Chronicle* ran its first story on the Salem murder, the Zodiac Killer dropped a letter to the paper into a corner mailbox in San Francisco. This was his first letter since he sent a note with yet another cipher to attorney Melvin Belli on December 20, 1969. "I have killed ten people to date," Zodiac boasted in the new letter. Only five of his victims had been confirmed (then and now). The serial killer didn't take credit for the Salem murder or even mention it, but he dangled the possibility that he could be responsible. Zodiac closed the letter with a sinister postscript: a hand-drawn diagram of a bomb.

"I hope you have fun trying to fygure [sic] out who I killed," he taunts. "Zodiac = 10. SFPD = 0."

By July 1970, SFPD homicide inspectors weren't 100 percent sure if the April 1970 murder of Robert Salem was the work of the Zodiac Killer or a twisted copycat. However, the arrests of two hippie-looking Satan cultists for a hit-and-run provided a break in the Salem murder case and revealed an even more heinous crime.

The hippies plowed the yellow Opel sportscar they'd stolen into a truck off Highway One just outside Big Sur on Monday, July 13, 1970. The Detroit tourist who was driving the truck wanted to get the hippies' insurance info. But they took off into the woods on foot. They didn't get far before highway patrolman Randy Newton caught up with Stanley Dean Baker, 22, and Harry Allen Stroup, 20, both from Wyoming. After being arrested, Baker was found with a recipe for LSD, a copy of Anton LaVey's *Satanic Bible*, and a human finger bone that had been gnawed on.

"I have a problem," Baker confessed to Newton. "I'm a cannibal." Baker went on to tell the officer that he had been electrocuted when he was 17. "I haven't been the same since," Baker explained.

The finger bone belonged to James Michael Schlosser, a 22-year-old social worker from Roundup, Montana, who'd picked up the pair while they were hitchhiking near Yellowstone Park. Baker repaid Schlosser's kindness by shooting him in the head while they camped on the banks of the Yellowstone River, but that was only the beginning. Baker dismembered Schlosser with a foot-long knife, and then cut out his heart and ate it right there in God's country. Grand theft auto was the least of Baker's crimes. Once in custody, Baker copped to killing and eating Schlosser and to murdering Robert Salem in San Francisco three months earlier. Baker told interrogators that that murder was part of a satanic ritual.

Baker claimed that he had acted alone when killing Schlosser, but Stroup's jury wasn't convinced that one man could accomplish the butchery of the 220-pound victim on his own. Stroup was convicted of manslaughter and served just two years for the crime.

When Baker testified during Stroup's trial, he said he was Jesus Christ and that he had killed Jimi Hendrix through a long-range hex. He also said that he killed and ate Schlosser in what the *Montana Standard* paraphrased as "an LSD-heightened rage at 'the establishment.'" When asked about the murder of Robert Salem, Baker pleaded the fifth. Baker also wouldn't say if he had cooked and eaten Salem's missing ear.

Baker served only 16 years of his life sentence and was released in 1986, eventually becoming a top salesman at a Minnesota sporting goods store until the tabloid TV show *A Current Affair* exposed him for his cannibal past. He died from liver cancer in Bemidji, Minnesota, in 1994.

Harry Stroup was convicted of selling meth in April 2007. When he was released again in July 2015, he had served more time for dealing drugs than for being an accomplice to murder and cannibalism. According to a July 3, 2015, *USA Today* article by James Schlosser's childhood friend Claire Baiz, Baker was never charged with the murder of Robert Salem, leaving open the possibility that the Zodiac Killer was responsible after all—at least officially.

## THE SANTA ROSA HITCHHIKER MURDERS

John Bly and Scott Bunting, both 17, were out for a Sunday afternoon motorcycle ride through a hilly stretch of road in Santa Rosa on March 6, 1972. They stopped to take a break in a spot overlooking a creek. One of them spotted what he thought was a mannequin in the creek bed below. When the boys realized they were actually looking at the naked dead body of a young woman, they hightailed it to the sheriff's office.

The murdered woman was Kim Wendy Allen, a 19-year-old Santa Rosa Junior College student. Sonoma County coroner Andrew Johansen determined that Allen died from asphyxiation by being slowly strangled by a cord or rope around her neck. Allen had been killed and dumped down the embankment about 24 hours before Bly and Bunting found her. Johansen also said there was evidence that Allen had been raped.

Allen was the first victim discovered in what's now known as the Santa Rosa Hitchhiker Murders, but she wasn't the first victim. Yvonne Weber, 13, and Maureen Sterling, 12, were the first girls to disappear. One of the girls' mothers dropped them off at the

Redwood Empire Ice Arena at 7:30 p.m. on February 4, 1972. When the mom returned to pick them up at 11 p.m., the girls were gone. The remains of Weber and Sterling weren't found until December 26, 1972. They weren't identified for another month.

From 1972 to 1979, the bodies of eight young girls were found dumped in deep embankments and creek beds in rural areas surrounding Santa Rosa. Jeanette Kamahele, 20, another Santa Rosa Junior College student, and Lori Lee Kursa, 13, a habitual runaway, both went missing in 1972. Carolyn Davis, 15, and Terese Walsh, 13, were found in 1973. A Jane Doe was found on July 2, 1979, around 100 yards from where Lori Kursa's remains were discovered. Most had been raped, and all had been found nude, except in the case of Jeanette Kamahele whose body was never found.

In 1975, with little progress in the investigation, Sonoma County sheriff Don Striepeke threw a Hail Mary pass and issued a report linking the Santa Rosa murders to the Zodiac Killer. In the Zodiac's last letter from January 29, 1974, the serial killer/gadfly took credit for 37 murders; only five victims had been attributed to him by authorities. Striepeke theorized that Zodiac was behind the Santa Rosa murders and several other similar unsolved killings throughout the western United States. During a press conference, Striepeke told reporters that they were dealing with a killer who "makes Juan Corona look like a piker."

Detective Sergeant Erwin "Butch" Carstedt, the investigator who developed this serial murder theory, also believed that the killer was leaving a trail of victims that formed a massive letter Z through California, Washington, New Mexico, Utah, and Colorado. Carstedt also said a symbol from "ancient English witchcraft" was formed from twigs and rocks near one of the body dump sites.

Somewhat coincidentally, Zodiac suspect Arthur Leigh Allen lived in a trailer in Santa Rosa close to where the bodies were found when he was studying biological sciences at Sonoma State from 1970 to '74. Allen had lost his teaching job due to accusations of child molestation, but he was later cleared as a Zodiac suspect through

DNA tests of confirmed Zodiac letters. Allen was arrested by the Sonoma County sheriffs for molesting a young boy on September 27, 1974. He served time at Atascadero State Hospital until August 1977.

Ted Bundy was also a suspect in the Santa Rosa Hitchhiker Murders, but he was ruled out on the basis of detailed credit card records showing he was in Washington State at the time of some of the disappearances. Bundy was responsible for some of the murders that formed Carstedt's massive Z, adding another bitter irony to this frustrating case.

With attempts to link the Santa Rosa Hitchhiker Murders to more notorious serial killers turning up fruitless, we are left with the more terrifying reality that there are even more people capable of such extreme violence.

## CHAPTER 13

# THE MURDER CAPITAL OF THE WORLD

### BROUGHT TO YOU BY THE PEOPLE OF THE FREE UNIVERSE

Sheriff's deputies were the first to arrive on Monday, October 20, 1970, at the scene of the fire at 999 Rodeo Gulch Road, a $300,000 flagstone home (over $2 million today) in the hills of Soquel overlooking Santa Cruz and the ocean. Things were odd about this fire from the beginning. Deputies had to push away a red Rolls-Royce and a black Lincoln that were parked across the driveway so fire crews could get in. Fire Chief Ted Pound went through the backyard to try to tap the home's swimming pool as a source of water to fight the growing blaze. He found something far worse than the fire there.

The body of Dorothy Cadwallader, a 38-year-old medical secretary, was floating in the pool. Beneath her were the bodies of homeowners Victor and Virginia Ohta and their two sons, Taggart, 11, and Derrick, 12. It was a massacre. All five victims had been shot in the back of the head, and their hands were bound with "colorful scarves." Three of the victims' faces were also covered by scarves.

"It was pretty awful," Santa Cruz County district attorney Peter Chang said, recalling the sight of young Derek Ohta being pulled from the pool. "He looked exactly like my son. I thought I was dreaming."

Dr. Victor Masashi Ohta was a prominent eye surgeon who had moved to Santa Cruz after being discharged from the Air Force in 1960. Virginia Ohta sang in a local choir and modeled gowns for a Santa Cruz Woman's Club fashion show only months before her death. Their two daughters, Taura and Lark, were fortunately both away at school when the rest of the family was slaughtered.

Making a strange case even stranger, a bizarre typewritten note was found on the window of the Rolls-Royce. "today world war 3 will begin as brought to you by the people of the free universe," the missive began, all in lowercase. The writer of the note promised "the penelty [sic] of death" to "anything or anyone who dose [sic] not support natural life on this planet." The note closed with a listing of tarot cards in bold print:

KNIGHT OF WANDS
KNIGHT OF CUPS
KNIGHT OF PENTACLES
KNIGHT OF SWORDS

The *Santa Cruz Sentinel* speculated that this was the work of a mystical cult akin to the Manson Family. Three "barefoot strange-acting people" who were seen at a Monterey restaurant were being sought for questioning. The two men and a woman asked the diner owner if he "served food in nature's manner." The woman was "waving a red wand and appeared to be in a semi-dazed condition."

There was also a similar slaying in Saratoga that same night: a gas station attendant was found shot in the back of the head with his hands tied behind his back. The hippies and the Saratoga murder turned out to be just real-life red herrings, however.

Down the hill from the Ohtas' opulent home was a rusty trailer surrounded by rickety cabins and a dry creek bed filled with broken-down cars. Scruffy and bearded John Linley Frazier had been living in a cowshed by his mother's trailer for the past four months as he descended into the delusions of paranoid schizophrenia. He murdered the Ohtas and Cadwallader believing that he had been chosen by God to save the environment.

Frazier had convinced himself that he was the John referred to in the New Testament's Book of Revelations and incorporated the occult into what Stanford psychiatrist Donald Lunde described as "a confusing system of delusional beliefs." Frazier saw his wife's and mother's desperate attempts to get him to seek therapy as a conspiracy against him and his mission. A week before the murders, he told his wife that "some materialists might have to die" for him to fulfill his destiny. Neighbors who had seen Frazier patrolling the wooded hills around his and the Ohtas' home with a gun reported their suspicions to police. Frazier had also been seen driving the Ohtas' station wagon after the murders. Police found Frazier asleep in his cabin on Friday, October 23, 1970, and arrested him.

After Frazier's arrest, the Catalyst, described by the *Sentinel* as "a hangout for hippie types," received several bomb threats as part of an anti-hippie backlash. A note left at a dress shop next door to the nightclub read, "The only good hippie is a dead one." A picture of a noose was drawn on the note next to the words, "reserved for hippies." The Catalyst is still there today and so are the hippies.

A jury found Frazier to be legally sane, and he was tried and convicted of five counts of murder. During his trial, he appeared with the left side of his head, beard, and eyebrows shaved bald, making him look like a deranged Batman villain.

Victor Ohta's mother and his daughter Taura both killed themselves in the wake of the murders, leaving Lark Ohta as the family's only survivor. "I heard that the killer felt that my parents were capitalistic pigs who raped the environment and needed to die," Lark Ohta told the *Chronicle* in 1990. "Yeah, my dad had expensive cars, but he cared about other people; he cared for their eyes for free if they couldn't pay."

Frazier died by suicide in Mule Creek State Prison in Ione, California, in August 2009.

The Ohta murders appeared to be an aberration to the people of Santa Cruz in 1970, but they were just the beginning.

## MURDER PREVENTS EARTHQUAKES

San Franciscans live with the knowledge that their city was once leveled by a massive earthquake. They also know that this will happen again; but when will the next "big one" be?

Reuben Greenspan, 67, emerged from his hermitage in the Arizonian desert like a prophet of old in late 1972 with his prediction that San Francisco would be laid asunder by a massive quake along the San Andreas Fault at 9 a.m. on January 4, 1973. Greenspan, a mathematician from Greenwich Village, had had some success predicting earthquakes since the 1930s by matching tidal data to the positions of the moon, sun, and the stars in relation to the Earth. Bruce A. Bolt, director of the seismographic station at UC Berkeley, called Greenspan's prediction "nonsense," and *San Francisco Chronicle* columnist Herb Caen denounced the latest prophet of doom as another of many "charlatans, fakes and liars." While Caen could convince San Franciscans not to call their city "Frisco," he couldn't stop them from getting panicky as 1972 drew to a close. State Farm reported increased sales of earthquake insurance, and several Bay Area residents planned to be out of town on January 4 just in case.

Herbert Mullin, 25, of Felton, California, near Santa Cruz, had a plan to avert the oncoming disaster. It involved murdering a lot of people.

"We human beings, through the history of the world, have protected our continents from cataclysmic earthquakes by murder," Mullin later explained. "In other words, a minor natural disaster avoids a major natural disaster."

On October 13, 1972, Mullin bludgeoned Lawrence White, a 55-year-old transient man, to death with a baseball bat in a secluded stretch of road in the Santa Cruz Mountains. Eleven days later, Mullin picked up Cabrillo College student Mary Guilfoyle hitchhiking. He stabbed her in the chest and the back and dumped her body in the mountains.

On November 2, 1972, Mullin stabbed Father Henri Tomei as he came out of the confessional booth at his church in Los Gatos. Tomei had fought the Nazis with the French Resistance during World War II, so he proved more combative than Mullin's previous victims. Even after being stabbed in the chest, Tomei kicked Mullin above the ear during a struggle over the blade. Mullin recovered the knife and stabbed the priest until he died. Since Tomei was killed on All Saint's Day, the press speculated that some kind of satanic cult was responsible.

Mullin was born on April 18, 1947, the 41st anniversary of the 1906 earthquake. Albert Einstein died on this date in 1955, an event Mullin later attributed to having psychically prevented him from being drafted and dying in Vietnam. Mullin had a relatively normal upbringing, but he started hearing voices sometime after high school. By the time he reached his mid-20s, those voices were telling him to kill. Before he committed his first murder, Mullin had been in and out of mental institutions in both California and Hawaii. Psychiatrists diagnosed him with severe paranoid schizophrenia. Unable to ignore Mullin's increasingly disturbing behavior, his parents sought to have him institutionalized, but Governor Ronald Reagan's mania for budget slashing had already gutted California's mental health care system. Mullin was allowed to roam free and unmedicated. He was even able to buy a .22 caliber handgun in December 1972 with no trouble at all.

January 4 came and went and San Francisco didn't crumble into the sea. Reuben Greenspan said that he had gotten his calculations wrong. Mullin believed that the murder spree was working, so he kept on killing.

Mullin murdered five people on January 25, 1973. His youngest victim that day was four-year-old Daemon Francis. Mullin later claimed that his victims had told him through telepathy that it was okay to kill them. On February 6, 1973, Mullin shot and killed four young men he came across in a campsite in the Henry Cowell Redwoods State Park. Mullin found a rifle among the dead men's belongings. He put it in his station wagon in case he needed it later.

A week later, Mullin was set to deliver a load of firewood to his parents' house when he heard his father's voice say, "Before you deliver the wood, I want you to kill me somebody." Mullin complied by shooting 72-year-old Fred Perez with the rifle he had pilfered from his last victims' campsite. After killing Perez, Mullin got back in his blue Chevy station wagon and calmly started driving to his parents' house to deliver the wood. He was caught by police a few minutes later.

Confronted with another, even more prolific mass murderer, Santa Cruz district attorney Chang described his beachside town as "the murder capital of the world."

Mullin confessed to killing 13 people in all and was sentenced to life in prison. But there were still other unsolved murders of college women that Mullin didn't cop to. As impossible as it seemed, there was yet another, even more terrifying serial killer stalking the hills and forests of Santa Cruz.

## THE COED BUTCHER

The Santa Cruz cops who drowned their sorrows at a dive bar called the Jury Room had always liked Edmund Kemper III. He may have been a little odd, but he was no hippie freak. He kept his brown hair and mustache neatly trimmed just like the policemen themselves did. Standing at six-foot-nine and weighing over 280 pounds, the cops gave Kemper the obvious nickname of "Big Ed." Kemper flattered his cop friends at the bar by telling them he would've joined the force himself if his extreme height wasn't over the limit for police work.

What the off-duty officers at the Jury Room didn't know about Big Ed was that he had murdered his grandparents in 1964 when he was 15 years old. Kemper had been sent to live with his paternal grandparents, Ed and Maud Kemper, at their ranch in the Sierra foothills when he was 13. Two years later, he shot his grandmother and stabbed her repeatedly for good measure. When his grandfather returned home, Kemper shot him too.

Rejected by the California Youth Authority because of the unusually violent nature of his crimes, Kemper was sent to the Atascadero State Mental Hospital. He was kept in the maximum-security facility until 1970, but received only minimum treatment while there. One can only wonder if so many future horrors could've been prevented with more attentive care.

As a child, Kemper made a game out of staging his own execution by writhing around in a chair as his younger sister pulled an imaginary lever of an imaginary gas chamber. When Kemper's sister accused him of having a crush on his schoolteacher, Kemper said, "If I kiss her, I would have to kill her first." When the family cat turned up butchered into pieces in a garbage can, Ed denied killing the pet, just as he had denied having cut the head and hands off his sister's new doll. Growing up with an authoritarian mother who shamed him at the slightest provocation made Kemper very good at deflecting blame.

After being released from Atascadero, Kemper moved into his hated mother's apartment in Aptos just outside of Santa Cruz. She worked at the new University of California campus there. She even got Ed a university parking sticker so he could park on campus, unwittingly giving him easy access to a large pool of potential victims.

Kemper began his killing spree on May 7, 1972, when he picked up Mary Ann Pesce and Anita Mary Luchessa, a pair of Fresno State students hitchhiking in Berkeley. He drove them to a secluded part of Alameda, decapitated them, and had sex with their corpses. He loaded the bodies in the trunk of his car and dumped them much closer to home on Loma Prieta Mountain in Santa Cruz County.

When women started disappearing from UC Santa Cruz and nearby Cabrillo College, UCSC warned its students to only get into cars displaying an official campus sticker—like the one Kemper's mom had gotten for him. Kemper killed and mutilated four more female students by February 5, 1973, when he shot Rosalind Thorpe and Allison Liu on campus. Because of that sticker, he was waved through a security gate with the corpses growing cold in the car.

On April 21, 1973, the day before Easter Sunday, Kemper bludgeoned his mother to death in their apartment. He then cut off her head and removed her larynx, throwing it down the garbage disposal.

"This seemed appropriate," he later told Stanford psychiatrist Donald Lunde, "as much as she'd bitched and screamed and yelled at me over the years."

After killing his mother, he called her coworker, Sara Taylor Hallett, and told her to come over. He strangled Hallett when she walked through the door so he could plant the alibi that the two women had gone on a trip for the holiday weekend. He left a note to taunt police, took the cash and credit cards from the two women's purses, and took off in his car with several loaded guns.

When he made it to Pueblo, Colorado, he pulled over to a payphone and called the Santa Cruz police to confess his crimes. He had to call three times before he could convince an officer that he was responsible for the grisly, unsolved murders of eight women, including his own mother. Kemper was arrested by Pueblo police on April 23, 1973, and sent back to California where he was tried, convicted, and sentenced to life imprisonment.

"If I killed them, they couldn't reject me as a man," Kemper later said of his victims. "It was more or less making a doll out of a human being . . . and carrying out my fantasies with a doll, a living human doll."

After his arrest, the Associated Press revealed that Kemper was engaged to a 17-year-old girl from Turlock that he'd met on the Santa Cruz beach. The teen's parents sent her away so she could recover from finding out that her fiancé was a monster.

In March 1977, Kemper sought permission to have a surgeon "reroute the electrical circuits in his brain" that compelled him to kill. The news stories on the killer's strange plea caught the attention of Hollywood agent-turned-producer Kevin Casselman who announced plans to produce a major motion picture on Kemper.

"It would have to be one of the most ghoulish films ever made, for ghoulish people," prosecutor Peter Chang told the *Santa Cruz Sentinel.* "Even if you minimized everything he did, it would be so ugly," Chang added. "It gave me nightmares for a week after I heard his confession. It's so gory, it's pornography."

Neither the film nor the surgery ever happened, but Kemper has now attained a certain level of media stardom through Cameron Britton's Emmy-nominated portrayal of him in the much-binged Netflix series *Mindhunter*. Kemper was also quoted by Christian Bale's character in *American Psycho* (2000), though Bale's sociopathic Wall Street banker misattributes the line to Wisconsin necrophiliac Ed Gein. Kemper has been eligible for parole several times during his imprisonment but has told his attorney that "he's just as happy going about his life in prison."

## CHAPTER 14

# DEATH TO THE FASCIST INSECT THAT PREYS UPON THE LIFE OF THE PEOPLE

### CINQUE

Donald DeFreeze was born into what would be a large African American family in Cleveland on November 15, 1943. He was the eldest of eight children. His mother was a nurse. His father was a toolmaker who beat his kids when things turned bad. DeFreeze stayed away from school rather than have to explain the bruises and cuts he got when his dad beat him with hammers and baseball bats. DeFreeze later told a state psychiatrist that his father had tried to kill him three times. He dropped out of school in the ninth grade and ran away to Buffalo where he joined a gang called the Cracked Skulls. He got arrested for busting into parking meters and boosting a car. From there, DeFreeze piled up criminal records in four states before he was 30, but he never seemed to spend much time behind bars.

DeFreeze was busted with homemade bombs in both New Jersey and Los Angeles in the 1960s. He was also arrested for stealing cars, possessing stolen guns, kidnapping, shaking down a prostitute, holding up a synagogue caretaker, and bank robbery. Psychiatrists in

Ohio recommended that DeFreeze be locked up because his "fascination with firearms and explosives made him dangerous." A California probation report said that he had "strong schizophrenic potential."

Despite such damning assessments, "when [DeFreeze] was convicted or suspected of serious crimes he was placed on probation or charges were dropped," according to the *Los Angeles Times*. DeFreeze's attorney, Morgan M. Morten, said that it was "indicated that [DeFreeze has] been cooperating with police." Louis E. Tackwood, a Black collaborator with the LAPD's criminal conspiracy section who later turned radical, said that DeFreeze was recruited by the LAPD's "Black Desk" to report on African American militant activity. A lot of the guns that DeFreeze stole ended up being distributed to rival Black nationalist organizations with the full knowledge of his contacts in the police department. The LAPD later declined to talk about it. DeFreeze's luck ran out when he was wounded in a shootout at a Bank of America branch in Los Angeles on November 17, 1969. He was sent to the California state prison in Vacaville for that.

While at Vacaville, DeFreeze was befriended by Colston Westbrook, a linguist with a penchant for macramé outfits and harsh language who oversaw the Black Cultural Association (BCA) at the facility. Prior to his role in the California prison system, Westbrook worked in Vietnam during the war for Pacific Architects and Engineers, a private contracting firm that provided cover for the CIA's Phoenix program. According to a May 17, 1974, *New York Times* article, the Phoenix program "included assassination teams."

Westbrook's BCA at Vacaville introduced Black prisoners to white citizens who were sympathetic to the Black cause. Most of them came from in and around UC Berkeley. Among the white Berkeley radicals that DeFreeze met through the BCA were Patricia "Mizmoon" Soltysik, Camilla Hall, Willie Wolfe, Russ Little, Nancy Ling Perry, and Angela Atwood. Most were middle-class or even upper middle-class. Wolfe was the son of a wealthy Pennsylvanian doctor. Perry's father managed a furniture store in Santa Rosa. Ling

Perry and Soltysik had been cheerleaders in high school and Atwood was a drama nerd. These once popular kids turned misfits later served as DeFreeze's loyal foot soldiers in something called the Symbionese Liberation Army (SLA), a 1970s fever dream with revolutionary ambitions that never numbered more than a dozen recruits. Despite its unimpressive size, the SLA pulled off the most notorious kidnapping since the disappearance of the Lindbergh baby.

In Vacaville, DeFreeze changed his name to Cinque after Joseph Cinqué, the West African man who led the revolt on the slave ship *La Amistad* in 1839. Even though DeFreeze was less than a model prisoner, he was permitted to have sex with Soltysik and other leftist women in the prison's conjugal trailers. He also sold weed and pills to his fellow inmates and split the take with the guards.

Brad Schreiber, a former improv comic from Burlingame, wrote a book in which he argues that DeFreeze was groomed by Westbrook to escape prison and infiltrate the radical left. Jeffrey Toobin, a shunned CNN legal analyst, dismissed this idea as laughable in a book of his own. Either way, DeFreeze was transferred to Soledad in 1972 where he just walked out an open door, hopped a fence, and headed for Berkeley without anyone going after him.

## MARCUS FOSTER

Marcus Foster became the first African American superintendent of the Oakland school system in April 1970. He had come west after running schools in Philadelphia where he had a proven track record of cutting the dropout rate and boosting grades—especially in predominantly Black schools where his success served as a symbol of what was possible.

"Young Blacks must be able to see themselves able to be what they want to be," Foster said in 1970. "You don't learn the basics if you don't see yourself as able to master them, if you don't see yourself powerful enough to do the job. If people see themselves as beautiful people, then they begin to act as beautiful people."

Foster's powers of persuasion were such that he was able to convince Robert Blackburn, his deputy superintendent in Philadelphia, to make the move to California with him. Foster was a Black man from a lower-class background; Blackburn was a white former Peace Corps volunteer who grew up with all the advantages that white privilege and a middle-class upbringing could give him. The two couldn't be more different on paper, but both men saw education as their cause.

Foster and Blackburn were leaving a school board meeting at 7 p.m. on November 6, 1973. As the two men crossed the parking lot, Blackburn noticed a pair of figures leaning against an administration building. Blackburn then heard something that sounded like firecrackers or cherry bombs.

"The two figures were crouching, and I saw flashes from the muzzles of their guns," Blackburn recalled in 2002.

Nancy Ling Perry, the official propagandist for the cult-like SLA, missed with her first shot but then hit Foster in the leg. Patricia "Mizmoon" Soltysik was supposed to take down Blackburn, but she was out of position, forcing Donald DeFreeze to blast the deputy superintendent with both barrels of his shotgun.

"I stumbled down the side of the car, into a narrow alley, stumbling and reeling," Blackburn said. A thick leather appointment book he had in his overcoat pocket minimized the amount of buckshot he took. Blackburn still clutched the keys to the education building. He was able to unlock the door and get himself to safety.

Foster was reaching for his car door when Soltysik walked towards him calmly and filled him full of the cyanide-tipped bullets that became the SLA's gruesome signature. The trio of assassins then fled two blocks to where SLA members Russ Little and Joe Remiro were waiting for them in a getaway car.

Foster was dead before the ambulance had even made it to Oakland's Highland Hospital. Blackburn was in slightly better shape, but only slightly. His heart stopped three times as a team of surgeons led by Dr. Coyness Ennix worked all night to keep him alive. Being shot by DeFreeze's shotgun instead of Soltysik's poison-dipped bullets may have been what kept Blackburn alive. He survived the attack, but lost his spleen and suffered from severe nerve damage.

The next day, an SLA communiqué taking credit for the Foster assassination arrived at Berkeley radio station KPFA. The memo labored over by SLA propagandist Nancy Ling Perry stated that a warrant calling for Foster's "execution by cyanide bullets" had been issued by "The Court of the People." They had assassinated Foster because they believed he had supported student ID cards that Perry referred to in her leaden revolutionary prose as an "Internal Warfare Identification Computer System." In reality, Foster had opposed the program and had navigated school board members and other stakeholders away from it.

But the complexities of democratic governing appeared to be beyond the grasp of the SLA, which saw Foster only as a reactionary stooge and Blackburn as a CIA agent because of his time spent with the Peace Corps. Perry and the SLA closed their memo with a rallying call that would become all too familiar in the coming months: "DEATH TO THE FASCIST INSECT THAT PREYS UPON THE LIFE OF THE PEOPLE," it stated in all-caps.

Like Zodiac before them, the SLA members were media trolls as much as they were murderers.

## OSCEOLA AND BO

It was after 1 a.m. on January 10, 1974, and SLA getaway drivers Russ Little and Joe Remiro—aka Osceola and Bo—were lost in a tangle of East Bay cul-de-sacs on the other side of the Caldecott Tunnel. They were searching for the SLA safe house on Sutherland Court in suburban Clayton, but they kept driving their van back and forth down Sutherland Drive in neighboring Concord.

Long before the advent of GPS, Little turned down one street and circled back to the wrong Sutherland only to start the whole monotonous cycle over again. Concord police officer David Duge spotted their slow-moving van. He let it go the first couple of times he drove past it, but it only looked more suspicious when it crossed his path again. Figuring it might be involved with an ongoing series of burglaries, Duge pulled the van over. He questioned Little, who identified himself as Robert James Scalise.

Remiro got out of the van. Duge recognized the bulge around Remiro's waist as the outline of an automatic pistol and raced back to his car to call for backup. Remiro had served two tours of duty in Vietnam; he was probably the most dangerous member of the SLA. Remiro drew a .380 Walther pistol and shot through the window of Duge's patrol car. Duge ducked and fired back. He missed Remiro, but his shot grazed Little's shoulder. Remiro took off on foot as Little sped away in the van.

Everything was quiet by the time Duge's backup arrived, but Little was still lost. He drove back to the scene of the shootout and was quickly stopped by the gathering of cops. Inside the van, police found three guns and a stack of SLA leaflets. Remiro was caught four hours later hiding in a yard just two blocks from the hideout he was looking for. His Walther automatic was later identified as the same gun used to murder Marcus Foster.

At 6:21 that evening, a fire was reported at 1560 Sutherland Court, two blocks from where the van was stopped. After making short work of a blaze that fizzled out before it started, the firemen found what the *Chronicle* called "a clumsy attempt at arson," along with still more Symbionese Liberation Army literature, the typewriters and mimeograph machines used to produce it, and lots and lots of bullets. Neighbors noticed a young couple who lived in the house packing up a car and driving away just before the fire. Neighbors remarked that the occupants of the house "seemed unemployed."

With Bo and Osceola arrested, Cinque felt it was time for the SLA to carry out the kidnapping that they had been planning. It was supposed to be their less violent follow-up to the Foster assassination to prove that the SLA was still a force. They now hoped they could exchange their hostage for their incarcerated comrades.

They couldn't, but they still succeeded beyond their most demented imaginings.

## TANIA

The heavily armed detachment of the Symbionese Liberation Army stormed the apartment at the back of the wood-shingled townhouse at 2603 Benvenue Avenue in Berkeley at 9:17 p.m. on February 4, 1974. Angela Atwood, aka General Gelina, bluffed her way past the front door by saying she'd been in a fender bender. Field Marshall Cinque and new SLA recruit Bill Harris, aka Teko, pushed their way in behind her. Cinque yelled for a safe, but the SLA wasn't after cash. They were after her.

She was Patricia Campbell Hearst, a 19-year-old media heiress and a living embodiment of California history itself. An avenue bordering the University of California at Berkeley and several buildings on its campus where she studied art history were named for her family. Her great-grandfather George Hearst mined the Comstock Lode in Nevada and became one of the richest men in America in the process. Her great-grandmother Phoebe Apperson Hearst was a philanthropist, feminist, and UC Berkeley's first woman regent. Patricia's grandfather William Randolph took his parents' fortune and used it to build a media empire and a massive castle overlooking the Pacific Ocean in San Simeon, California. Her father, Randy Hearst, wasn't quite the captain of industry as his forbears, but he was still publisher of the *San Francisco Examiner* at a time when that really meant something. And her mother, Catherine, followed in great-grandmother Phoebe's footsteps as a regent of the University of California System, which included UC Berkeley as well as UCLA and several other campuses throughout the state.

On the night of the home invasion, Patricia's somewhat less prestigious fiancé and former high school math tutor, Steven Weed, pleaded with the intruders that he didn't have a safe. He begged them to take his wallet. Cinque belted him across the head with a leather sap filled with lead. Patricia fled to the kitchen in the back of the apartment. Atwood caught up with her and shoved a .45 in her face. Not far behind, Harris, a gun-obsessed Vietnam vet, pushed Patricia face first down on the floor and sat on her with his knee in her back. Patricia twisted around to take a look at her attacker. "Don't look at me!" Harris shouted and slammed her face down on the floor. Patricia continued to struggle, making it hard for Atwood to hogtie her with nylon cord.

When Weed recovered from Cinque's blow, he bum-rushed Harris but was knocked to the floor. When Weed got up again, he bolted out the backdoor, through the yard, and over the fence, leaving Patricia behind. On their way out, Cinque fired his submachine gun at curious neighbors, but no one was injured. Harris dragged Patricia to the stolen Chevy Impala outside, stuffed her into the trunk, and then into a smelly closet in Daly City where she remained for 57 days.

"I was alone there with the stale musty odor of sweat and filth," Patricia recalled. "I might as well have been in an underground coffin." Patricia had grown up in a mansion in Hillsborough, the San Francisco peninsula's most exclusive enclave. She went on hunting trips in San Simeon and swam in Hearst Castle's lavish Roman pool during family vacations, a luxury reserved for the Hearst family even after the estate became a state-run park. She was born into wealth and power, and now she was powerless. As far as the SLA were concerned, she was a prisoner of war.

Her world was reduced to that closet; Patricia's captors shrunk it even further by keeping her blindfolded. She cried so much, her blindfolds were soaked with her tears as soon as they tied a fresh one to her head. She was only allowed to leave the closet for bathroom breaks, during which she was always chaperoned by an SLA member who called her a "bourgeois bitch" as she peed.

And the humiliations were combined with incessant threats. Cinque told her she'd be the first to die "if the motherfucking pigs come charging in here."

"As soon as the shooting starts, we'll come in here and waste you," he added.

Over the days and weeks that followed, the rest of the SLA told her she'd be shot on the spot just in case she hadn't heard it the first time. When this army of eight carried out war-games in their suburban single-family hideout, they spat "rat-tat-tat" outside of that closet door making the machine-gun sound that little boys make when they play soldier during recess. Rat-tat-tat. First to go. Shot on the spot. Rat-tat-tat.

After four days of captivity, the SLA turned the closet into a recording studio and had Patricia tape a message to give her family proof of life. "Mom, Dad, I'm okay," she said in a dull monotone as she fought back tears through the entire address. After the recording, Cinque felt up her breast and scolded her for daring to question Mizmoon during one of their bathroom chats. He pinched her nipple brutally and grabbed her crotch. "I felt frozen in the dark, stunned. My whole body felt icy numb," she recalled. After Cinque left, she "cried hot tears of humiliation and fear."

"Being helpless, I had sensed the ever-present possibility of sexual abuse," she continued. "But this was a clear, overt threat of what I could expect if Cin became angry with me for any reason."

Cinque raped her sometime in early March after Patricia had been held in the closet for a month. "Cin came into the closet, shut the door, and said, 'Take off your clothes,' and he had me," Patricia wrote. "I lay there like a rag doll, my mind a million miles away. It was all so mechanical and then it was over. I said to myself, rationalizing again, 'Well, you're still alive.'"

Around the same time that Cinque raped her, Patricia submitted to Willie Wolfe, aka Cujo or Kahjoh, in her closet prison. Patricia liked Wolfe as much as she could like any of her abusers. He spent hours at the edge of the closet softly reading to her from *The Communist Manifesto*, Carlos Marighella's guerrilla warfare handbook *For the Liberation of Brazil*, and his favorite quotes from Chairman Mao about dying for the cause. While he later gave her an Olmec monkey charm to show his affection, she remained blindfolded through the ordeal. She could not see his face. She had no agency. She could not consent. He had raped her as much as Cinque had.

After weeks of enduring mental, physical, and sexual abuse, Cinque floated the idea to Patricia of her joining the SLA. "You're kinda like the pet chicken people have on a farm," he said. "When it comes time to kill it for Sunday dinner, no one really wants to do it."

"I knew that the *real* choice [emphasis hers] was the one in which Cin had mentioned earlier: to join them or be executed," she wrote. "They would never release me. I knew too much about them. He was testing me and I must pass the test or die."

The FBI hadn't come to her rescue. Her dad, Randy, had failed to negotiate her release even with the millions he had put into the People-in-Need food program to meet the SLA's ever-shifting demands, and her mom, Catherine, pissed off the SLA even more by accepting a reappointment to the University of California Board of Regents from Ronald Fucking Reagan. Without having much of a choice, she

FBI

Security cam photo of Patricia Hearst, aka Tania, and Donald DeFreeze, aka Field Marshall Cinque, holding up the Hibernia Bank on April 15, 1974.

joined with her captors on March 31, 1974, and became the latest foot soldier in the Symbionese Liberation Army. After spending 57 days in musty closets in Daly City and then San Francisco, the blindfold finally came off and she could see her captors-turned-comrades in all their grotesque squalor. She had won that much at least.

Three days later, the SLA made their latest acquisition official by releasing a tape where Patricia called her father "a corporate liar" and proclaimed she had joined her captors in a revolution that never really started. "I have been given the name of Tania after a comrade who fought alongside Che in Bolivia," she explained. "I embrace the name with the determination to continue fighting with her spirit." To drive the point home, the media-savvy SLA also released a snapshot of Hearst/Tania clad in fatigues and cradling a carbine in front of a sigil that bore the image of a multiheaded cobra that looked like it was designed by Jim Steranko for a *Nick Fury, Agent of S.H.I.E.L.D.* comic book.

Courtesy of the Daly City History Guild

The SFPD wanted poster for Donald "Cinque" DeFreeze, Patricia Hearst, and the rest of the Symbionese Liberation Army following the Hibernia Bank robbery on April 15, 1974.

The newly christened Tania was photographed again on April 15, 1974, as she helped her new SLA compatriots rob the Hibernia Bank on Noriega Street in San Francisco's Sunset District. In a series of black-and-white photographs captured by the bank's security cameras, Tania was front and center. She looked the part of the revolutionary with her M1 carbine in hand, even though she quickly realized that the gun was inoperable. And behind her were Cinque on one side with Perry on the other, their submachine guns at the ready to mow down their new recruit if she went off script.

"This is Tania . . . Patricia Hearst," she said when she remembered her lines. "First person puts up his head, I'll blow his motherfucking head off!"

On the day that Patricia was allowed to take off her blindfold, and her captors christened her as Tania, Cinque had talked to her in a sweet voice.

"The people love you, Tania," he said softly. "You've given up your past life to become a freedom fighter, and they love you for that. You're a symbol of hope for them, Tania."

And two weeks later at the Hibernia Bank, she was Tania, the freedom fighter, the symbol of hope. She was living her life like the original Tania who'd fought alongside Che, but she would still be the first to die if anything went down.

Shot on the spot.

Rat-tat-tat.

CHAPTER 15

# KILLING GERALD FORD

Gerald Rudolph Ford Jr. became vice president when his predecessor Spiro Agnew resigned in disgrace on October 10, 1973, following a bribery scandal. Ford became president less than a year later when Richard Nixon resigned in disgrace on August 9, 1974, during the Watergate investigation. Ford's unlikely presidency is best remembered for the time he fell down the Air Force One stairs during a diplomatic visit to Austria. In the early days of *Saturday Night Live*, Chevy Chase's impression of Ford consisted of nothing more than a series of pratfalls before emerging from the stage floor with the familiar "Live from New York . . ."

Ford was hardly the kind of transformative figure to inspire one potential assassin, let alone two of them. But in September 1975, he survived two different assassination attempts in as many weeks.

## SQUEAKY FROMME

On September 5, 1975, President Ford walked across the lawn of the

California State Capitol grounds on his way to meet once and future governor Jerry Brown. A crowd gathered to see the accidental leader of the free world. No one in Ford's security detail noticed a petite redhead in a kind of nun's habit standing only two feet from the president until she pulled a Colt .45 automatic from an ankle holster underneath her crimson robe.

"I saw a hand coming up from behind several others in the front row, and obviously there was a gun in that hand," Ford recalled.

Secret Service agent Larry Bruendorf grabbed the woman and disarmed her before she could fire off a shot. Fortunately for the president, she'd forgotten to cock the gun and load a round into the chamber.

"Why are you protecting him?" the woman screamed as Bruendorf spun her to the ground. "He's not even a public servant!"

"Her eyes just had this sort of glaze, like a person in deep shock, totally oblivious to what was going on," eyewitness Alex Saldamando

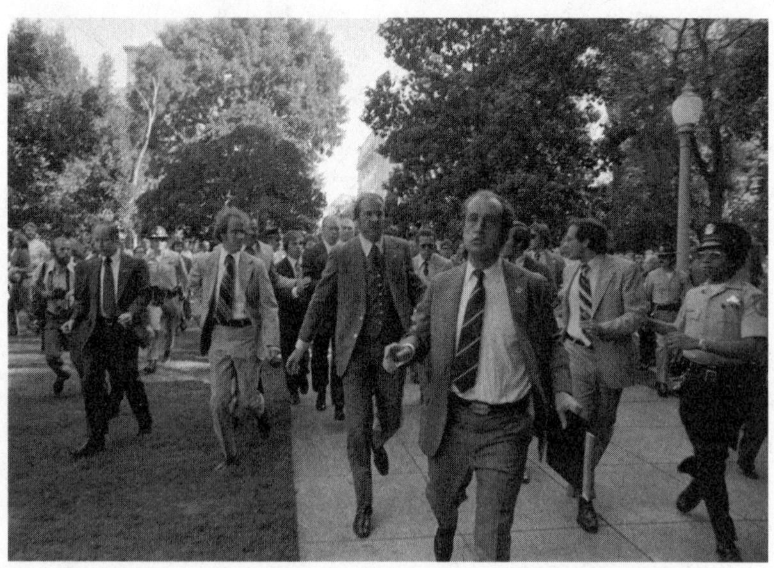

Courtesy Gerald R. Ford Library; photographer: Ricardo Thomas

**Secret Service agents rush President Ford towards the California State Capitol after Manson devotee Lynette "Squeaky" Fromme tried to shoot him in Sacramento on September 5, 1975.**

told the *Los Angeles Times*. "They slammed her up against the tree and frisked her."

Ford soldiered on and addressed the California legislature as planned. The topic of his speech was crime in the streets.

The would-be assassin was Lynnette "Squeaky" Fromme, a woman described by Manson prosecutor Vincent Bugliosi in his bestseller *Helter Skelter* as the "undisputed leader" of the Manson Family outside of prison. She still believed in Charlie and reportedly wrote him almost every day.

Manson had found Fromme crying on a bench in Venice Beach in 1967 after a fight with her domineering father. Manson charmed her with talk of prison, the Haight, and fate bringing them together.

"The way out of a room is not through the door," Manson told Fromme. "Just don't want out, and you're free."

"No one had ever treated me like that before, not pushed me around, so I just picked up and went," Fromme later explained. "A dog goes to somebody who loves it and takes care of it."

Fromme followed Manson back to the Bay Area where she became the second member of what would later be known as the Family after Mary Brunner, a UC Berkeley librarian. The polyamorous trio first lived in Berkeley before moving to a flat at 636 Cole Street in San Francisco, half a block from Haight Street. The Victorian house is now a popular walking tour attraction thanks to the Family's short stay there.

Fromme returned to Southern California with Manson in late 1967 when things got too violent in the Haight even for them. She lived in squalor out on the old movie sets at Spahn Ranch with the rest of the burgeoning cult, and even performed sexual favors for the octogenarian George Spahn to keep the Family in the rancher's good graces. Fromme squealed when Spahn touched her, so he started calling her Squeaky. The rest of the Family picked up on this, giving her a nickname worthy of a gangster's gun moll when the Manson Family made national headlines.

Like other women in the Manson Family, Fromme dove in supermarket dumpsters for discarded food and sang backup vocals when Manson auditioned for Hollywood music producers. When the rock stars and record producers weren't around, Manson would yank hard on Fromme's hair if he felt she wasn't giving him her undivided attention during his extended rants on Helter Skelter, the racial apocalypse he believed was prophesied by the Beatles' *White Album*. As bad as Fromme and other Manson women had it, poor Mary Brunner had it much worse. Manson hit Brunner, knocked her down, and kicked her while she was on the floor as an example to the other women. Manson had convinced his followers that they would rule the world by his side after Helter Skelter went down. The occasional beating seemed like a small price to pay for a piece of global domination.

Fromme wasn't there on August 9, 1969, when Tex Watkins stabbed Sharon Tate 16 times while the pregnant actress cried for her mother during the Cielo Drive massacre. She was also back at the ranch the very next night when Charlie, Linda Kasabian, and a bunch of other freaks crammed themselves into a pickup truck and drove out to Los Feliz to carve up Leno and Rosemary LaBianca. Family member Ruth Ann Moorehouse later speculated that Manson "sent out the expendables" to commit these murders. Fromme was too important for these ad hoc homicides.

When Manson, Susan Atkins, Patricia Krenwinkel, and Leslie Van Houten were indicted for the Tate-LaBianca murders in 1970, Fromme was free to work the outside. She ran errands for Manson's defense attorney and wrote the liner notes to a vinyl pressing of Charlie's demo tapes. Fromme also sat on the sidewalks outside of the L.A. County courthouse as the trial went on, posing for pictures and telling passersby that "Charlie is all about love." She seemed so pleasant to be around that no one paid any attention to the X she had carved in her forehead to match Manson's.

Fromme was arrested with several others in Stockton in 1972 after the body of James Willett was found buried near a fire trail in Guerneville. Willett and his wife, Lauren, had been living with Fromme and an odd mingling of Family and Aryan Brotherhood members. Fromme was released for insufficient evidence. Lauren Willett later turned up dead in what was claimed to be a demonstration of Russian roulette.

In 1973, Fromme moved into a small apartment in Sacramento to be closer to Manson while he was incarcerated at Folsom State Prison. She lived with Sandra Good, another Family burnout who still clung to the idea that Charlie was the son of God. When state prison officials denied their repeated requests to visit their leader, they channeled their energies into a twisted kind of environmental activism.

"We're waiting for our lord, and there's only one thing to do before he comes off the cross, and that's clean up the Earth," Fromme said in July 1975.

Fromme and Good wrote letters to corporate execs, threatening them with assassination if they didn't stop polluting the planet. Then on a Friday morning in September, Fromme decided to take more direct action. She picked up a 60-year-old surplus .45 she was borrowing and went out to meet the president.

Investigators determined that Fromme's attempt to shoot Ford, who'd served on the Warren Commission investigation into the assassination of JFK, wasn't part of any greater conspiracy. Letters from Manson seized from Fromme's apartment made no mention of the president. Fromme acted alone, just like Lee Harvey Oswald had in 1963, at least as far as Ford was concerned. Ford was always a staunch proponent of the lone gunman theory.

During her trial, Fromme refused to walk to the courthouse, forcing federal agents to carry her into the courtroom like a baby. She was sentenced to 15 years to life for trying to kill the president. In December 1987, she escaped into the mountains around Alderson Federal Prison for Women in West Virginia. A maintenance supervisor and a records supervisor helping with the search recaptured her after she had been on the lam for two days.

Fromme was released on parole in 2009.

## SARA JANE MOORE

In the days after Squeaky Fromme had pulled a gun on him, President Ford remained undeterred as he headed into an election year. Ford had neither been elected as president nor vice president. He ascended through the fallout of scandals and then compounded the air of illegitimacy that hung over his shaky presidency by pardoning Nixon and other Watergate coconspirators. Winning the White House in 1976 was his one chance at electoral legitimacy, so he went on with his schedule of "contacting the American people as I travel from one state to another" as if no one had tried to shoot him.

Ford was in California again on September 22, 1975, to address a labor organization at the St. Francis Hotel at Union Square in San Francisco back when Republicans addressed labor organizations. Ford left the meeting using a freight elevator and banged his forehead on a heavy metal door. The resulting gash across his balding dome was obvious. White House Chief of Staff Donald Rumsfeld and Ford's other handlers worried that the press would see it and report that Ford had fallen down again, giving *Saturday Night Live* some new material. Chevy Chase loomed large over the Ford Administration.

When Ford emerged from the hotel's Post Street entrance, he paused to wave at the crowd of potential voters who had gathered on the sidewalk.

Oliver "Billy" Sipple had been waiting for three hours that day in the hopes of seeing the president. When Ford waved at the crowd, Sipple, a "husky" ex-Marine and Vietnam vet, saw a woman pointing a chrome-plated .38 right at the president.

"I screamed 'gun' as loud as I could, and grabbed her arm," Sipple told the Associated Press. "I seen a gun and dived for it. I don't even know what I felt."

The woman squeezed the trigger as Sipple lunged at her. A shot whizzed past the president, followed by another. Secret Service agents shoved Ford and Rumsfeld into a waiting limousine.

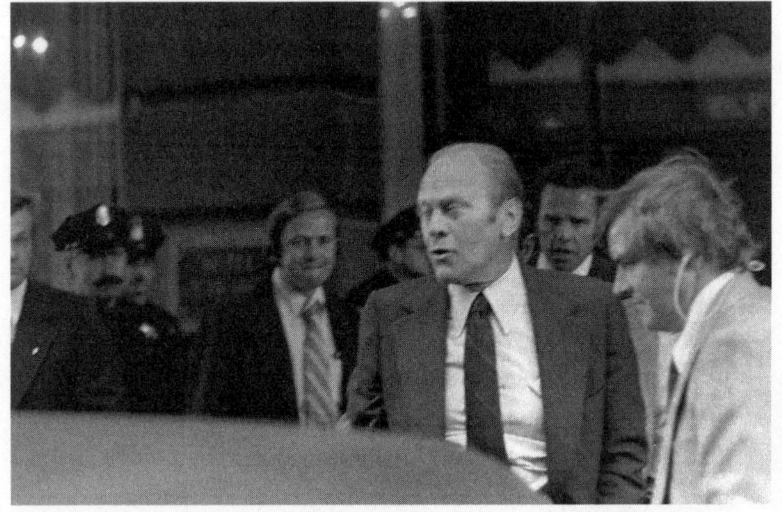
Courtesy Gerald R. Ford Library

President Ford winces at the sound of a gunshot as Sarah Jane Moore attempts to shoot him in front of the St. Francis Hotel in San Francisco on on September 22, 1975, just 17 days after Squeaky Fromme tried to kill him in Sacramento.

Ford was rushed to the airport and the security of Air Force One. As much as Ford may have wanted to get the hell out of California, he had to wait on the tarmac for three hours while First Lady Betty Ford wrapped up an event in the Peninsula suburbs. In those days before smartphones made news inescapable, Betty Ford boarded the plane unaware that her husband had been shot at again.

"I think it was Rumsfeld who finally told her that someone took a shot at the president," White House Press Secretary Ron Nessen recalled. "I can tell you that quite a few martinis were consumed on the flight back."

Ford's second would-be woman assassin in two weeks was just as strange as the first, if not even more so. Sara Jane Moore was a middle-aged mom with a son in private school. She was also an FBI informant with ties to the Symbionese Liberation Army.

Moore had even been questioned by local police and Secret Service agents two days before the president's visit after she had told San Francisco police that she might try and "test" the president's security team. Police lieutenant and future San Francisco mayor Frank Jordan confiscated a .44 caliber handgun from Moore, but federal agents deemed her "not of sufficient protective interest to warrant surveillance" and let her go. Nobody bothered to search her home.

"Apparently, she was able to get another gun," Jordan quipped the day after the assassination attempt.

Moore later told the *Berkeley Barb* that the gun she used to try to shoot Ford and the one that was confiscated were both purchased from a Danville gun collector as part of an ATF sting operation. Moore was first recruited as an FBI informant when she volunteered for People-in-Need, a food distribution program funded by the Hearst family to appease SLA demands and earn Patricia's release.

"I was intrigued by the whole thing," Moore later said about informing for the FBI. "It was like a B-movie. I was really enjoying myself."

Moore worked as what the FBI referred to as "a possible security informant" from June 1974 to June 1975, but was let go for telling an underground newspaper about her double life. "She was compensated for her expenses," according to an FBI statement.

In the days leading up to her shooting at Ford, Moore found herself an outcast from both law enforcement and the radical organizations that she had snitched on. When Patricia Hearst was finally apprehended by police and FBI agents in San Francisco on September 18, 1975, it looked like Moore's B-movie life as a double agent was over and done, but she had other ideas. She decided to shoot the president outside the St. Francis Hotel as "an ultimate protest against the system."

"I'm glad he didn't die," Moore told the *Los Angeles Times* in a jailhouse interview two days after the shooting. "I did want to be prevented," she added. "I don't like to kill people."

Moore was sentenced to life in prison for attempting to assassinate the president. Just like Squeaky Fromme before her, Moore also escaped from Alderson Federal Prison for Women in West Virginia, only to be found hitchhiking by police. She was released on parole in 2007 at the age of 77.

Oliver Sipple, the man who saved the president, was outed as a homosexual by Herb Caen in the *San Francisco Chronicle* on a tip from Harvey Milk. Milk believed that revealing this hero's sexual orientation would help win respect for gays and lesbians in the military, but Sipple had not come out to his family. Sipple instead found himself alienated and had to face the PTSD from his service in Vietnam all alone.

"If I were a homosexual or not, it doesn't make me less of a man than what I am," Sipple told the press at the time. Sipple received no hero's welcome to the White House Rose Garden, and a letter of thanks came only weeks later. Sipple died in his apartment on Van Ness Avenue in 1989 at the age of 47 after years of alcoholism. The letter from the White House was still among his prized possessions.

The double assassination attempts sparked off a new round of debates on gun control that proved just as frustrating then as they are today. "The attempted assassination is likely to start a new congressional debate on gun control, but it is already clear there will still be opposition to controls," an unnamed writer for United Press International wrote.

"It's something you learn to live with," Betty Ford said after the first attempt on her husband's life.

Ford did start wearing a thin bulletproof vest after the second assassination attempt. He lost the 1976 presidential race to Governor Jimmy Carter of Georgia on November 2, 1976. A stunned President Ford gave a solemn concession speech the next day. His voice hoarse, he surrendered the podium to First Lady Betty Ford, who expressed his thoughts for him. As she read her husband's letter to President-elect Carter, the news camera zoomed in on Ford as the survivor of two presidential assassination attempts fought back tears.

## CHAPTER 16

# RAINBOWS AND LEATHER

### THE LAVENDER PANTHERS

The Reverend Ray Broshears, an ordained minister and gay rights activist with a mustache to die for, was beaten senseless on July 4, 1973. He had called the police earlier on "some young toughs" who were lighting fireworks outside of his Helping Hands Gay Community Service Center.

The police showed up and didn't do much except tell the toughs who had called them. Once the cops took off, the toughs went to work on the reverend in what turned out to be an origin story worthy of a superhero movie.

Two days later, Reverend Ray (as he preferred to be called) took a page from San Francisco's vigilante history as he brandished a rifle at a press conference where he announced that the Lavender Panthers would be patrolling Polk Street and the Tenderloin armed with sawed-off pool cues. According to an Associated Press story that ran in the *Los Angeles Times*, Broshears was "flanked by two 'drag queens' armed with rifles and pistols."

Pat Rocco & ONE Archives at the USC Libraries

Reverend Ray Broshears, leader of the Lavender Panthers, an LGBTQ+ vigilante group that patrolled Polk Street and the Tenderloin armed with sawed-off pool cues in the mid-1970s.

"We deplore violence, but we must meet force with force," Broshears said, clad in a clerical collar with a crucifix hanging around his neck. "Never again will a gay person be beaten without retaliation."

Described a few months later by *Time* magazine as "a stiff-wristed team of gay vigilantes," the Lavender Panthers numbered "21 homosexuals, including two lesbians who are reputedly the toughest hombres in the lot."

"All of the Panthers know judo, karate, Kung Fu or plain old alley fighting," according to *Time*.

Those martial arts skills came into play in a gay-bashing incident described in *Time*: some young homophobes started pushing around a pair of men leaving the Naked Grape, "a well-known gay bar." Broshears and the Panthers pulled up in a gray VW van "and lit into them."

"We didn't even ask questions," Broshears said. "We just took out our pool cues and started flailing ass."

The SFPD permitted the pool cues at least for a while, but forbade the Lavender Panthers from carrying firearms. Broshears did, however, keep a shotgun in his office that he boasted would "leave a hole in a man big enough to drive a tank through Georgia." Broshears also encouraged people in the LGBTQ+ community to keep guns in their homes for self-defense.

Before starting the Lavender Panthers, Broshears formed the Gay Activists Alliance in 1971 and was one of the founders of San Francisco's first gay pride parade in 1972. He also performed some of the city's first same-sex marriages for three lesbian couples that same year. Although the marriages weren't legally recognized, the act garnered Broshears a bit of publicity at the time, just as the Lavender Panthers did a year later.

While Broshears was effective at gaining attention, he was viewed with suspicion by other factions of the LGBTQ+ rights movement. According to author Christina B. Hanhardt in *Safe Space: Gay Neighborhood History and the Politics of Violence* (2013), Broshears was rumored to have been an FBI informant and even involved in the assassination of JFK. Broshears did testify against an alleged associate of Lee Harvey Oswald, pilot David Ferrie, during New Orleans district attorney Jim Garrison's hearings on the JFK assassination. He also knew Sara Jane Moore, would-be presidential assassin and known FBI snitch.

In the end, Broshears was just as alienated from the emerging homosexual middle class in the Castro as those on Folsom Street and the Tenderloin that he served. "Many of the city's affluent gays do not like the idea of hard-eyed homosexual toughs causing commotion in the streets," according to *Time*.

The Lavender Panthers dissolved in 1974. Broshears attempted to revive his modern-day vigilance committee in 1979, but he could no longer get the attention of the press or of a changing LGBTQ+ community.

Broshears died in relative obscurity from a cerebral hemorrhage on January 10, 1982.

## THE DOODLER

At 1:25 a.m. on January 27, 1974, a man called the San Francisco police.

"I believe there might be a dead person on the beach at, right across from Ulloa Street, Ulloa Street, if you follow the street right down to the water," the caller said. "I thought I saw somebody lying there but I didn't want to get too close to him because you never know what could happen, okay?"

When the dispatcher who took the call asked for the man's name, he politely declined. "I just wanted to let somebody know," he said. "Maybe he needs help or something, but I just felt it was my duty to report it."

After the call, police found the body of Gerald Earl Cavanaugh on Ocean Beach as the tide threatened to carry the corpse out to sea. Cavanaugh had been stabbed 17 times in the chest, back, and stomach. The coroner's report described the 49-year-old furniture finisher as "never married," implying that he was homosexual.

Cavanaugh was the first known victim of the "Doodler," a serial killer who preyed on gay men in the Castro in 1974 and 1975. Also called "The Black Doodler" because of the color of his skin, he met his victims in bars and restaurants and charmed them by drawing their likenesses on cocktail napkins or whatever was available. Once the Doodler made it home with his intended victim, he'd stab him to death and then dump the body on the beach.

The sheer number of brutal murders of gay men in San Francisco during those years makes the Doodler's body count hard to ascertain. *The Encyclopedia of Unsolved Crimes* (2009) by Michael Newton credits the Doodler with as many as 14 murders. However, Elon Green, in his exhaustive 2011 history of the serial killer in *The Awl*, only attributes five known kills to him, which still matches the number of known victims killed by the Zodiac Killer or Jack the Ripper.

But even with his own pulp villain name, the Doodler remains obscure. There are no bestselling books detailing his still-unsolved crimes being made into major motion pictures or true crime documentaries parsing the details of the case on basic cable networks. However, Inspector Dave Toschi (the cop Mark Ruffalo played in 2007's *Zodiac*) did investigate a series of "S&M slayings" of gay men in the mid-'70s; those murders also remain unsolved and are attributed to yet another serial killer, who picked up often leather-clad men in Ringold Alley by Folsom Street.

The Doodler killed three men in 1974 and two in 1975. His last known victim was Harald Gullberg, a 66-year-old sailor. His partially decomposed body was found on June 24, 1975, on the Lincoln Park golf course that overlooks the ocean.

Six months later, on January 19, 1976, the *San Francisco Chronicle* finally mentioned the case in a front-page story titled "Sado Murder Horror" in a two-tone font that made it look like the poster of a grindhouse horror movie. By this time, 17 gay men had been murdered in San Francisco since 1974 by the Doodler and other suspects. A day later, in a follow-up story titled "The Gay Killers," the *Chronicle* published a police sketch of the Doodler that depicted a young African American man with wide cheeks accentuating an almost pointy chin.

By 1977, police had a good suspect for the Doodler murders, and they also had witnesses who could identify him. One Los Angeles man recalled a night when he had gone home with a young Black man matching the Doodler's description, but decided to leave when a knife fell out of the man's coat. Other survivors of brutal attacks by the Doodler were described in a July 1977 AP story as "a well-known entertainer" and "a diplomat." The problem for police was that none of these witnesses would testify for fear of being outed.

Harvey Milk, then described as "an advocate of homosexual rights," gave his thoughts on the reluctance of witnesses to go on the record in the Doodler case. "I can understand their position," Milk told the AP. "I respect the pressure that society has put on them."

**The original SFPD forensic sketch of the Doodler from 1975 and an updated version from 2018 to show what the serial killer who once stalked the city's Gay community might look like now.**

"They have to stay in the closet," Milk added.

All the years of beatings and entrapment by San Francisco police also deterred the LGBTQ+ community to participate in the investigation. Without any witnesses willing to go on the record, the Doodler suspect walked.

In 2018, San Francisco Police Inspector Dan Cunningham reviewed the Doodler case and dug up DNA evidence from at least one murder scene alongside new information from the foreign diplomat who survived being attacked by the Doodler. On February 6, 2019, Cunningham held a press conference announcing a $100,000 reward for information leading to the serial killer's identity plus an updated police sketch of the suspect, 45 years after he dumped his first victim at Ocean Beach.

"It's baffling, frustrating. But I've been digging around for a year, looking into a lot of different places, and we've made some headway," Cunningham told the *Chronicle*. "I do believe this can be solved."

## THE OSCARS STREAKER

David Niven struck a serious tone as he took the podium at the Dorothy Chandler Pavilion in Los Angeles during the 1974 Academy Awards ceremony.

"If one reads the newspapers or listens to the news, it is quite obvious that the whole world is having a nervous breakdown," the London-born star of *The Guns of Navarone* observed. A moment later, artist Robert Opel streaked across the stage buck-naked as if to prove Niven right.

Opel, his shaggy hair and mustache making him look like the most 1974 thing ever, flashed a peace sign as he ran across the TV camera frame, his junk bouncing up and down with each stride. The live audience both gasped and laughed, the band struck up a couple of bars of "That's Entertainment," and Niven recovered by making a quip about "shortcomings." The show went on. *The Sting* won Best Picture.

Instead of being taken to jail, Opel was whisked off backstage for a press conference. "People shouldn't be ashamed of being nude in public," Opel remarked, standing in front of a towering Oscar statue. "Besides—it's a hell of a way to launch a career."

That career didn't have much time left, however. Just five years later, Robert Opel was gunned down in his San Francisco art studio.

Opel moved to San Francisco from Los Angeles after serving four months in county lockup for stripping naked in front of police chief Ed Davis to protest the closing of nude beaches.

"The climate appears more conducive to civilized behavior," Opel said about his new home. Opel opened Fey Way Studios at 1287 Howard Street in March 1978. With its exhibitions of works by Tom of Finland and Robert Mapplethorpe, Fey Way was an out gay art studio at a time when gay art was only shown in gay bars, even in San Francisco. Opel's gallery was dismissed as "a sex shop" by mainstream newspapers when it was mentioned at all.

Opel also published a sex zine called *Finger* and produced a play titled *The Heartbreak of Psoriasis* starring Divine. Ever the provocateur, he staged a mock execution of Harvey Milk assassin Dan White at UN Plaza during the Gay Freedom Day Parade on June 24, 1979, despite reportedly being warned not to by San Francisco police.

Around 9 p.m. on Sunday, July 8, 1979, Opel was entertaining his friends Anthony Rogers and Camille O'Grady at Fey Way when a pair of men armed with a pistol and a sawed-off shotgun showed up demanding drugs and money. Opel was known to supplement his artist's income by selling amphetamines and PCP, but he didn't have any drugs in the studio that night.

"Get out of my space," Opel said, standing his ground.

"I'm gonna blow your head off," the man with the pistol said.

"You're going to have to," Opel replied. "There's no money here."

O'Grady and Rogers, who were being held in a backroom by the man with the shotgun, then heard a shot followed by the thud of Opel's body hitting the floor. Opel had taken a bullet to the head. The bandits fled as other tenants in the building came down the stairs to see what was going on. The men made off with only $5 and a camera. Opel was pronounced dead at 10:40 p.m.

O'Grady, an artist herself as well as "The Leather Queen of Folsom," drew sketches of the robbers and handed them over to police along with information told to her by a musician friend of Opel's. Working from this and other tips, homicide inspectors soon identified the holdup men as Maurice J. Keenan and Robert Kelly. The duo was arrested along with Keenan's wife, Linda Holt, at San Francisco International Airport on July 10 as they were trying to flee to Miami.

Keenan, who had beaten up and shot (but not killed) another man during a meth binge only three days before killing Opel, escaped from jail three times before the close of his murder trial. This, and homophobic behavior from police clerks, has fueled speculation that Opel was killed as a part of a police conspiracy. However, Bay Area county jails experienced a wave of escapes at the time. Keenan was one of 12 inmates who broke out of San Francisco's Hall of Justice at gunpoint on April 29, 1980. Of those 12, five including Keenan had escaped before.

As the triggerman, Keenan was given the death penalty, but the sentence was overturned on appeal in 2000. He is now serving a life sentence.

Robert Opel lives on as the go-to image of '70s craziness in TV news segments.

## THE BARRACKS

The Barracks at 1147 Folsom Street between Seventh and Eighth Streets was a two-story BDSM wonderland with theme rooms that catered to every fetish imaginable. After opening in 1971, the bathhouse quickly established itself as one of the biggest and best-known clubs on Folsom's "Miracle Mile," a stretch of nearly 30 different leather bars and clubs in South of Market in the 1970s. The club closed down in 1976 and was being redeveloped into a hotel in 1981, until somebody lit a match and the whole thing went up in flames.

The fire started in the Barracks around 2 a.m. on Friday, July 11, 1981. The flames quickly spread through the warehouses and flats that crowded Hallam Street and Brush Place, a pair of dead-end alleyways that fed onto Folsom. Jonathan Gilcrist, a motel clerk, saw the growing blaze while he was walking down Folsom. He charged onto Hallam and yelled for people to get out of their homes.

"Fire started coming out of the windows," Gilcrist told the *San Francisco Chronicle*. "The next thing you know, a vacant hotel across the alley was on fire. Then everything was on fire."

A group of elderly retirees, who lived in the area because of its cheap rent, fled from their flats only to find themselves trapped between pillars of flame and the concrete wall of a warehouse. Bill Livingston, who lived in a former furniture factory at the end of Brush Place, rushed downstairs to open his large steel garage door so people could escape through his live-work space.

"They were very disoriented," Livingston said. "The heat and smoke were tremendous."

Dean Chambers, a 29-year-old waiter, watched the fire from his flat on Langton Street, just doors away from the blaze. "It was like *Gone with the Wind*," Chambers said. "Flames were shooting from buildings just yards away."

Fire crews had to dodge flaming debris from the collapse of the Barracks just after they arrived on the scene at 2:15 a.m. Fire Chief Andrew Casper deemed that this was "more than a fire."

"It was a conflagration," he told reporters.

Residents told the first responders that some people may have been chained up in S&M slave quarters that dotted the neighborhood and unable to escape. Firefighters told the Associated Press that they found "a bed with hooks, chains and manacles at the back of one building."

"Homosexuals dressed in leather and chains were among those who watched thick smoke from the blaze darken the sky," reported the AP.

Chief Casper believed that the fire could have been fueled by large quantities of butyl nitrate, aka Rush, that may have been stored there. One of the apartments destroyed by the fire was owned by the company that produced the chemical "particularly popular among gay men" to "produce an intense orgasm," according to "health officials" quoted by the *Chron*. This was the third fire to consume buildings owned by the manufacturer of Rush in two years.

Photographs of the inferno's aftermath look like something from the firebombing of Tokyo during World War II, but surprisingly nobody died in what was dubbed the costliest fire since the 1906 earthquake. Five firefighters were injured in the blaze that damaged or destroyed 27 buildings and left 119 people homeless.

In the end, no evidence of Rush was found in the charred wreckage, but the fire still looked very suspicious. A day after the disaster, police arrested Otis J. Bloom, a disgruntled housepainter from Millbrae on suspicion of arson.

Bloom was upset after losing some tools near the Barracks, telling a construction worker in the area that "this place is just going to burn to the ground." According to a confession later played in court, Bloom left a nearby bar called the Stable to stuff a stack of newspapers in the door of the defunct bathhouse. He then returned to finish his beer and lit the fire sometime after last call.

"I don't really know if I did it intentionally or what," he confessed. "There is a lot of things I've done but that I never knew or realized I had done." Bloom was sentenced to seven years in prison in May 1982. He died on March 19, 2015.

While Folsom Street's Miracle Mile of gay leather bars was already on the wane when the Barracks burned down in 1981, the AIDS crisis devastated the community by the end of that decade. The SF Eagle on 12th Street still survives though, and the Folsom Street Fair gives us a glimpse of the neighborhood's glorious history of hedonism on the last Sunday of every September (newer pandemics permitting). As for the Barracks, the Bloodhound (a faux dive bar popular with the bridge and tunnel crowd) and an America's Best Value Inn now occupy the space that once housed so many dungeons.

## CHAPTER 17

# THE GOLDEN DRAGON MASSACRE

The war for the narrow streets and alleys of San Francisco's Chinatown started on Chinese New Year 1972 when gangster Joe Fong broke from the powerful Wah Ching gang to start his own mob made up of both foreign- and American-born Chinese. He called his gang the Chung Yi, but they were better known on the streets as the Joe Boys. A year later, Fong was 19 years old and already serving a life sentence in state prison for murder and conspiracy. The war went on anyway.

The two gangs and their allies battled for control of protection rackets and firecracker sales. Nearly 50 lives were lost during the five years that the war raged down Grant Street and along Pacific Avenue. And just when it seemed like it would never stop, it all came to a bloody end after three holiday long weekends during the summer of 1977.

Memorial Day kicked off the summer vacation season in San Francisco with the usual fog on Monday, May 31, 1977. A day later, 20-year-old Kin Chuen Louie left his Telegraph Hill apartment at 2:15 p.m. Louie had come a long way since getting shot in the shoulder during a brawl at the YWCA on Clay Street in September 1975. He'd then been a leader of the Hop Sing Boys, a gang that ran with the Wah Ching. Now he was a member of the Hop Sing Tong, the fraternal organization that publicly denied all ties to the street gang named after it.

Moments after leaving his apartment, a teenager with a gun chased Louie up Kearney. Louie made it into his red car parked near Green Street. He slammed it into reverse, pushing the car parked behind him into a telephone pole. Louie didn't get the chance to put his car in drive before the hitman emptied 12 slugs from his .380 Walther pistol, killing him. The police never found the gun or the killer.

Violence erupted again on the Fourth of July when the Wah Ching marched on the Ping Yuen projects, a 433-unit housing complex along Pacific Avenue, its name meaning "tranquil garden." The Wah Ching wanted their cut of the holiday's firecracker sales. The Joe Boys were there, and they didn't want to give it to them.

"It was Dodge City in Chinatown," former Joe Boys member Bill Lee wrote in his gangland memoir, *Chinese Playground* (1999). "Weapons were drawn and gunfire erupted, with gangsters running up and down the street, ducking behind cars and into doorways, blasting one another."

During the melee as the sound of gunshots blended with the perpetual pop of Independence Day firecrackers, 17-year-old Felix "Tiger" Huie of the Joe Boys was shot in the back. He was later found dead in a pool of his own blood in a courtyard of the Ping Yuen projects. Two other Joe Boys and a Hop Sing Boy were injured.

Shortly after Huie was buried, Joe Boys visiting his grave found that other Joe Boys graves had been vandalized.

"Those assholes are fucking up the plots and pissing on the headstones," Joe Boy Peter Ng told Bill Lee. "What happened to the code, man?"

"It was now open season and 'no-holds barred'—no rules, no honor, no mercy," Lee recalled. "At stake was the control of Chinatown;

independents against the Chinese underworld, and there were scores to settle."

The five-year feud had finally come to a head, and Labor Day was just around the corner.

Tom Yu was a boss in the Joe Boys gang. He plotted the Golden Dragon Massacre to get revenge for Tiger Huie and end the Wah Ching for good. It ended the Joe Boys instead.

On Saturday, September 3, 1977, Yu gathered his crew at a house in Pacifica, a coastal suburb on the southern end of San Francisco. Yu was over 18, but his boys were younger. This was by design. Yu figured they'd only do a year of juvenile detention if they got busted—no matter what they'd done. The war for Chinatown in the 1970s was fought by child soldiers.

The boys got their stash of guns out of the closet. They drank beer, smoked weed, and waited by the phone. Yu got the call he was waiting for at 2 a.m. on September 4, the day before Labor Day. Wah Ching chief Michael "Hot Dog" Louie and Frankie Lee of the Hop Sing Boys were chowing down on Hong Kong noodles at the Golden Dragon Restaurant on the corner of Washington and Grant. It was time to roll.

Melvin Yu (no relation to Tom Yu) prepared to do the most damage by taking the .45 automatic rifle. Curtis Tam grabbed the sawed-off shotgun, and Peter Ng packed a standard shotgun and a .38 handgun. The boys piled into a four-door Dodge Dart that Peter Cheung had stolen earlier with this moment in mind. Tom Yu stayed behind in the burbs while his brother, Chester, got behind the wheel.

Open as late as 3 a.m., the Golden Dragon was a popular place to cap off a night of bar hopping, and its upstairs hall played host to nearly 10 years of Chinatown wedding receptions and rehearsal dinners. By the time the boys made it there at 2:40 a.m., there were as many as 75 diners between the restaurant's main floor and mezzanine level. Chester double-parked the Dart and left it running while the gunmen slipped nylon stockings over their heads and stormed the restaurant. One of Hotdog Louie's men saw them coming.

"Man with a gun!" he yelled in Cantonese. The Wah Ching and Hop Sing Boys—Raymond "Shrimp Boy" Chow reportedly among them—hit the floor. The other diners didn't speak Cantonese. They were all still in their chairs when Martin Yu opened fire with the high-powered automatic rifle, spraying the main floor with a hail of bullets.

Tam and Ng blasted the mezzanine with their shotguns. Tam later claimed he didn't kill anyone and fired his gun into an empty booth in the confusion. When later asked why he hadn't left the house in Pacifica when the shooting was being planned, Tam said, "I don't know my way around there. They don't have BART or a bus."

To survivors, the shooting seemed to last forever, but it only took a minute. When the smoke cleared and the killers took off back for Pacifica, five people were dead with 11 wounded. None of them were gangsters. It was the most deadly mass shooting in San Francisco history until the tragedy at 101 California in 1993.

Among the dead was Wong Fong, a 48-year-old waiter with seven children. Before a bullet had severed his spine, he had been looking forward to his first day off in two weeks. The other murder victims were Paul Wada, a law student at University of San Francisco known for volunteer work; Denise Louie, who was visiting Wada from Seattle; Calvin Fong, a Riordon High honor student; and Donald Kwan, a steel worker from West Portal. Surprisingly, there were two off-duty cops in the Golden Dragon when the gunfire erupted. Neither of them could get off a shot during the shooting. There were just too many people in the way.

With Chinatown becoming a ghost town as tourists stayed away, Mayor George Moscone offered a $25,000 reward for information leading to convictions in the Golden Dragon case. The reward was soon increased to $100,000. By March 1978, an informant collected the cash, and the three gunmen and several accomplices were arrested and later convicted. The underage killers were all tried as adults. Curtis Tam was convicted on a lighter charge of second-degree murder in exchange for testifying against his accomplices. He was released from prison in 1991. Retired police sergeant Daniel Foley called Tam "the one person in that whole crowd that had a conscience."

Melvin Yu, the Joe Boy with the machine gun, was paroled from state prison in 2015. The feds tried to deport him back to China, but China wouldn't take him. With nowhere else to send him, Yu was back in San Francisco's Chinatown by October 2015.

"It will take me a few lifetimes to make amends," Yu told the *Chronicle*.

Peter Ng was convicted on five counts of first-degree murder. He will be eligible for parole again in 2020 after being rejected eight times already. Tom Yu attempted to cut an immunity deal with the district attorney's office, but any plea bargain was refused once it was determined that Yu had masterminded the massacre even though he had been over 10 miles away from the Golden Dragon when it happened. Yu was convicted of five counts of murder, 11 counts of assault, and two counts of conspiracy. He was sentenced to life in prison. He has been rejected for parole nine times.

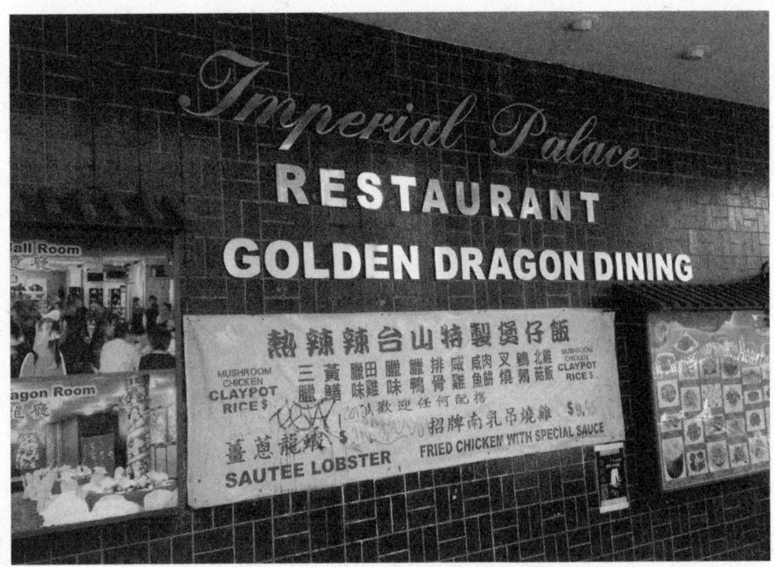


Bob Calhoun

Now called Imperial Palace, the site of the worst gangland massacre in San Francisco history still cops to its Golden Dragon past on its storefront.

The Joe Boys dissolved after the convictions in the Golden Dragon Massacre case. This left the Wah Ching unchallenged in Chinatown, except by the San Francisco Police Department's Asian gang task force, which was established following the Golden Dragon killings.

The Golden Dragon reopened soon after the massacre but closed at 10 p.m. every night, leaving the late-night trade to Sam Wo's on Washington Street. The restaurant shut its doors for good (kind of) in January 2006 due to mounting health violations. It soon reopened as the Imperial Palace, which now proclaims "Golden Dragon Dining" in gold letters on its familiar green-tiled storefront. The paint is old and the dining room is cluttered. Plush booths no longer line the mezzanine. A flatscreen video monitor is now mounted high on the wall, facing the main dining room, showing a security cam's view of the restaurant's front doors, and the street just beyond them.

## CHAPTER 18

# THE LAST VICTIMS OF JONESTOWN

### GUYANA

On November 19, 1978, a small Guyanese military detachment marched through the foreboding jungle towards the Peoples Temple Agricultural Project, an American farming community known as Jonestown. The troops, accompanied by 20 teenaged trainees, had just come from the narrow airstrip at Port Kaituma where they'd found a bloodbath. U.S. Congressman Leo Ryan of San Mateo and four others had been shot dead by the followers of the Reverend Jim Jones, who had established the nearby 3,800-acre agricultural project in 1974 with the blessings of the Guyanese government. As the men of the Guyanese Defense Forces closed the distance to Jonestown, they feared they'd find themselves in a firefight. What they found there, however, had them longing for a shootout instead.

The grounds of the Jonestown compound were covered in corpses. The bodies of Jones and his followers were already bloated from the jungle's intense heat and humidity, even though they had been dead for barely a day. A handful of the Peoples Temple members, including Jones himself, had been shot. The rest of the 909 victims died from drinking a grape-flavored drink spiked with potassium cyanide. At least 300 of them were children, and many of them were babies.

The press called the tragedy the "Jonestown Massacre," and they spun it as a cautionary tale about the Svengali-like Jones—always shown wearing oversized shades and looking like a brooding Elvis impersonator—who exerted total control over a legion of brainwashed followers who would do anything at his command. They "drank the Kool-Aid," spawning a trope that has lingered in the American zeitgeist despite its inaccuracies. First, the punch wasn't Kool-Aid, but Flavor Aid, a cheap knock-off. Second, many people tried to escape into the jungle but were forced back to the vats at gunpoint by Jones's security team—the true fanatics there. Those who drank the poison willingly did so after weeks of sleep deprivation and forced labor broke down their resistance.

"It's easier to believe that over 900 people died in Jonestown, including about 300 innocent kids, because they were all foolhardy and stupid, and trusted somebody who clearly they should not have trusted," said Jeff Guin, author of *The Road to Jonestown: Jim Jones and the Peoples Temple* (2017), a much-needed reexamination of the Jonestown story. "The tragedy goes greater when you realize why they were there and how, in the end, they were willing to give up their lives, even though it wasn't because they believed in Jim Jones anymore. But because they thought there was just nothing else for them."

The Reverend James Warren Jones took an unlikely path to prominence. He was a white minister to a mostly Black congregation in 1950s Indianapolis, a Midwestern city with very Southern policies on race. As a voice for the powerless, Jones became a driving force for integration in the Indiana capital by 1960. His successes continued when he moved the Peoples Temple to Northern California in the mid-1960s, after an *Esquire* article convinced him that Mendocino County was where he and his church could survive the nuclear Armageddon he had prophesied. With new members drawn to Peoples Temple by its combination of old-time religion, Black gospel, and a hip message of "apostolic socialism," Jones was able to recreate a social safety net at a time when Governor Ronald Reagan was tearing California's apart. Peoples Temple members handed over their paychecks and the deeds to their houses to fund senior homes, daycare centers, and medical clinics. And through their selfless toil, they hoped to create a world free of racism and materialism.

"Nobody joined Peoples Temple to get anything," Guinn said. "They were willing to give up material things to try to make it a better world for everybody, and that, to me, is the definition of tragedy.

"I mean, you have people walking around San Francisco who say they wouldn't be alive today without Peoples Temple and their drug programs." Guinn added, "Peoples Temple really did do all these fine things."

Nicolas Martin

By 1978, the once-thriving Fillmore district was plowed asunder by racist urban renewal policies, making what was left of the community susceptible to the promise of the Reverend Jim Jones's Peoples Temple at 1859 Geary Boulevard, San Francisco.

By the early 1970s, Peoples Temple expanded into cities throughout California and moved its headquarters from sleepy Ukiah to 1859 Geary Boulevard in San Francisco next door to the Fillmore Auditorium. With so many Black churches in the Western Addition neighborhood leveled by bulldozers, Peoples Temple offered hope to the African Americans who had hung on through urban renewal, and Jones's church soon became a political force in the city. If you were a politician or activist and you needed hundreds or even thousands of people to march in a protest or get out to vote, Jones could provide that for you. For the city's aspiring progressive powerbrokers such as California Assemblyman Willie Brown and State Senator George Moscone, an alliance with Peoples Temple proved indispensable. And this partnership paid off in 1975 when Peoples Temple mobilized enough votes to make Moscone the

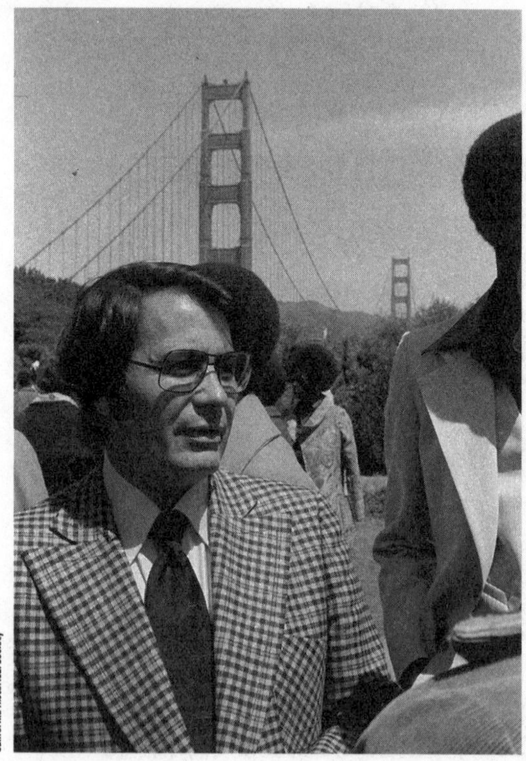

California Historical Society

The Reverend Jim Jones of the Peoples Temple with the Golden Gate Bridge in the background on Memorial Day, May 30, 1977. He would coerce hundreds of his followers to drink poisoned fruit punch during the Jonestown Massacre before the end of the following year.

mayor of San Francisco, transforming what was a relatively conservative city dominated by business interests and Democratic machine politics into the liberal bastion we know today.

And Jones's growing influence in San Francisco was felt on a national level. Jane Fonda and her activist husband, Tom Hayden, attended Peoples Temple services in Los Angeles. In 1976, presidential candidate Jimmy Carter's wife, Rosalynn, and his vice presidential pick, Walter Mondale, both met with Jones when they swung through San Francisco on the campaign trail (something Jones used to impress officials in Guyana). Unfortunately, greater power for Jones meant more power for him to abuse.

There were early warning signs to be sure, such as Jones's childhood penchant for staging funerals for roadkill, or his performance of faked faith-healings he learned on the rural revival circuit, but things kept getting more bizarre. At Peoples Temple Planning Commission meetings, Jones maintained his own fight club and laughed through the beatings as worshippers were forced to box each other as punishment for any perceived shirking of duties. Sexual relations within married couples was forbidden as being "counter revolutionary," while Jones felt free to use other people's husbands and wives for his own gratification.

For children, there was an Orwellian torture chamber called "the Blue Eyed Monster" where all of their worst fears came to life. When that no longer seemed sufficient, children were dropped down a pit that Jones named "Bigfoot" in a nod to pop culture trends of the time. The increased brutality led to some defections—and even some key ones—but most of Jones's followers stuck with Peoples Temple in the hopes that this was just a rough patch, and the pastor they thought they knew would come back to them.

"It was like the frog in the pot of water," Jonestown survivor Tim Carter explained. "If you drop him in the water that's already boiling, he'll try to hop right out. But if you put him first in a pot of lukewarm water and then turn up the heat little by little, he'll stay in the pot even though he's finally being boiled to death."

That pot was boiling over in 1977, and Jones couldn't keep accounts of mounting abuse from making their way to the public even with Willie Brown owing him favors and Peoples Temple attorney Tim Stoen moonlighting in the San Francisco District Attorney's Office. With an exposé in *New West* magazine about to hit the stands in July, Jones and his core followers fled to the "promised land" in Guyana, a small South American country that was happy to have an American commune near its disputed border with Venezuela.

Jones was hard enough to avoid at the church in San Francisco, but in Jonestown he was everywhere. His amphetamine-fueled harangues were broadcast through the camp's loudspeakers in what sounded like a poetry slam from the ninth circle of hell. With pressure mounting back in California, Jones declared what he called "White Nights" during which his followers must stay on edge for days watching for CIA or mercenary raids that never happened, but were always coming. With everyone calling Jones "Father," what he did to these people was child abuse writ large, and across several generations all at once. He employed the abuser's tools of beating, negging, gaslighting, and isolation and had at least 100 snitches on hand to keep everyone else in line; to mix the cyanide with the Flavor Aid and make sure everyone drank it.

They wheeled out the metal drums filled with dark liquid on February 16, 1978. Jones told them the drink was poisoned. They drank it anyway, hoping to just get things over with after months of hard labor in what had become a brutal plantation. But the punch was fine and nobody died that day. It was all just a dress rehearsal for the horrors to come. And Jones's "revolutionary act of suicide" finally came on November 18, 1978, after Congressman Ryan had left for that airfield. The drums were wheeled out once again, but the punch was poisoned this time. The Peoples Temple members drank it one way or another, and they died. But the deaths didn't stop then and there on that improbable farm in the unforgiving jungle. Jonestown was a lingering tragedy in more than just a spiritual sense. People connected to Jones kept on dying months and years after the last body came back from Guyana.

## PEOPLES TEMPLE HIT SQUADS

In November 1969, Elmer and Deanna Mertle took a three-and-a-half-hour ride in a crowded school bus from Berkeley to Redwood Valley, north of California's wine country, to see this exciting new minister of a small Disciples of Christ Church. The Mertles had been married for a little over a year, and their long commutes to work were already putting a strain on their relationship. Both had children from previous marriages, and Deanna felt she was struggling to hold their new family together. She hadn't been to any kind of religious services in over a year when some friends suggested taking this unusual day trip. Deanna thought that church may be what she needed.

The minister was Jim Jones and the church was Peoples Temple. During the service, worshippers waited in a long line to praise their minister for his Christlike powers.

"My pastor, Jim Jones, healed me of cancer," an elderly Black woman said before she broke out into song. Another woman claimed that she walked away from an auto accident unscathed because of Jones's love, and another said she witnessed Jones bring a man with "a mark on his forehead that looked like a bullet hole" back from the dead.

While Deanna was impressed with how well behaved children were during the long service, and how Black and white people worshipped together so freely, she was put off by all the boastfulness. She didn't think she'd return, but she and Elmer couldn't stop thinking about what they'd witnessed. To remind them, their mailbox was soon crammed full of handwritten letters from Peoples Temple members thanking them for stopping by and inviting them to come again. One church member even sent a box of homemade chocolates. Elmer and Deanna ate the chocolates.

They both started to have strange dreams about Jim Jones. In one of Deanna's dreams, Jones was a giant whale that swam frantically in a small pond to protect a pair of tiny fish from harm. "Twice while I was at work, I had actually felt as if Jim Jones were in my head and I were looking out at the world through his eyes," she later wrote.

After six weeks, she'd forgotten her misgivings over Jones and his odd congregation. "Instead of thinking about the puzzling miracles," she recalled, "I was recalling the beauty of Black and white people living together without any barriers between them." Elmer and Deanna returned to Redwood Valley. As they stepped inside the wooden barn of the church, Jones walked right up to them.

"I'm so glad you returned," he said with a warm smile. "We were all hoping you would."

At a time when shunning materialism to live in communes was becoming a part of American life, the Mertles joined Jones's flock and soon had a miracle of their own. Shortly after they moved to Ukiah to be closer to their new church, Deanna convinced herself that her six-year-old son Eddie had developed an irregular heartbeat. Although doctors never diagnosed or treated the condition, she believed that Reverend Jones had miraculously cured it through telepathy.

"From that day forward, Eddie was able to play as hard as any boy," Deanna wrote. The Mertles were soon let in on the grift, but they believed that stooping to old carnie tricks was justified by the cause. They stole mail from prospective Peoples Temple recruits and gave private letters to Jones so he could appear to be clairvoyant when he met with them later. The couple was appointed by Jones to the Peoples Temple Planning Commission, a select group that debated new Peoples Temple business in marathon sessions where the reverend often boasted of his sexual exploits. The Mertles were frogs in the pot of water.

Deanna believed that Jones had saved Eddie, but the savior became the boy's tormentor as all the Mertle children were subjected to the beatings and sleep deprivation that were a routine part of life in Peoples Temple. In 1974, Deanna and Elmer had finally had enough of the abuse after Jones forced them to watch their 16-year-old daughter Linda get whacked 75 times with a two-foot-long "spanking board" after she was caught hugging a friend who was branded a "traitor" to the church.

"I bowed my head and squeezed my eyelids together until they hurt wishing I could shut out the horrible scene, as well as my guilt over being helpless," Deanna recalled. Linda screamed as Jones counted each whack. By 60 whacks, Deanna felt she was going to throw up as Linda's body writhed from the impact. "Oh God," she thought, "just let it be over, please, and I'll leave this place and never return."

After the 75th blow, someone jammed a microphone in Linda's face. "Thank you, Father," she said before a guard helped her walk to the restroom. After the ordeal, a Peoples Temple lawyer demanded that the Mertles sign a release form stating that they gave Jones permission to have Linda beaten. There were six guards in the room with them. They signed the release.

The Mertles defected from Peoples Temple and changed their names to Jeannie and Al Mills, hoping to make a fresh start. In the months after leaving, the newly named Mills family was subjected to scare tactics from Jones and his followers. Threatening notes were left on their doorstep. Jones's personal bodyguards stalked them. Peoples Temple members even set off a bomb in the Bank of America branch where the couple kept a safe deposit box—or at least took credit for the bombing—in another note left on the Millses' front porch.

"We saw you two near the bank last night," the note read. "We know where you keep your belongings."

But Jeannie and Al Mills were formidable opponents. They established the Human Freedom Center to help other ex–Peoples Temple members readjust to society and put political pressure on Jones through the Concerned Relatives organization. They also went on record in *New West* magazine's exposé of the abuses happening inside their former church. Their efforts led San Mateo Congressman Leo Ryan to make his ill-fated fact-finding mission to Guyana in November 1978, which ultimately sparked off the Jonestown apocalypse. Jones blamed them for Ryan's visit in what is now referred to as the "Death Tape." Before Jones was shot in the head either by himself or one of his followers in Guyana, he issued a chilling warning to Deanna with the moans of his condemned flock audible in the background.

"The people in San Francisco will not—not be idle," Jones said. "Now, would they? They'll not take our death in vain you know."

Although Jones died in a jungle 4,500 miles away on November 18, 1978, the Millses didn't feel safe. The couple grew nervous as the one-year anniversary of the Jonestown Massacre approached. "The people in San Francisco" that Jones spoke of were just across the Bay from the Millses' Berkeley home. Were any of them still loyal to Jones? Would they still kill for him? There was every reason to believe they would, considering what played out in Guyana.

In the citywide chaos that had followed the assassinations of Supervisor Harvey Milk and Mayor George Moscone on November 27, 1978, rumors swirled that a Peoples Temple hit squad was responsible. Jonestown had happened just nine days earlier. It seemed plausible that Temple mercenaries were behind the City Hall shootings before aggrieved ex-supervisor Dan White emerged as the culprit. The urban legend of Peoples Temple hit squads haunted the Bay Area in the waning days of the 1970s.

November 18, 1979, Jonestown's one-year anniversary, came and went without incident. The Mills family breathed a sigh of relief; they appeared to be safe from the horrors of their past. But their respite was short-lived.

On February 27, 1980, Jeannie and Al Mills were found murdered in their suburban home. Their 15-year-old daughter, Daphne, was rushed to Alta Bates Hospital only to die two days later. All of them had been shot execution style in the head with a .22 caliber pistol.

That apocryphal Peoples Temple hit squad quickly became the culprits in the public's imagination, but police had a suspect much closer to home: Eddie Mills.

Eddie, 17, was home watching TV the night the rest of his family were slain in other rooms of their modest cottage home. Eddie claimed he didn't hear the gunshots. None of the Millses' neighbors did either, giving the teenager's story a shred of believability. One neighbor also reported seeing a van leaving the neighborhood around the time of the murders, stoking speculation that Jones loyalists had stealthily executed most of the Mills family. Despite being found with gunpowder residue on his hands, Eddie wasn't arrested for the murders until December 2005 when he was detained by customs officials while reentering the country from his home in Japan. Berkeley cold case investigator Russ Lopes believed he had put together an airtight case against Mills. However, with just 48 hours to charge Mills with murder, Alameda County prosecutor Chris Carpenter didn't feel his office had time to review the evidence, so he cut Eddie loose.

"Eddie Mills gets away with murder, and it's outrageous," Lopes raged in the *Oakland Tribune*.

"Even if you're not absolutely, 100 percent sure you'll win at trial, you take it to trial and let a jury decide," Lopes later told the *San Francisco Chronicle*. "Weaker cases have gone to trial."

Linda Mertle, Eddie's sister whose extended beating in 1974 caused her family to leave Peoples Temple, spoke out in support of her brother's innocence. "I'm just glad [Eddie's] home," she told the *Oakland Tribune*. "My personal opinion is it's an easy way out. They don't want to do the footwork to find out who really did this."

And who really did it? Without the closure of a trial and conviction, nobody really knows for sure. Berkeley police closed the case, but the murder of Al, Jeannie, and Daphne Mills remains a mystery.

Eddie Mills returned to Japan where he now lives with his wife and two children.

## THE MAZOR FILES

Joseph Mazor was like a character straight out of a film noir. He was a disbarred lawyer and con man who served time for passing bad checks before he somehow got a private investigator's license and opened his own San Francisco detective agency. He claimed that the 1970s detective show *The Rockford Files* was based on him, although this was probably another lie like the stationery he used that said his agency had offices around the world. The *Examiner* described him as "husky, tough talking," and he sometimes wore an eyepatch. Mazor was probably chasing what he thought was an easy mark when he inserted himself into the Peoples Temple saga in 1977. While there are at least a couple of kids who didn't die in Guyana because of him, so many more probably did as a result of his working both sides against the middle.

Mazor first reached out to Jeannie Mills (Deanna Mertle) in August 1977. Although Mills had been out of the Peoples Temple for three years, she was still concerned for the well-being of Candy and Carl, two children she'd grown close to who were in the custody of foster homes run by Temple members. Mazor promised that he could deliver the children to Mills and only charged a $1 retainer for the service. When Mills asked why he would do this, Mazor told her that "getting children back to their rightful guardians was his specialty."

Although Mills later wrote that "a warning bell should have rung" in her head after her initial meeting with Mazor, the private dick made good on his promise and brought the children to her only days later. Mazor even had the children's biological mother on hand to sign temporary custody of Candy and Carl over to Jeannie and Al Mills.

"We had to admit that he was fast," Mills wrote in *Six Years with God: Life Inside Rev. Jim Jones's Peoples Temple* (1979), her memoir published only months before her still-unsolved murder.

Mazor may have been effective, at least initially, but his shady past was used to discredit Mills and the Concerned Relatives organization she had founded to bring attention to the abuses at the Peoples

Temple. In a September 23–29, 1977, *Berkeley Barb* piece, reporter Art Silverman pilloried Mazor for "at least eight arrests in three states" and hiring "one of San Francisco's largest public relations firms" to "coordinate a publicity campaign against the [Peoples] Temple and its minister." The *Barb* piece was so in the bag for Jones that it was included in a Peoples Temple flyer accusing Mazor of being "a special agent for Interpol—the Nazi-infested international criminal police organization begun in Hitler's Germany."

Despite the denunciations, Jones later warmed up to Mazor and had the detective visit him in Guyana in September 1978. At Jonestown, Mazor told the reverend how he had led an expedition of armed mercenaries to the edge of the settlement to snatch children and return them to relatives in the United States. This story was probably all bullshit, but it deepened Jones's already bottomless paranoia just two months before he ordered the mass suicide. Whether Mazor cozied up to Jones as part of a scheme to rescue more children or had really sold out his Concerned Relatives clients is impossible to determine in a scheme that is either byzantine or completely ad hoc. Both Jones and the Concerned Relatives came to rely on Mazor for information on what the other side was up to, and both felt like they were being played.

After the Guyana tragedy, Mazor found himself with an odd specialty of working cases involving American religious groups in Latin American countries. While searching for four missing American Jehovah's Witnesses in Mexico, he was beaten badly by drug traffickers and had to have a plate put in his head, making his already volatile personality even more erratic.

On November 15, 1985, nearly seven years to the day after the Jonestown tragedy, Mazor's wife of just one year, Nancy Lou Mazor, called the Taraval police station at 3:30 a.m. "I just shot my husband," she said. "If you don't get here in a hurry, I'll do it again."

Officers arrived at their apartment on La Playa Street, and Nancy Lou met them at the door with a .22 pistol in her hand. Mazor was found dead on the bed with a bullet in his chest. Nancy's 13-year-old son from a previous marriage heard his mother and stepfather arguing before he went to sleep but told officers he hadn't heard the gunshot. Neighbors heard a scream about a half hour before police arrived.

Nancy insisted on being booked under her birth name, Nancy Lou Thompson. Adding an extra level of strangeness, she retained Jim Jones's former attorney Charles Garry to defend her. "[Mazor] came at her," Garry told the *Chronicle*. "He goes wild sometimes." Nancy Lou said that, in the past, Mazor had threatened to kill her and her son and throw them in the Bay, but she wouldn't say much more about what led up to the shooting. She was acquitted of killing her husband in August 1986.

## THE SCHOOL SHOOTING

Tyrone Mitchell was a member of the Peoples Temple in 1978, but he didn't make it to Guyana. His fiancée, Marylou Hill, had problems with her passport. Mitchell stayed behind with her. This saved his life, but nearly his entire family had already joined Reverend Jones at his Peoples Temple Agricultural Project. Mitchell's parents, four sisters, and one of his brothers all died at Jonestown on November 18, 1978. They were among the bloated bodies shown in aerial shots on network newscasts. Mitchell was already a disturbed man before the Jonestown Massacre. He was even more so after it. His fiancée later told the *New York Times* and other news sources that Mitchell suffered "a nervous breakdown" after the tragedy. "He was never the same after that," she told the *Los Angeles Sentinel*.

After Jonestown, Mitchell rented a room in a two-story Victorian in the South Central Los Angeles neighborhood that he'd grown up in and started buying guns. He had several shotguns and an AR-15 assault rifle with a banana clip that held 30 rounds. His room was right across the street from the 49th Street Elementary School. He had a great view of the playground from his front window.

Roderick Martin, who grew up with Mitchell in South Central, told the *Sentinel* that Mitchell "had this fixation about guns."

"He would take a Daisy air rifle and shoot at buses," Martin said. "He would shoot over in the playground after all the kids had gone home from school. He would shoot at people's windows and just up in the air."

At 2:23 p.m. on Friday, February 24, 1984, the final bell had just rung at 49th Street Elementary. Mitchell opened fire from his apartment as children flooded the playground. His barrage lasted 10 long minutes—enough time for him to fire 60 rounds from his AR-15 and several shotgun bursts into the schoolyard as teachers directed screaming kids back into the school buildings. The children who couldn't make it inside took cover behind trees and trash cans. Shala Eubanks, 10, was shot dead that day. Ten other children and two adults were injured from gunshots and shattering glass. Carlos Lopez, 24, who was shot twice while walking past the school, died eight weeks later from his wounds.

The SWAT team closed off the neighborhood. A team of officers trained to deal with standoff situations was brought in to coax Mitchell out of the house. They were unsuccessful. After four hours, the SWAT team stormed the house after pounding it with 16 canisters of tear gas. They found Mitchell dead from a self-inflicted shotgun wound.

In something that is depressingly familiar in today's America where mass shootings like this are nearly everyday occurrences, the news coverage focused on calls for increased mental health care services and not on how Mitchell amassed his arsenal in the first place.

To mark the one-year anniversary of the shootings, the *Los Angeles Times* touted a plan by police and mental health officials "that they hope will prevent similar tragedies." The February 24, 1985, article, "County to Assist Police with Mentally Ill," detailed coordination with mental health officials and greater training in dealing with the mentally ill for police officers.

"This will give us a better chance of spotting Tyrone Mitchells beforehand and preventing some of them," Commander James Jones of the LAPD told the *Los Angeles Times*.

"We won't catch all of them, but if we can prevent just one incident like the school shooting . . ." Jones added before trailing off.

Unfortunately, 30 years later, preventing just one mass shooting is no longer enough.

## CHAPTER 19

# THE WHITE WORKING CLASS

### TWINKIE THE KID

Dan White resigned from the San Francisco Board of Supervisors on November 21, 1978. It was a sudden move. He hadn't really consulted with anyone on this except his wife, Mary Ann. White wrote a letter of resignation by hand and had his assistant, Denise Apcar, deliver it to Mayor George Moscone.

White's phone was already ringing off the hook by the time he got home from discussing his resignation with the mayor. His constituents in the Excelsior, Crocker Amazon, Portola, and Visitacion Valley neighborhoods were pissed. They were the firemen whom White used to work with at the Moscow Street fire station; the policemen he worked with before that; the residents of the Hahn Street projects whom White grew up across the street from; the people who ran little shops on San Bruno Avenue; and the young African American men from the Sons of Sunnydale street gang he played tackle football with.

They were forgotten people living in a southern swath of the city that was shrouded by the peaks of San Bruno Mountain and ever-persistent fog. It was the last piece of San Francisco before you got to Colma, the land of the dead, the end of the line. These people scraping by in cheap apartments and moldy tract homes all campaigned for White and propelled him to an upset victory for District Eight supervisor's seat in 1977. They believed in him and he had let them all down.

Under pressure, White asked Moscone to return his resignation letter, but it was already too late for that. The Board of Supervisors had voted to accept White's letter, making it a part of the official public record. White no longer represented his people in District Eight. Of course, Moscone could just reappoint White to the board. While Moscone had been amenable to letting White take back his letter when both men thought that was all it took, now Moscone told Dan he'd have to think it over, and the mayor already had a lot on his mind.

They were still counting the bodies at the Peoples Temple Agricultural Project in Guyana when White staged his little retirement drama. Moscone had appointed Jim Jones to a seat on the San Francisco Housing Authority, and now it looked like the reverend had ordered his followers to kill San Mateo Congressman Leo Ryan and gulp down cyanide-laced grape punch in a sweltering jungle. Moscone was dealing with the aftermath and bracing for the shitstorm. The people of District Eight would have to wait as they always had, leaving Dan White to do nothing but brood. And brooding was something he excelled at.

Things were so much easier for White when the toughest thing he had to do was rush into burning buildings to save mothers and babies. He didn't even have to climb a ladder the day this regular-duty heroism landed him in the *Chronicle* on August 5, 1977. White and another firefighter took the elevator to the 17th floor of the Geneva Towers, a neglected and crime-ridden pair of high-rises not far from where White grew up. Once at the 17th floor, the firemen knocked down the door of the fiery unit with a sledge hammer and led Essie Franks and her baby to safety from a blaze set by the woman's abusive ex-boyfriend. People cheered White for that. Hell, they elected him for it.

When White became a supervisor, he could no longer fight those fires. He had to resign from the fire department due to conflict-of-interest rules. His annual salary went from a fireman's $36,000 to a supervisor's $9,600, and he and Mary Ann had their first child on the way. To compensate for this, the city's business interests set up White, who they thought would be a conservative tie-breaking vote, with the Hot Potato stand at Pier 39. But slinging spuds for tourists was time-consuming and undignified. It also made a working-class hero into a total sellout.

As a politician, Dan White campaigned on homophobic dog whistles aimed at the resentments of Irish and Italian Americans who bought their homes in Crocker Amazon back when real estate agents wouldn't sell to Black people. "I am not going to be forced out of San Francisco by splinter groups of radicals, social deviates, and incorrigibles," he said in an early version of his stump speech. Yet once in office, the Vietnam vet from a large Irish-Catholic family (nine siblings!) with a dead and decorated firefighter father often voted with Harvey Milk, the liberals' standard bearer and the most prominent out gay politician in the country.

"Dan had more in common with Harvey than he did with anyone else on the board," said Roy Sloan, the gay political consultant who engineered White's successful campaign. White and Milk were both proud of their military service. They both wanted to stick it to the man, although just who the man was probably varied. And they both benefited from liberal reformist Mayor Moscone moving the selection of San Francisco's supervisors from citywide votes to district elections, a radical makeover of the city's political system that resulted in the board's first Black woman, Chinese American, and openly-gay supervisors. White and Milk were able to win their respective elections with just the Irish and Italian hardhats from the Excelsior or the growing LBGTQ population in Milk's Castro without having to appeal to the vast middle-class blandness of the Sunset District as every supe candidate had had to do in previous elections.

During a committee vote, White supported Milk's Gay Rights Ordinance to ban discrimination based on sexual orientation, and he convinced board president Dianne Feinstein to appoint Milk as the chairman of the Streets and Transportation Committee. Things went south in April 1978, when White believed he had Milk's vote to block the Catholic Church from building a youth campus for violent juveniles in the Portola. Milk, however, refused to go totally NIMBY and voted in favor of it with the other liberals. Making things even more humiliating, White had invited several Portola residents to City Hall to witness what he thought would be his crowning achievement.

"White came up to me right afterward and says, 'I guess a leopard never changes its spots,'" retired judge and former supervisor Quentin Kopp told *SF Weekly* in 2008. "He was mad. Very mad."

The Catholic boy opposed Mother Church, and the gay civil rights leader—one of the "social deviates" no less—sided with her. Nothing made sense to Dan White anymore except his deep sense of betrayal. He spent the rest of his short stint on the board thwarting Milk's and Moscone's lefty agendas out of pure spite by becoming that tie-breaking conservative vote.

"Harvey was no longer a friend, and it wasn't any fun anymore," Sloan recalled. "It was all 'no' votes on the parades and anything else Harvey wanted."

White was already withdrawn before he formally withdrew from the board. When he'd campaigned in 1977, he looked like a Kenner action figure brought to life. He had the square jaw and the immovable coiffure of the Six Million Dollar Man in his red tracksuit, or maybe Big Jim, a 12-inch piece of plastic that Wikipedia describes as "an average Caucasian male with no other distinguishable characteristic, except having a permanent good attitude and joy for life." By the fall of 1978, White resembled a man who always had headaches and had run out of shaving cream several days earlier.

During the weeks leading up to his resignation, White stopped keeping office hours at City Hall and stopped sleeping with Mary Ann at home. He mostly wallowed on the couch reading Jack London novels of rugged men struggling against nature. He no longer worked out and his diet went to shit. He guzzled Coca-Cola and gorged himself on Twinkies, the cream-filled treats cranked out of the Hostess factory on 16th and Mission Streets by union bakers who probably lived in District Eight. "You'll get a big delight out of every bite of Hostess Twinkies," promised the then-ubiquitous comic book ads in which the Hulk just needed some of that golden sponge cake to give him the strength to defeat the Roller Disco Devils. But all Dan White got out of his new Twinkie diet was his dead father's saggy jowls. He could not deal with those jowls.

Mary Ann urged her husband to see a doctor so he could at least start sleeping again. "No," he replied. "I can do it all myself." Men

Mike Weiss, Double Play Collection; San Francisco History Center, San Francisco Public Library

Dan White flexes his tattooed arm sometime before his depression-fueled junk food binges.

didn't ask for help back then. They held it all inside until they totally lost their shit, and Dan White was progressing according to plan.

Soon, everyone was a snake and White was the city's own Saint Patrick. The ever-expanding list of serpents included the voters in District Eight who tried to recall him for not doing his job; Goldie Judge, his original campaign manager who couldn't deal with his shit anymore; and Milk, Moscone, and the entire leftward side of the San Francisco political establishment. "They're snakes," he said whenever any of them were mentioned. "They're all snakes."

Nobody bothered to tell White that he wasn't getting his old job back, but he figured it out from a Thanksgiving Day *Chronicle* article and a phone call the following Sunday from Barbara Rush of CBS News asking for a comment on being passed over by the mayor. The next morning, on November 27, 1978, White cleaned himself up and put on his best suit. His assistant, Denise, was going to pick him up and take him to City Hall before the press conference where Moscone was going to announce White's replacement. Denise thought White was going to deliver a petition with 1,000 signatures from District Eight voters supporting his reappointment, but White had something else in mind.

As he got dressed, he strapped on his old Remington service revolver from his police days and put several hollow-tipped shells in his coat pocket along with the folded-up dust jacket to *Ireland: A Terrible Beauty* by Jill and Leon Uris, an oversized doorstopper that might be the most depressing coffee table book ever published. Jacket copy that must have resonated with White promised "the much-storied Ireland of peat fires and pubs" along with "the tragedy of Ulster, a province ripped apart, where fanatical zealots perpetuate the Reformation under the haranguing of hate mongering preachers." On the back cover, a boy in short pants no older than nine glowered at the camera. Holding a metal pipe, the kid was ready for a fight, or maybe even a centuries-old conflict.

After being dropped off at City Hall, White avoided the metal detectors by entering the building through a large back window that was often used as a shortcut by supervisors. He went upstairs and asked to meet with Mayor Moscone. White had to wait as Moscone talked over Christmas shopping with California assemblyman Willie Brown, another object of White's ire. When the future mayor Brown left Moscone's office through a back door, he didn't realize how lucky he was.

White was summoned into the mayor's office, and Moscone gave him the bad news that he wasn't being reappointed to the board. To ease the blow, the mayor poured White a shot of whiskey. In return, White drew his gun and pumped five rounds into the mayor. White reloaded his gun and ran down the hall to the supervisors' chambers where he emptied his revolver into Harvey Milk. With both of his victims, White put extra slugs through their skulls at close range, execution style.

White fled from City Hall and called Mary Ann from a payphone at the Doggie Diner on Van Ness Avenue and met her at St. Mary's Cathedral on Gough Street and Geary Boulevard. "I shot the mayor and Harvey," he said. Together, they went to SFPD's Northern Station on Fillmore where White turned himself in. As an ashen Dianne Feinstein—who had just become mayor of San Francisco via tragedy—met with reporters at City Hall to announce that Milk and Moscone had been killed by their former colleague, police drove White to the Hall of Justice where he sobbed his way through a 25-minute confession conducted by Inspectors Edward Erdelatz and Frank Falzon.

"I could see the game that was being played," White said, choking back snot and tears. "They were going to use me as a scapegoat, whether I was a good supervisor or not, was not the point. This was a political opportunity and they were going to degrade me and my family and the job that I had tried to do and, and more or less hang me out to dry.

"Didn't even have the courtesy to call me or tell me that I wasn't going to be reappointed," White complained. "Then ah . . . I got kind of fuzzy and then just my head didn't feel right . . ."

Dan White confessed to breaking every oath he had ever taken but maintained that he hadn't planned on shooting anyone. It helped that he was among friends. He and Falzon grew up in the same neighborhood and went to St. Elizabeth's grammar school together. When White was a cop, they were teammates on the SFPD softball team.

With his strict moral code, White was a misfit when he'd been on the police force, but he was treated like a celebrity by the stream of visiting cops and the deputies who guarded him at the county jail while he awaited his trial. Stopping by an inmate's cell was against all regulations, but regulations didn't apply to White while he was in custody. White had free use of the phones and always had plenty of books to read and roast beef sandwiches to eat along with an open-ended prescription of Dalmane, a powerful sleeping pill with hypnotic qualities. While White visited with his old police pals, he seemed like one of the guys, but once they left, he went back to reading books about Irish martyrs that fed his fantasy that he was among their number.

Six months later, in May 1979, Dan White was tried before a jury that was just as white and working class as he was. In a diverse San Francisco, the jury contained no African or Asian Americans, and the only potential juror identifying himself as gay was removed after a challenge from the defense. Many of those who made the cut were related to people who worked in law enforcement or the fire department. One even described himself as a retired cop. If District Attorney Joe Freitas and Deputy D.A. Tom Norman weren't going to deviate from their regular playbook of rejecting Black and gay jurors, defense attorney Douglas Schmidt was more than happy to let them impanel the jury he was hoping for.

In spite of its magnitude, the trial was a brisk one, lasting 11 days. During hours of expert psychiatric testimony on White's junk food addiction, satirist Paul Krassner jotted down "Twinkie defense" and then skewered the notion in his snark-filled court dispatches for the *San Francisco Bay Guardian*. Once Herb Caen name-checked it as "the Twinkies Insanity Defense" in his mega-popular *Chronicle* column, the phrase became a sugary bookend to "drinking the Kool-Aid." But just as there wasn't any Kool-Aid at Jonestown, the effect of Twinkies on the outcome of the Dan White trial was just as fallacious.

The turning point in the trial—if there even was one—came when Deputy D.A. Norman put Frank Falzon on the stand. The inspector was the prosecution's lead investigator during the trial but seemed more like a defense character witness that day as he called White "a man among men." By most accounts, Falzon was a good detective, but he never should have been put in this position: his friendship with White should have kept him off the prosecution's team. However, it wasn't like anyone else associated with the SFPD would have been any better. Moscone tried to make the department less homophobic and racist, and the rank and file hated him for it. Norman dug the hole even deeper by having Falzon play the tape of White's confession in the belief that it would prove that the slayings of Milk and Moscone were premeditated murder. Instead, several of the jurors wept along with White's analog sobs. The jury picked by the prosecution to be tough on crime had gone soft on the defendant.

And the jurors cried again as their verdicts were read after six days of deliberations on May 21, 1979. With White's Ken doll looks and his rock-ribbed biography, that jury of his peers—in the extreme—was swayed by the defense's case that the defendant suffered from diminished capacity and didn't know what he was doing as he pulled the trigger over and over again. So, for gunning down their mayor and a major civil rights leader, they found Daniel James White guilty of two lesser counts of manslaughter.

Anything less than a life sentence was unacceptable to the city's LGBTQ+ community, but now Harvey Milk's assassin was going to be eligible for parole in just five years. Making everything even more galling, the triumph of Dan White's legal team was delivered on the eve of what would have been Milk's 49th birthday, and all the planned celebrations on Castro Street that went along with it.

"Faces were sullen, the atmosphere suddenly Southern and heavy," Herb Caen wrote following the verdict in what may be his best column. "You could almost imagine lynch mobs. People stood on downtown street corners, talking about the Verdict That Shook the World, or parts thereof. Matters that had seemed so pressing only the day before—the gas crisis (fake or real?), the Giants (weak up the middle?), *Apocalypse Now* (triumph or tragedy?)—faded away. The sound of sirens waffled continuously, from Hunters Point through the Castro to Polk. The city of love was undergoing another agony of hate, doubt and confusion. . . . If ever the stage was set for a confrontation, it was the Dan White Verdict."

## WHITE NIGHT RIOT

At the end of that November day when Dan White shot Milk and Moscone, gays and lesbians gathered in the Castro and marched down Market Street to Civic Center. It was a path that Milk, "The Mayor of Castro Street," had led marchers down so many times before. With Milk gone, at least some of that burden fell on future AIDS activist Cleve Jones, who had worked for Milk as a student intern.

"What I remember the most is the extraordinary silence," Jones wrote in his memoir, *Stitching a Revolution* (2000), "beyond a faint tramp of shoes on asphalt, there wasn't a sound to be heard."

After the crowd got to Civic Center, Joan Baez sang "Swing Low, Sweet Chariot," and Jones, Feinstein, and others made speeches that weren't particularly memorable. "It was anticlimactic," Jones wrote. "The silent march itself had been the most eloquent expression of our grief."

Things weren't so quiet on May 21, 1979, after the news of diminished capacity defenses and two counts of manslaughter for White hit the evening news broadcasts. Jones addressed a growing and angry crowd in the Castro through Harvey Milk's battered bullhorn.

"Today, Dan White was essentially patted on the back," Jones said. "He was convicted of manslaughter—what you get for hit-and-run."

DAN WHITE
GETS
SPECIAL TREATMENT!
WHY?
BECAUSE:
-HE'S AN EX-COP?
-HE'S A "FAMILY MAN"?
-HE'S WHITE?
-HAS FINANCIAL PROBLEMS!?
-HE EATS JUNK FOOD!?
WE DENOUNCE
TRIAL & VERDICT!
PROTEST!
8 PM - NIGHT OF VERDICT
- STEPS OF CITY HALL
BRING CANDLES IN MEMORY OF :
Lesbian & Gay mens CoaLition Against The Death PenaLty

California Historical Society

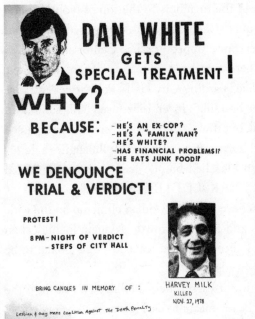

A flier for a protest at San Francisco's City Hall planned for after the announcement of a verdict in the trial of Dan White for the assassinations of Supervisor Harvey Milk and Mayor George Moscone. San Francisco's LGBTQ+ community was so angered by the light manslaughter conviction that the protest exploded into the White Night Riot on May 21, 1979.

Jones was at City Hall on the morning of the double assassination. He stood next to Dianne Feinstein and stared at Milk's bloody body as brain tissue seeped out of the hole in his skull that White had put there. Jones summoned this sad, gruesome memory after the verdict as he stood at the intersection of Castro and Market. "I saw what Dan White's bullets did," Jones said. "It was not manslaughter, it was murder."

Once again, thousands coalesced in the Castro and began marching up Market Street. This time, chants of "Murder! Murder! Murder!" and even "Kill Dan White!" were punctuated by the percussive tone of the self-defense whistles that gay men carried back then to call for help when attacked by gay-bashers and cops who not only resembled Dan White but probably played on the SFPD softball team with him.

"It was eerie and frightening to see familiar faces so distorted by anger as to be nearly unrecognizable," Jones recalled. "Everyone wanted blood, wanted revenge."

Jones intended to lead the marchers to the top of Nob Hill and then down to Union Square, the route Milk often used to tire out a heated crowd, but everyone stopped at Civic Center and went no farther. It wasn't long before rocks started flying from the crowd, forcing a line of riot police guarding City Hall's Polk Street entrance to take shelter inside the building's foyer. Jones used Milk's bullhorn to try to calm the crowd, but it was taken away from him and passed around. When the bullhorn got to Amber Hollibaugh—a feminist lesbian activist with bleached-blonde hair—protestors started chanting, "LET HER SPEAK! LET HER SPEAK!"

"I remember being relieved to see a woman climb up on the wide railing beside the stairs and face the crowd," Maggie Jochild, then with Lesbians Against Police Violence, recalled. "She looked to be working class and clear-headed."

"It's time we stood up for each other," Hollibaugh said into the bullhorn. "That's what Harvey meant to us. He wasn't some big leader. He was one of us. I don't think it's wrong for us to feel like we do. I think we should feel like it more often!"

Every line of Hollibaugh's speech was met with cheers and the shrill punch of the whistles. "Tell the truth!" one man yelled.

"Don't you listen to anybody who tells you you don't need to fight back," Hollibaugh continued.

The crowd responded with a prolonged chant of "FIGHT BACK! FIGHT BACK! FIGHT BACK!"

The cheers and chants from the crowd grew so loud that they drowned out the end of what Jochild described as "one hell of a speech."

"And then all hell broke loose," Jones said, although it's doubtful that things would have gone down any differently no matter who had that bullhorn.

Protestors tore the ornate brass work from the facade of City Hall's entrance and used the broken pieces of metal to break the glass windows. Gay men in leather chaps ripped parking meters out of the sidewalk and used them as battering rams, as the police watched from behind doors that couldn't hold up for much longer.

Liberal supervisor Carol Ruth Silver got smacked in the head with either a brick or bottle as she tried to calm the crowd and had to be taken to Saint Francis Hospital. Mayor Feinstein observed the chaos from her second-story office as her constituents below pelted her workplace with newly purchased trash cans and flaming bundles of newspapers. She considered addressing them but decided against it.

"I would have been a lightning rod," Feinstein later said. She opted to call in for police reinforcements from the burbs instead.

At one point, a squadron of police riding three-wheeled motorbikes attempted to mount a counterattack but were met by what Jochild described as gays and lesbians "on the big motorcycles they rode in every Freedom Day Parade."

"Most of these queers were big, especially the women; most of them had on leather," Jochild recalled. They revved the engines of their big hogs and the police retreated down Grove Street. "I've often wondered if I just imagined this whole episode," Jochild said. "Fortunately, I had companions with me who saw the same thing."

Things got more violent after the protestors were joined by angry young men from surrounding neighborhoods who weren't necessarily gay or even sympathetic to the LGBTQ+ cause. By 10:30 p.m., the first of several police cars parked on McAllister Street was torched.

"The flames from the eight burning police cars bathed the City Hall dome in an eerie flickering light and their sirens screamed like dying animals until melting down silenced them one by one," Jerry Carroll wrote, reporting for the *Chronicle*.

After the close of the White trial, Paul Krassner went home and got high. He was writing about "the ridiculous verdict" for the *Bay Guardian* when reporter Mike Weiss called and told him about the riot. Krassner took a cab to Civic Center and arrived in time to see the cops finally emerge from City Hall.

"They ran out like hell for revenge," Krassner recalled. "The police were running amuck in an orgy of indiscriminate sadism, swinging their clubs wildly and screaming, 'Get the fuck outta here, you fuckin' faggots, you motherfuckin' cocksuckers!'" Krassner took some very precise baton shots to his ribs that broke bones, punctured his lung, and caused him a lifetime of pain. Two *Chronicle* reporters and a TV journalist were also clubbed by cops in the melee, and one officer dented in the hood of *Chron* photographer Jim Storey's car, which was being used as the newspaper's command vehicle.

Police launched canisters of tear gas into the crowd, and then a line of riot cops bearing clubs and plexiglass shields swept through Civic Center Plaza. As protesters fled down Market Street, the police broke ranks to pursue them.

"At times a single demonstrator would find himself isolated, and a group of officers would club him to the ground and handcuff him to await a patrol wagon," Katy Butler wrote in the *Chronicle*.

Back in the Castro, cops stormed the massive Elephant Walk bar on the corner of Castro and 18th Streets, beating everyone inside. Jones had made his way back to his neighborhood by this time to see "the shadows of people being knocked down and punched and kicked" in what was Harvey Milk's favorite bar and is now named after him.

In an uncredited editorial, the *Bay Area Reporter*, the newspaper of record of the Bay Area's LGBTQ+ community, tried to make sense of what is now known as the White Night Riot: "With the assassination of Harvey Milk, who in the past—time after time—turned angry crowds into peaceful demonstrators, no Gay leader has emerged with enough affection and charisma to turn events around. Hence, to this writer—what happened, happened—perhaps not appropriately, but predictably. The Gay community was pushed too far."

"To many, the destruction of property was a futile response," the editorial writer added. "It accomplished nothing. Except, satisfaction."

The closure of Castro Street for the planned celebration of Harvey Milk's birthday still took place the next day even though Mayor Feinstein had considered calling in the National Guard. San Francisco's gays and lesbians weren't able to take power with their siege on City Hall, but they would never be truly powerless again. Milk had given his life to win them a seat at the table. They weren't giving it back.

## THE PAIN AND TROUBLE I'VE CAUSED

O.J. Simpson—another son of San Francisco's southern fringes who would find himself at the center of a controversial murder trial—held the Olympic torch aloft as he ran up a hillside stretch of the Pacific Coast Highway in Malibu on the morning of July 21, 1984. Although he'd been retired from the NFL for five years by then, Simpson resembled something out of Leni Riefenstahl's *Olympia* by way of a Hertz rent-a-car commercial as he bounded past thousands of spectators who crammed themselves onto crumbling seaside cliffs to cheer him on. At the top of the hill, Simpson handed the torch to Michael Bailey, a seven-year-old with cerebral palsy, who pushed himself through a kilometer of Ocean Avenue in Santa Monica in a custom-made walker as Simpson whispered encouragement in his ear.

"It took Bailey more than 15 minutes to finish," the *Los Angeles Times* reported. "When he was done, the boy seemed overcome by exhaustion, his cheeks flushed, his brow covered by perspiration."

"He's been practicing for weeks," Bailey's mother said.

Seven days later, square-jawed gold medal winner Rafer Johnson carried the torch up mechanical steps that rose before him at Los Angeles Memorial Coliseum. At the top of this feat of mechanical engineering, Johnson stood and faced the crowd and put the torch to the gas-powered Olympic rings above him. President Reagan and First Lady Nancy beamed from the press box as the flames traveled through the rings and set the Olympic cauldron ablaze. It was morning in America. The games of the XXIII Olympiad had begun.

Sometime after that but before Lionel Ritchie performed an extended version of "All Night Long" at the games' closing ceremonies, Dan White met his old friend Frank Falzon at a Los

Angeles café. White had served his five years at Soledad State Prison and was paroled to what the *Chronicle* called "the sprawling anonymity of Los Angeles County." During their lunch meeting, White filled his old friend in on details of the shooting of Milk and Moscone that he forgot to mention when he first confessed to the crime in 1978.

"I was on a mission. I wanted four of them," White said, letting Falzon know that his capacity wasn't all that diminished when he went to San Francisco's City Hall to discuss getting his old job back. White told Falzon that he had planned to murder two other public officials that day that he thought had plotted against him.

"Carol Ruth Silver—she was the biggest snake of the bunch," White explained, "and Willie Brown. He was masterminding the whole thing."

"I felt like I had been hit by a sledgehammer," Falzon later said. "I found out it was a premeditated murder."

Falzon told his colleagues in SFPD's homicide unit about his conversation with White, but none of these revelations ever made it to a parole board. Despite psychiatric testimony during his trial that he suffered from clinical depression, White had not received any treatment for his mental health issues during his incarceration or parole. And when his parole was done in January 1985, he was free to go anywhere he wanted. Mayor Feinstein warned her former board colleague not to return to San Francisco, for his own safety as much as anyone else's. "It is my belief that your return would seriously jeopardize you, your family and your home," Feinstein wrote in a letter hand-delivered to White by San Francisco police chief Cornelius Murphy during a meeting in an LAX coffee shop in October 1984.

Feinstein held a press conference on January 7, 1985, after White was already a free man. "There is a generally held belief the sentence was a very short one," Feinstein said. "Two very fine people are dead. I'm hopeful people will be able to say, 'Let's put it behind us.' At the same time . . . the situation has the potential to be a violent one."

White didn't heed the warning. After struggling to write his long-rumored book in Ireland for a couple of months, he came back to the family's white stucco home on Shawnee Avenue in the Excelsior District, then a last bastion of the white working class in San Francisco. (The white working class loves its last bastions.) Yet even in those fog-soaked slopes where avenues named after nations (France, Persia, Russia) crisscrossed streets named for European capitals (London, Lisbon, Moscow), White couldn't escape being the "Gayslayer," a title bestowed upon him in shit-disturbing columnist Warren Hinckle's book of essays by the same name. White had become the city's boogeyman and a specter haunting his own backyard—not far from where the feds had busted Patricia Hearst and where Penny Bjorkland had pumped 18 homemade slugs into August Norry.

The violence against White that Feinstein predicted came to pass but not in the form of vigilantes or pissed-off protestors. On Monday, October 23, 1985, Dan White waited for Mary Ann to leave for work in the morning and then drove the family's 1970 yellow Buick LeSabre into the garage. He lined the car's windows with towels, taped them in place to get a good seal, and ran a green garden hose from the exhaust pipe into the cab. He sat in the driver's seat, revved the car's union-made big-block V8 engine, and inhaled the carbon monoxide until his last polluted breath.

A little before 2 p.m., White's brother, Tom, found him dead in his car, clutching pictures of his family. The 39-year-old killer of men and hopes left notes for his brother, wife, and mother. "I'm sorry for all the pain and trouble I've caused," White wrote in the letter he taped to the windshield for his brother to find.

In the car's cassette deck, police found a tape of an Irish ballad called "The Town I Loved So Well," a lament for an Irish town torn apart by occupation and rebellion. With its lyrics of "men on the dole" playing "a woman's role" and "armored cars and bombed out bars," Susan Sward and Mark Z. Barabak of the *Chronicle* called the song "a haunting echo of the way White viewed changes in San

Bob Calhoun

The modest home on Shawnee Avenue in San Francisco's Excelsior District where Dan White killed himself by revving the engine of his yellow Buick LeSabre to fill the garage with carbon monoxide as he listened to an Irish ballad called "The Town I Loved So Well."

Francisco." Even as he died, White's sentimentality for a dreadful conflict that he was never a part of convinced him of his own martyrdom—even though he was the one who wore the jackboots and raised the truncheon.

He was the martyr-maker, never the martyr.

## CHAPTER 20

# THE FACE OF THE GIRL IN ROOM 24

The San Francisco police weren't much help when Valerie McDonald disappeared after leaving her North Beach apartment with a majorly shady character on November 9, 1980. Officers told McDonald's friend that she had to wait 72 hours before they could file a missing person's report. With McDonald still missing a week later, her parents, Dee Dee and Robert Kouns, flew down from Oregon. The cops told them that Valerie had probably taken off for Vegas. McDonald's friends and family had a whole clique of suspects for detectives to question, but they seemed uninterested in the case until evidence uncovered after a fatal shootout in British Columbia forced them to take notice.

McDonald was an aspiring actress and filmmaker, and her striking looks and beautiful features came with a little bit of an edge. "She was the original goth girl," said Eddie Muller, Bay Area author, film presenter, and founder of the Film Noir Foundation. "At least that's how I see her in my memory."

"She even wore a cape," Muller added. "But the most memorable thing was her aura; she floated. Never a fast move. She seemed ethereal. Everyone was aware of her, at all times. When she walked by, everybody noticed. She radiated a kind of mysterious vibe."

Muller and McDonald both studied narrative filmmaking with experimental director George Kuchar at the San Francisco Art Institute in the late 1970s. Muller even wrote "a silly script" about sisters who hunted vampires that he wanted her to act in. "I wanted to be her friend," Muller recalled, "but she ran with a different crowd. Unfortunately, drugs were involved."

After graduating from the San Francisco Art Institute in 1978, McDonald decided to stay in the city for a while. She waited tables and worked the occasional acting gig to make ends meet. She moved into the Tower Apartments above Mooney's Pub on Grant Avenue in June 1980. A few weeks later, a new manager took over McDonald's building. Something about the new building super left her scared, and it got even worse when he hired on a couple of his pals to help run things.

The men in charge of the Tower Apartments were violent criminals who'd met while rotating through San Quentin. Phillip A. Thompson, the new building manager, was released from Quentin early on a work furlough after serving time for assault with a deadly weapon, forgery, and receiving stolen goods. His long rap sheet also included two rape charges from the early 1970s. Once Thompson landed the job at the Tower Apartments, he made the place into a kind of halfway house for his big house buddies. John Gordon Abbott became the building's assistant manager on August 26, 1980, after also being released on work furlough. They were soon joined by Michael John Hennessey, the youngest of the bunch, who was on parole after serving a term for burglary.

While Thompson set everything in motion, Abbott was the mastermind of the criminal operation being planned from McDonald's apartment building. Abbott was a British national who grew up in

Canada, spoke fluent Japanese, and possessed a genius level IQ of 160. He was the son of John Abbott, a marketing economist for the United Nations, and Dr. Ursula K. Abbott, a former UC Davis professor who now has an annual genetics symposium named after her. Abbott himself dropped out of Davis and turned to crime. He was sent to prison after a shootout with police in 1976 that left his younger brother, Michael, dead. In prison, Abbott met Thompson. The two were hardly model prisoners. They ran various scams there, and even escaped from the place, but were released early anyway.

Before she disappeared, Valerie told a close friend that she had seen her building's new supers engaging in "Satanistic [sic] activities" and partying down with "large bowls of cocaine." She knew she had to get away from these guys, but they knew just how to get to her. On November 9, 1980, McDonald was packing up her apartment with a friend when Hennessey stopped by and offered her a bit part in a Dustin Hoffman movie being produced by Dino De Laurentiis, the mega producer who gave us *Flash Gordon* (1980) and *Conan the Barbarian* (1982). Hennessey claimed he was supplying the set with blow, and said that McDonald was perfect for the part of a pretty blonde victim of a serial killer, who was being hunted by Hoffman. It sounded sketchy as all hell but also somehow plausible. Two years earlier, Hoffman had starred in *Straight Time*, a gritty parolee drama based on the novel *No Beast So Fierce* by Edward Bunker, a reformed convict who had become San Quentin's youngest inmate when he was just 17 years old.

While Hennessey may have recycled prison yard gossip about Hoffman and *Straight Time* to sound convincing, it also helped that he was the right lure. Compared to his pals, he came off as the good one, and McDonald even said she liked him. Hennessey also offered to pay McDonald $200 up front with more to come. While that may not seem like a lot now, McDonald was only paying $100 a month in rent back in 1980, making this equivalent to $7,000 in today's San Francisco. With her move out of the Tower Apartments, McDonald really needed the money. She also couldn't resist the idea of scoring her big break.

McDonald left with Hennessey. She was never seen alive again.

The men suspected of kidnapping McDonald were able to get out of town before an uninterested SFPD was goaded into any kind of action by her parents. Abbott, Thompson, and Hennessey arrived in British Columbia near Abbott's hometown on November 22, 1980. Thompson didn't stay up north very long before he headed back to the Bay Area. But he took their only set of car keys with him, forcing his partners to hire a local locksmith to get into their green Chevy Monte Carlo. When the locksmith tried to test the new keys on the trunk, Abbott put his hand over the lock and wouldn't let him open it.

Abbott had the car towed to a transmission shop in Trail, B.C., on November 24. A day later, he and Hennessey pulled two large duffel bags and a box of papers out of the trunk. When the men showed up to pick up the car the following day, plainclothes Mounties were waiting for them. Abbott and Hennessey opened fire, hitting Royal Canadian Mounted Police constable Jim Lark in the leg. Like Abbott's brother before him, Hennessey was killed in the shootout. Abbott may have been a genius, but he wasn't much for keeping his partners alive.

Nobody knows who tipped off the Mounties about Abbott and Hennessey, although Davis police did contact Canadian authorities in 1978 when Abbott had escaped from prison. "It is my belief that Mr. Abbott should be considered very dangerous and would kill without hesitation," Detective Sergeant John Parsons wrote in a prophetic letter to the RCMP.

When police searched Abbott and Hennessey's apartment in Rossland, B.C., they found Valerie McDonald's voter registration and unemployment cards, and one other ghastly piece of evidence: a receipt from San Francisco dated November 5 for 11 bags of cement, two bags of plaster, a tub, and a hoe. Robert and Dee Dee Kouns, McDonald's parents, feared that the men were planning to dispose of a body in the days before their daughter disappeared. Police also found long strands of strawberry-blonde hair that could have come from McDonald in the trunk of the Monte Carlo.

After Abbott was arrested in Canada, San Francisco police finally got interested in the case. On January 17, 1981, they raided a warehouse in Hunters Point used by the gang. Thompson was arrested during the raid, but he wasn't held for anything to do with McDonald's disappearance.

In the warehouse, investigators found files with plans for a string of elaborate heists throughout the Bay Area, including a pair of robberies that had been perpetrated by Thompson on December 24 and 30, 1980, a month after the Canadian shootout. Thompson had kept ominous records on UPS drivers, including the ages of the drivers' children and the routes they took to go to school. Pillow cases were dropped over the UPS drivers' heads and they were driven to the warehouse and robbed.

According to the *San Francisco Examiner*, Abbott and Thompson used robberies to get seed money to buy guns to sell to right-wing militias in El Salvador and cocaine cartels in Bolivia and Colombia. Thompson's ties to the CIA and other federal agencies went from wild conspiracy theory to reported fact, and it was even revealed that he worked as a driver for the Nixon campaign in 1972.

"That's something that always puzzled me," San Francisco burglary inspector Neil Jordan told the *Examiner*.

"We had a statement from Abbott acknowledging his and Thompson's complicity in at least three robberies, and evidence to tie them to three others," Jordan added, before noting that other Bay Area jurisdictions never moved to prosecute. It was also puzzling to Jordan that Abbott and Thompson got out of San Quentin early on work furlough less than two years after escaping from prison and setting up a burglary ring while they were on the lam.

"Why did [Thompson] get out so early? I don't know," Jordan said.

Despite being held in jails nearly 1,000 miles away from each other, Abbott and Thompson both denied any guilt in the disappearance of Valerie McDonald. Without a body or a murder weapon, they weren't charged in the crime.

"She was just the face of the girl in room 24," Thompson told the *Examiner*.

A creepy line in a poem found in Abbott's journals seized by Mounties seemed to tell a different story, however. "The Ice Maiden in her fallen beauty also what a dream," Abbott wrote. "Flying in the air flowing with the stream."

In 1991, a human skull and pieces of torso were found on the floodplain of the Kettle River just outside of Danville, Washington, near the U.S.-Canada border. J.R. Sharp was a volunteer deputy with the Ferry County Sheriff's Office when the bones were first examined and stored in the basement evidence room, but he stayed with the case even after they failed to match a nearby missing person case.

"The driving factor was we had some human remains in our evidence room and a family out there," Sharp told the *Seattle Post-Intelligencer* in 2003. "It's our responsibility to that family to do all we can to make an identification."

After becoming the only full-time detective on the eight-deputy force, Sharp successfully petitioned the Ferry County Commission for $3,000 to hire a forensic anthropologist to reexamine the bones. They already knew the bones belonged to a woman, but now they were able to peg her age at 25 to 35. She was also of European and possibly part Asian ancestry.

Sharp sent out an alert with the new information through Washington state's Homicide Investigation Tracking System. After sorting through 100 calls from police agencies throughout the Pacific Northwest, he got a request for dental records from California's Missing and Unidentified Persons Unit in 1999. Eighteen months later, on November 22, 2000, California authorities called the Ferry

County Sheriff's Office with a positive identification of those bones. The Jane Doe who had been packed away in a box since 1991 was Valerie McDonald.

The identification of their daughter's remains gave Dee Dee and Robert Kouns a sense of closure but not justice. The men they were positive had murdered Valerie—John Gordon Abbott and Phillip A. Thompson—still weren't charged with the crime. Furthermore, it was unlikely that a small "department out here in the sticks working on a shoestring budget," as Detective Sharp described it, would ever be able to connect that box of bones to a murder in faraway San Francisco to the satisfaction of a 21st-century jury.

Thompson and Abbott had committed so many crimes that they couldn't escape punishment entirely. Abbott served eight years in a Canadian prison following the 1980 shootout with Mounties. He was released in 1989 and then deported to the United Kingdom. In the early 2000s, Thompson was serving an 18-year sentence for kidnapping and grand theft for the spate of mail robberies that he masterminded from the same Hunters Point warehouse where he and his cohorts had likely murdered McDonald. Thompson had received a stiffer sentence than Abbott, but he was eligible for parole by 2003.

This was especially galling to the Kounses, who had spent the two decades following Valerie's disappearance advocating for victim's rights in Oregon. The couple founded an advocacy group called Crime Victims United and campaigned successfully for the passage of Measure 11, a 1994 Oregon ballot initiative that set some of the harshest mandatory minimum criminal sentences in the country. While such "tough on crime" statutes have come under scrutiny with our nation's exploding prison population, looking at the Valerie McDonald case makes it easy to understand how we got here.

While Thompson had escaped being indicted for the murder of Valerie McDonald, another cold case caught up with him. On June 19, 1971, the body of Betty Cloer, a 21-year-old mother, was found by two young girls on horseback in a field near Sacramento. Cloer had been beaten, raped, and shot three times. Police were given a description of the man she went out dancing with the night before, but they never found a suspect. In late 2003, sperm found on Cloer's clothes was matched to Thompson by a new round of DNA testing. Thompson was charged with the murder by investigators from the El Dorado County Sheriff's Office on the day he was scheduled to get out of prison. He was found guilty of first-degree murder on April 8, 2008, and will likely spend the rest of his life behind bars. He is currently incarcerated in the California Medical Facility in Vacaville.

John Abbott, the mad genius, got off more lightly. In 2012, *Investigate Magazine* found Abbott living in a tiny village in New Zealand where he had amassed millions of dollars in property, paying for all of it in cash. He was soon barred from reentering New Zealand and Australia after authorities in those countries learned of his ultra-violent past. He fled to the U.K. but is now reportedly in Japan where he has taught English for years.

Adding an extra level of despair to a story that hardly needs it, Detective J.R. Sharp, aka Carroll Sharp Jr. (the nominal hero of this chapter), resigned from the Ferry County Sheriff's Office in 2006 during an FBI probe into allegations that he had inappropriately touched troubled teenage boys living in his home during what the *Spokesman-Review* of Spokane, Washington, described as "informal wrestling sessions."

But the Valerie McDonald case had other twists and turns that fall somewhere outside of its already crooked narrative. On December 31, 1980, Ines Sailer, a 23-year-old German kindergarten teacher, celebrated the coming of the new year at a party in San Francisco's Richmond District. On January 1, 1981, she was found dead nearly 60 miles away in a carport in San Jose. Sailer had been sodomized and shot five times in the body and the brain with a small caliber handgun. Police believed that she had been murdered somewhere else and then dumped there.

Stranger still, investigators found a slip of paper in Sailer's wallet with Valerie McDonald's name and phone number written on it. The Sailer murder took place more than two weeks before the raid on the Hunters Point warehouse that led to Phillip Thompson's arrest for his UPS delivery truck robbery spree. While Thompson had murdered and raped before, this wasn't proven until much later. It could not be ascertained if he was ever a suspect in the Sailer investigation.

But in another carport a little over a year after the Sailer killing, Dawn O'Malley stood by while her fiancé, David Wallace, parked his car in their San Francisco apartment building on February 20, 1982. Melvin Forte, a steely-eyed career criminal, came up behind O'Malley and shot her in once in the back. Forte then plugged Wallace in the head as he got out of the car. Wallace fell to the floor, dead.

O'Malley was found and rushed to the hospital where medical personnel accidentally broke her finger while removing the diamond engagement ring that Wallace had sold his Austin-Healey sportscar to buy for her. After surviving the shooting, O'Malley cloistered herself away at her parents' house for five months.

"I had no one who could understand what I was going through," O'Malley later recalled. "I didn't know anyone who witnessed the murder of someone they loved."

The day after shooting O'Malley and Wallace, Forte robbed a business in Milpitas and continued his crime spree with armed robberies in Los Altos and Burlingame, where he shot a security guard with the same gun he'd used to kill Wallace. Forte was found with the gun when he was later arrested in San Francisco. He was sentenced to life in prison based mostly on the ballistics evidence. While at San Quentin, Forte tutored inmates and played in a jazz ensemble. He also tried to strangle a prison librarian.

In 2006, San Jose detectives tested physical evidence found on Sailer's clothes and body 25 years earlier, and matched it to a sample in a state database. Melvin Forte was the man who raped her. Police were also able to determine that Forte had once worked at the Langendorf

Bakery in San Jose, and also had relatives there, giving him knowledge of the area where Sailer's body was found.

"Working and homicide is two different things," Forte said in the opening statement of his trial. The killer acted as his own attorney, and things didn't go very well for him. Forte undid his own defense while grilling Barbara Kelch, the apartment manager who found Sailer's corpse.

"I remember seeing you," Kelch said under Forte's cross-examination. Apartment records for the complex where Sailer was found were long gone by the time of the trial, but Kelch was able to establish that Forte had lived in the building. "I didn't recall you until I saw you today," Kelch said. "I'm an artist. Details are important to me."

The jury brought in a guilty verdict in less than three hours. Dawn O'Malley was able to confront her fiancé's killer during the sentencing phase of the trial. Forte referred to himself in the third person as he questioned his one-time victim.

"Okay, what did you do when the person shot you?" Forte asked.

"You shot me," O'Malley replied, as jurors visibly winced.

Forte was given the death penalty on May 6, 2011. He now sits on San Quentin's death row.

While one interpretation of the DNA evidence may indicate that Forte had an accomplice in Sailer's murder, he botched his case so thoroughly that this avenue was never explored during the murder trial. And we are just left to speculate on who that accomplice could be, although Thompson's modus operandi and the scrap of paper that connected Sailer to McDonald present us with one suspect. Was Forte part of the crew that helped Thompson carry out the mail truck heists and other far-worse crimes? Only two men can answer that, and they're both spending the rest of their rancid lives in California correctional facilities.

For Eddie Muller, the memory of Valerie McDonald is not one that will ever fade. He became obsessed with the case about 15 years ago when the cop who worked her missing person's case and the private eye whom her family hired when she went missing crossed his path. “These people just appeared in my life,” Muller explained. “It didn’t feel like a coincidence because it happened within a few weeks of my having a dream about Valerie, after not thinking about her for more than 20 years.” Muller dove into researching the case, but like everyone else drawn to it, he found it to be “hell’s rabbit hole.”

“She was, sadly, the Black Dahlia of my generation,” Muller said. “I’m still haunted by her story.”

## CHAPTER 21

# THE HUCKSTERS

### BYE, KIDS

Ed Barbara of Furniture USA was the Bay Area's undisputed king of commercial interruptions in the 1970s and '80s. No commercial break during my childhood was safe from his rapid-fire promises of easy credit, made as he floated ethereally across rows of flimsy bed sets through the magic of a really obvious green screen.

"No cosigners, no credit references necessary," he proclaimed before closing each 30-second spot with his trademark catchphrase, "Bye, kids," just to add an extra bit of creep factor.

Barbara's ads may have been a constant nuisance, but no one forgot them. A whopping 95 percent of San Jose State students knew who Ed Barbara was in a 1980 survey.

"The secret to success is to irritate the public," Barbara said during a 1980 interview. "I learned many years ago that to be remembered, you have to irritate."

"No one forgets his worst enemy," Barbara added.

For those clamoring to buy a new fridge from their worst enemy, Barbara was their man. After conquering the South Bay's distressed credit market, Barbara set his sights on Wall Street, or at least the pink sheets. In 1984, Barbara founded Dynapac Inc., a strange conglomerate that included an automatic sofa bed company and a televised bingo scheme.

"There will be no cost of money or consideration on the part of the players," Barbara claimed in a September 4, 1984, press release for Intercom Network Bingo, which he assured investors was a "true mania with continued rapid growth."

But Barbara really became the Wolf of El Camino when Dynapac bought a 50 percent interest in the Ladder Ranch gold mine close to (and I'm not making this up) Truth or Consequences, New Mexico. Celebrity attorney and Zodiac Killer pen pal Melvin Belli wrote a letter urging potential investors not to miss out on Dynapac's mother lode, and the company projected gold production worth $93 million in 1985. Shares surged from $2 in late 1984 to $8.32 by February 1985. The problem for investors was that Dynapac's projections were more than a little bit off. They were out-and-out lies.

According to an April 1986 investigative report by new-fangled CNN (back when they did investigative reports), Dynapac workers salted the Ladder Ranch mine with outside ore to fool investment analysts. Barbara denied the accusations, but David Fingado, a former assayer for the mine, told CNN in an August 9, 1986, report that Barbara was lying. Fingado died in a suspicious car crash five days later.

In early October 1986, the SEC charged Barbara and several of his business associates with fraud. Barbara went on the lam. Furniture USA filed for bankruptcy by the end of the month, citing over $3.3 million in debts. Not surprisingly, the furniture chain's biggest creditors were KTVU Channel 2 and KOFY TV 20, the local stations that constantly ran his annoying ads.

While Barbara's South Bay furniture empire was crumbling, he started a new one in Vancouver, British Columbia, with some of the

$2 million he'd swindled from Dynapac investors. After establishing himself in Canada, Barbara bilked his new customers out of $50,000 for furniture that was paid for but not delivered.

Barbara was arrested in mid-1987 in Vancouver, Washington, and extradited to New Mexico where he finally stood trial. A jury convicted him of a dozen counts of fraud and racketeering in July 1988, but somebody in the Santa Fe court system thought it was a good idea to let a guy famous for saying "Bye, kids" out on bail. Barbara skipped again, forcing the judge to sentence him in absentia to 19 and a half years in state prison. Barbara reportedly died of cancer in Florida while still on the run.

Despite dominating local airwaves for over a decade, little remains to mark Barbara's broadcasting legacy but some old message board threads and a summary of a 1989 *Unsolved Mysteries* segment about him. The most fitting memorial to Ed Barbara is an f-bomb laden spoof commercial where he lets us know what he really thinks of all his "lazy bastard" customers, which will hopefully always be streaming on YouTube.

"You know why you people can get credit at Furniture USA?" he asks, shaking his finger at the camera. "Because I'll break your fuckin legs, you son of a bitch, if you don't pay! You understand?

"Get your ass down here today. Remember. No cosigners and no credit references."

Bye, kids.

## THE CARPET KING

"Wild-Eyed" Leon Heskett was the self-proclaimed Bay Area "Carpet King" in the 1960s and '70s. He ruled his discount empire from his bright yellow Carpet Coliseum store in Oakland, which was once described as "the most horrible thing I have ever seen" by an unnamed speaker during a Burlingame Planning Commission meeting in 1973. Heskett's newspaper ads boasted "The West's largest carpet inventory" over a publicity photo of Heskett standing proudly next to towering shelves filled with rolls of rugs.

While business appeared to be booming through the '70s, it all went up in smoke (literally) on February 17, 1982, when a six-alarm fire gutted Heskett's flagship Oakland store. UPI reported it took 85 Oakland firefighters to combat the blaze that was easily seen from San Francisco.

"What the hell can you say?" Heskett said. "When you work for 30 years to build a business, and it's gone in 30 minutes."

Arson was suspected, and Heskett was quick to blame Cary Cheifer, "an irate customer" who, according to Heskett, had threatened to kill him and run him out of business only days earlier. Cheifer was hauled in for questioning by police but was cleared as a suspect after taking a polygraph test.

It turned out that Heskett himself had set the blaze with the help of two store employees. And once Heskett became a firebug, he couldn't stop. The huckster also planted a pipe bomb in the Piedmont home of his former attorney, Robert K. Lane. Fortunately, Lane was able to stamp out the fuse before the device went off. Heskett turned himself in and was later charged in the attempted firebombing.

For whatever reason, Heskett wasn't indicted for arson, but he was instead convicted of 11 counts of mail fraud for letters he sent to the TransAmerica Insurance Co. to collect $1.2 million in claims from burning down his own store. Heskett, looking "pale and weak," according to the *Chronicle*, was sentenced to eight years in prison on April 25, 1985. He was also ordered to repay his insurance company. Tyrone David, one of Heskett's accomplices, drew a five-year sentence.

After Heskett was initially indicted in 1984, Cary Cheifer, the man whom Heskett tried to frame two years earlier, sued the deposed carpet king for slander and malicious prosecution. Heskett didn't show up to the hearing, and Cheifer won a default judgment, giving him $250,000 in damages and $1 million in punitive damages. Heskett later tried to appeal the ruling citing that he couldn't make the hearing because he was in jail at the time, but the court of appeals ruled that Cheifer was still entitled to the award.

Heskett died on December 17, 2006. He is buried in the Sacramento Valley National Cemetery in Dixon, California. His gravestone reads, "I love you every day in each and every way."

## GET A BIKE!

Matthew's TV and Stereo on the gentle incline at "Top of the Hill, Daly City" didn't have a whole lot of floor space, but it was kind of a big deal. The Monkees signed autographs there before playing a sold-out show at the Cow Palace in the 1960s. Michael Dorn from *Star Trek: The Next Generation* pushed 8-track players there in the 1970s when he went to San Francisco State. But owner Steven Matthew David achieved his highest level of local fame in the 1980s when he bombarded the local airwaves with TV ads offering free bikes with 25-inch Zenith TVs and Sanyo car stereo systems. "Get a bike!" David exclaimed as he hovered over his store's stacked inventory via green screen as triumphal stock music set an upbeat tone. David paid $90 to $120 for the 15-speeds, and that cost was all passed back to the customer, but David maintained that no one seemed to mind.

"Over the years, we've moved 150,000 bikes," David boasted to the *Examiner* in 1992. "Three percent of the people in the Bay Area are riding around on bikes they bought from us."

But all that sweet coin from moving Fisher cassette decks wasn't enough for him. He wanted to get in on the original tech boom coming out of Cupertino, so he hatched an ingenious—and illegal—scheme that actually bit into Steve Jobs's bottom line.

In March 1984, David conspired with John Lynch, an employee of the archdiocese of San Francisco, to purchase 2,700 Apple computers using the institution's educational discount. The computers were supposed to go to Catholic schools, but only 450 Macs made it to classrooms while David moved the rest out of his Computer Connection store in San Francisco at full price.

"We're painfully aware of it and are trying to resolve it," Reverend Miles Riley, a spokesman for the archdiocese, told the *Chronicle* after learning of the scam. "We want to pay back what is owed and make amends."

According to the *Examiner*, David also billed Apple $100 per computer in service fees, claiming his company installed the contraband Macs at the schools. Apple estimated it lost more than $700,000 from the scam. David and Lynch were indicted on fraud charges by the San Francisco District Attorney's Office on May 15, 1986. While David was still pleading not guilty, Lynch copped to the rip-off and was sentenced to three years' probation, 500 hours of community service, and a $500 fine. By August, David pleaded no contest and was required to return more than $860,000 in cash and computers to Apple, a company now valued at $1 trillion that has avoided paying billions in U.S. taxes by storing its cash offshore.

The Apple scam wasn't David's first brush with the law over his business practices. In March 1974, San Mateo's and San Francisco County's district attorneys charged David and Bay Area disc jockey Tom Campbell for using what the *Examiner* called "bait and switch" tactics. David and Campbell advertised impossibly low prices on products that were conveniently out of stock as a way of luring customers into the store. David paid an out-of-court settlement of $80,000.

After paying back Apple in 1986, David closed down his Computer Connection store, but Matthew's TV and Stereo kept on going until November 1992 when now-defunct national chains like Circuit City and the Good Guys drove him out of business.

"I'm tired of doing this," David told the *Examiner* as customers mobbed his store one last time. "I've lost interest. What am I going to feel when I close the door here for the last time? Nothing but relief."

In 2003, David still owned the building at 6400 Mission Street that once housed his retail empire, but the storefront had become what Daly City officials deemed "an eyesore." David agreed to clean up the place in August 2003. "I'm indeed embarrassed and ashamed to be down here," David said, appearing before Daly City officials. "I agree with the staff that the building looks terrible and I apologize."

Today the building is home to a One Dollar Only store, where several items go for more than a buck.

## SEVERED PENIS, FILM AT 11

They were called the KGO Cowboys, a local news team dressed like Wild West outlaws riding into a ghost town on horseback in a 1970s TV spot so ridiculous that it reportedly inspired the newsman brawl in *Anchorman: The Legend of Ron Burgundy*. Leading this gang of teleprompter-reading desperados was Fred Van Amburg, the lead anchor of KGO's *News Scene* from 1969 to 1986. Known to viewers as just "Van Amburg," he pioneered the "happy talk" TV news format, where the newscasters bantered back and forth between stories that were all too often as gruesome as the Zodiac and the Zebra murders.

Sometime around 1974, KGO's ratings-topping news style made national waves when Van Amburg hyped footage of a severed penis found on the railroad tracks of the West Oakland train yards. In a 1974 *60 Minutes* story on the emergence of tabloid TV journalism, Mike Wallace reported that 55 percent of KGO's *News Scene* broadcasts were made up of "fire, crime, sex, accidents, tearjerkers, and exorcism stories"—the old media equivalent of clickbait. When Wallace asked about the severed penis, Van Amburg replied, "We didn't just cut that thing off and put it out there," and noted that somebody was the victim of this attack.

And Van Amburg still had pride in KGO's scoop decades later. "You'll have to admit that the backlighting when the cop held up that baggie with the evidence was dramatic," Van Amburg later boasted to a Broadcast Legends meeting held in San Francisco in 1995.

Pat McCrystle, the KGO news photographer who captured the image of the dismembered member for Bay Area viewers, recalled the incident in a comment on Rich Lieberman's *415 Media* blog.

"I made sure that I filmed it with the beautiful background of the 'city' behind the big baggie with the little wiener going in it," McCrystle wrote. "I bet I ruined lots of dinners that evening for the 6:00 news."

While the castration became a national symbol of TV news excess, details of the crime and its victim go unremembered. Who was the unwilling castrato? Who cut off his dick, and why? Did the man survive being castrated? Was his sex organ surgically reattached? Searches of the digital archives of the *Chronicle*, *Examiner*, and *Oakland Tribune* turned up no reporting of the incident beyond mentions of the media uproar it caused. As for Van Amburg, he rode this brand of reporting to paydays reportedly as high as $1 million a year, and a whopping 50 percent ratings share of Bay Area television viewers. While he was riding high, he never apologized for his news judgment.

"You know that transsexual who wants to play tennis [Dr. Renee Richards]? Well, if I had it my way, we'd spend the whole sports segment of the news on that story because that's the future, that's the trend. Not runs, hits and errors," he told the *Examiner* somewhat prophetically in 1976. Van Amburg was thrust into retirement when KGO refused to renegotiate his contract for undisclosed reasons in 1986, and he never worked in TV news again. He died at his home in El Cerrito, California, on June 22, 2017.

## CHAPTER 22

# THE OUTSIDE LANDS

### A CLUMP OF SHRUBBERY

In 1865, San Francisco was barely removed from its early days of sidewalks built from tobacco crates laid out over mud, but city leaders had already started planning for its grand park. They brought in Frederick Law Olmsted to have a go at converting the windswept sand dunes of an area called the Outside Lands into something on par with the Central Park that he designed for New York. After totally missing the redwoods and seeing no trees "of beautiful proportions near San Francisco," Olmsted was out. Tasked with planting the trees that Olmsted didn't find and making what would become Golden Gate Park out of a 1,017-acre rectangle that stretches from Ocean Beach to the Haight-Ashbury was William Hammond Hall, the park's first superintendent. And starting in 1870 and continuing through the 1880s, he and his successor, the hard-drinking horticulturalist John McClaren, were pretty successful in making a tightly hemmed yet sprawling arboretum out of what had previously been a habitat for sand fleas.

After 20 some odd years of meticulous landscaping, all those newly planted trees came to provide excellent cover for corpse disposal and lonely suicides. The body of a well-dressed young man was found covered in blood and lying in "a clump of shrubbery" near a casino that was once in the park on July 14, 1891. Railroad worker D.C. Butler was found dead in the bushes near the south drive in November 1895. The body of a hide dealer named Charles Rosenberg was found in some bushes near Strawberry Hill in June 1898. Bodies always seemed to be found in bushes or shrubs grouped in "clumps" as if the *Chron*, *Ex*, and *Call* had convened a joint style-guide meeting on how to describe the most popular piece of park scenery for cadaver discoveries. That is, unless the bodies were found floating in the park's picturesque man-made lakes and ponds, or the few that were left in outhouses and commodes.

While the 1890s were the boom years for finding dead people in the park, joggers (so many joggers), rangers, and picnickers have been stumbling upon corpses lying around clumps of shrubs ever since. Starting in 1981, Golden Gate Park played host to three of the strangest body dumps in its 150-year history.

## CHICKEN WINGS AND BLOODY STUMPS

On Sunday, February 8, 1981, the headless body of an African American man was found wrapped in a sleeping bag near Alvord Lake in Golden Gate Park, not far from where Haight Street ends at Stanyan. Police couldn't locate the victim's head, but they did discover a chicken wing and two kernels of corn jammed into the bloody neck stump. A slaughtered chicken was also found 50 yards from the corpse. Police speculated that either a very sharp axe or a machete was used. A deputy coroner called the cut "very clean."

Fingerprints identified the headless man as LeRoy Carter Jr., a 29-year-old petty criminal with a bit of a rap sheet, but nothing that should've made him a candidate for human sacrifice. Because of the ritualistic nature of the killing, the case was given to Inspector Sandi

Gallant. She had recently handled local investigations in the wake of the Jonestown Massacre in Guyana. Without knowing it, she had become the department's resident expert on religious extremists. With the dead chicken in mind, Gallant reached out to Charles Wetli, coroner of Dade County, Florida, and one of the country's top experts on Santeria, a religion brought to the Caribbean by enslaved West Africans that's a little heavy on the use of poultry. Wetli told Gallant that the murderer would return the severed head to the scene of the crime in 42 days to complete the ghastly ritual.

"We literally were laughed at by our homicide investigators, and our chief of detectives," Gallant later recalled in the *Los Angeles Times*. As the 42-day mark neared, even Gallant was filled with self-doubt.

"Our problem was, even though our homicide detectives didn't buy it, my partner and I weren't out there doing surveillance on the 42nd day either," Gallant said. But sure enough, Carter's head turned up under a bush near Alvord Lake exactly 42 days later on March 22, 1981. The murder of LeRoy Carter Jr. remains unsolved.

Library of Congress

Alvord Lake in Golden Gate Park in a photo dated 1892. The park officially opened in 1870 and quickly became the place to discover dead bodies. The headless body of LeRoy Carter Jr. was discovered near here in 1981.

## THE BARRELS

The 55-gallon metal drums looked out of place. They were left in Golden Gate Park near a narrow jogging path about a mile from the ocean. Answering reports from concerned residents, mounted patrolman Bruno Pezzulich was the first to inspect the drums on May 3, 1983. He noticed that one of them was marked "Toxic Chemicals" and called the fire department. When one of the firefighters moved one of the concrete-sealed barrels, blood oozed out.

Chief Assistant Coroner Joe Surdyka had the drums thoroughly x-rayed and finger printed before he dared to open them. To open the drums immediately could have damaged "the integrity of any evidence on the outside," Surdyka explained to the Associated Press. Surdyka found the body of a fully clothed Black man in one drum and two naked white women stuffed in the other. There was a lot of blood in those drums, and the bodies were badly decayed. It took Surdyka a few days before he could determine that all three victims had died from gunshots to the back of their heads.

The male victim was Michael Thomas, 24. He had a record of robbery and drug arrests going back to 1977. The female victims were Phyllis Melendez, 24, and Brenda Oakden, 19. Melendez lived with Thomas and had been arrested five times for prostitution in 1982. Oakden went by the name of Brenda Rule in the city's punk rock scene and dated Mike Fox, the guitarist for the early hardcore band Code of Honor. Barry Ward—a prolific guitarist who has gigged with RKL, Crosstops, Me First and the Gimme Gimmes, and even Gwar—knew Brenda Rule. "I guess the question was why Brenda got caught up with that. Wrong place at the wrong time?" Ward said. "She wasn't a prostitute. Just a sweet girl that liked punk."

The investigation dragged on for months, but police finally made an arrest in August 1983 when they were able to match fingerprints found on the drums to Anthony "Jack" Sully, a former cop turned killer. Sully was a hard-looking man with a mustache and a receding hairline. He had served on the Millbrae police force from 1967 to

'74 before quitting to open an electrical contracting business in Burlingame. Sometime after turning in his badge, Sully developed a passion for torturing and murdering prostitutes while freebasing cocaine. He was linked to three other Bay Area murders, in addition to the bodies in the drums.

His first victim was Gloria Fravel, a prostitute who worked for an escort service run by Tina Livingston, a frequent accomplice of Sully's. According to court records, Sully tortured and raped Fravel in his Burlingame warehouse over the course of a weekend in February 1983. He occasionally took breaks from the mayhem to freebase coke with Livingston and another escort named Angel Burns. When Fravel's gag came loose and she started to scream, Sully killed her by yanking hard on a noose that he had tied around her neck. Sully and Burns dumped Fravel's body off to the side of Highway 35. Sully kept a newspaper article reporting the discovery of Fravel's body as a sick kind of trophy. He thought it was hilarious that the corpse was found by a butcher.

Sully then murdered Thomas, Melendez, and Oakden and stuffed them into drums. After that, he killed Barbara Searcy when she went to his warehouse to collect money he owed her. He showed Livingston the body and coerced the madam into breaking into Searcy's apartment to erase a message that Sully had left on her answering machine. Sully and Livingston then dragged Searcy's body behind his pickup truck to make it unrecognizable.

Kathryn Barrett, a drug dealer, was Sully's last known victim. Sully and his friend Michael Francis stabbed Barrett six times in the chest as Livingston watched. When Barrett didn't die from the multiple knife wounds, Sully slammed a sledgehammer into her face. Francis later said that "he could not forget the sound of Barrett's bones cracking."

When Sully was brought to trial in 1986, he entered a not guilty plea. His defense tried to paint Livingston as the murderer and mastermind of a plot to frame their client. Livingston cooperated with the prosecution, pleaded guilty to manslaughter, and served three years.

On June 3, 1986, Sully was found guilty on six counts of first-degree murder after a seven-week trial.

"You killed me for a crime I didn't commit," Sully yelled after the sentence was read. He then screamed obscenities as deputies dragged him out of the courtroom. He was sentenced to death just over a month later.

"I'm not a monster, a maniac nor am I subhuman," Sully, 41, said during a 40-minute speech at his sentencing hearing. Deputies lined the courtroom walls to guard against another outburst from the convicted murderer.

Sully appealed his verdict in 2013, but the court upheld his death sentence. He currently awaits his fate on San Quentin's death row.

## KILLING A KID FOR PROFIT

Suulan Chem, 37, and her nine-year-old son, Michael Nguyen, were pulling into the driveway of their white stucco home on 25th Avenue in the Sunset District at 12:25 a.m. on September 2, 1992, after a friend's birthday dinner. Three Asian toughs were waiting for them. One of the men put a gun to Chem's head and forced her to the ground.

"Be quiet," he commanded. "Make no noise, or we'll kill you."

The other men snatched Chem's purse and threw her boy into their getaway car. The men sped off while the mother screamed for help on the sidewalk.

Michael's battered body was discovered by a woman walking her dog just seven hours later in what the *San Francisco Chronicle* described as "a brush covered ravine" in Golden Gate Park. Michael was just a week away from starting the third grade at McKinley Elementary School in Duboce Triangle.

Chem and Michael's father, Thanh Nguyen, had fled Vietnam after the Fall of Saigon in 1975. Nguyen drove a cab for Luxor, and Chem tried her hand at several businesses that went down the drain. Neither of them had very much money, making them unlikely targets for kidnapping-for-ransom. A lie detector test cleared Chem of any involvement in her son's murder.

"At this point, I have no idea why the child was killed," homicide inspector Jim Bergstrom told the *Chron*, noting that the case was "very unusual." Mayor Frank Jordan had the city put up a $25,000 reward for information leading to an arrest in the case. "This is a heinous crime, and I want to use all possible means to apprehend the person or persons who committed this murder," he said in a statement released by his office.

Investigators came up with a theory that Michael's murder was ordered by loan sharks because of a $100,000 loan taken out by the sister of Chem's former boyfriend, Thaun Wu, 41. While the loan shark theory didn't hit the mark, it pointed police in the right direction.

Thuan Wu, aka Tom Wu, was an insurance salesman who had the habit of taking out big policies on unwitting friends and family members. He took out five policies worth a total of $750,000 on young Michael. Wu had known Michael since the boy was six. Michael's mother was unaware of the policies on her son, or of an additional $100,000 policy that Wu took out on her naming Wu's own teenage son as the beneficiary. It was later determined that Wu forged Chem's signature on the policies.

Wu also held a $100,000 policy on his sister, Nga Tuyet O, who died after a plunge off the Bay Bridge in 1991. Her death was ruled a suicide, so Wu couldn't collect. Wu held another $300,000 policy on his friend, Phoc Huyhn, who was shot five times after Wu invited him to a card game. Huyhn survived, depriving Wu of yet another big payout.

When police arrested Wu in a Marina District motel on January 28, 1993, the scam artist was wearing a hat and glasses in what police chief Anthony Ribera called "an obvious attempt to disguise himself."

Wu had planned to fake his own death by finding a corpse that looked like him in either China or Vietnam, burning the body, and then reporting it to the U.S. Embassy so he could collect on insurance policies he had taken out on himself. Wu then planned to alter his appearance by undergoing plastic surgery and take a new identity by entering into a sham marriage.

Police also arrested Victor Kiet Diep, 21, for the kidnapping and killing of Michael Nguyen. Diep was being held in the San Mateo County jail for a strong-arm robbery of a phone store in Foster City when he was arrested for the Nguyen murder. Chem identified Diep as the man who held a gun to her head. It is unclear from news reports if any other accomplices were ever charged in the abduction.

Wu and Diep were found guilty of first-degree murder and other charges on June 18, 1996. Wu was also found guilty of conspiracy to murder Phuoc Huynh, and Diep was convicted of using a firearm in the commission of a felony. Wu and Diep were later sentenced to life in prison without the possibility of parole.

## CHAPTER 23

# THE NIGHT STALKER IS BORN

By mid-August 1985, Richard Ramirez had murdered 13 people and raped several others in the Los Angeles suburbs. Since the beginning of his Southern California reign of terror in June 1984, the serial killer had almost as many nicknames as he did victims. The press and police referred to him as the "Valley Intruder" and the "Walk-In Killer," but none of his aliases inflamed the public imagination until he took a trip to San Francisco and became the "Night Stalker."

Ramirez had murdered four people and attacked four others in July 1985. He started off August by attacking a couple in Northridge on August 6. He then killed Elyas Abowath, 31, and repeatedly sodomized Sakina Abowath, 27, in the couple's Diamond Bar home two days later. Fearing that the Southern California media had raised too much awareness of him, Ramirez returned to his old hunting grounds in San Francisco's Tenderloin District where he had raped and killed nine-year-old Mei "Linda" Leung on April 10, 1984, before his more notorious killing spree. Ramirez had left Leung's limp body dangling over a pipe in an apartment building at 765 O'Farrell Street, where she lived with her parents and younger brother. Nobody had yet connected the murder of Leung in San Francisco to Ramirez's L.A. crimes, so he checked into the Bristol Hotel on Hyde Street in the Tenderloin sometime after August 8, 1985.

"The people we get here I would call third-class types," Bristol Hotel manager Alex Melnikov told the *San Francisco Chronicle* in 1985. "About 70 percent are on dope. I don't ask a lot of questions."

Ramirez left his room smelling like skunk and drew a pentagram on the bathroom door, which police later removed as evidence. On August 15, Ramirez burgled some jewelry from a house on Baker Street in the Marina. No one was home in the main house that night, but Ramirez also tried to enter the house's in-law unit where Rose Marie Ovian, 22, slept.

"He tried to get in my sliding glass door, because the screen was moved," Ovian, a relative of the burglary victim, later told the *Chron*.

Three days later, the serial killer spread terror in the Lake Merced area near San Francisco State University when he broke into the home of Peter Pan, 69, and his wife, Barbara, 64. Ramirez shot Peter in the head, killing him, and then shot Barbara and beat her savagely, leaving her for dead. The couple's son, David Pan, found his parents the next day after stopping by for a morning visit. The son had to force the door open to gain entry. Ramirez had ransacked the house and scrawled the words "Jack the Knife" (a quote from a Judas Priest song titled "The Ripper") and a pentagram on the Pans' bedroom wall in red lipstick.

On August 20, 1985, the *Chron* reported that the Pans might have been mistaken for the winners of a $1 million jackpot from playing slots in Tahoe. Two days later, Bay Area residents realized that the attack on the Pans was no ordinary botched robbery when the SFPD issued a statement saying that the same killer who'd been prowling the L.A. exurbs was a suspect in the Pan murder. The statement read, "Because of certain similarities between a murder case in this city and the recent serial murders in the Los Angeles area, investigators from both jurisdictions had a meeting to determine if the cases were related."

The statement went on to mention that police patrols had been "increased in certain San Francisco areas." After Ramirez's San Francisco homicide, the ever-sensational scribes at the now-defunct *Los Angeles Herald Examiner* decided that calling this serial criminal the "Valley Intruder" wasn't going to cut it anymore. The killer had gone statewide. After nixing names based on his preferred mode of entry, such as the "Screen-Door Intruder," the *Herald Examiner*'s editorial board decided to dub him the "Night Stalker," after a short-lived 1970s TV series where Darren McGavin played a grizzled reporter who investigated crimes committed by vampires and other monsters. Although there was no evidence that Ramirez actually stalked his human prey, and easy entry into homes appeared to be how he selected his victims, the paper called him the Night Stalker in its very next edition, and the moniker stuck.

The Night Stalker was born.

With the Night Stalker still thought to be in Northern California, San Francisco mayor Dianne Feinstein held a press conference on August 23, 1985. She almost ruined the whole statewide investigation in the process. Feinstein, who had come to power after Mayor Moscone was assassinated by former San Francisco supervisor Dan White on November 27, 1978, sounded stern enough as she addressed the murderer who had come to her city.

"This is a very serious situation. The killer goes into a home at night and kills . . . at random," the future senator said. "Somewhere in the Bay Area, someone is renting a room, an apartment, or a home to this vicious serial killer. I am hoping that people will look at this composite drawing," she continued, holding up a police sketch of the suspected Night Stalker, looking far uglier than Ramirez turned out to be. The drawing depicted the killer with a mop of curls topping off a long face filled with rotten teeth, and showed none of the demonic sex appeal that would later stir the passions of so many jailhouse groupies. However, anyone who had lived to describe Ramirez had also survived being beaten and raped by him. What they saw was a monster—not a rock star.

If Feinstein had just offered her office's $10,000 reward for the capture and conviction of the Night Stalker and stopped there, she would have made a stirring statement. But she went on to describe the evidence that tied together so many crimes throughout the state. She spoke of how ballistics tests matched the gun used in San Francisco to the same one used in two of the killings in Los Angeles. She also mentioned a unique pair of Avia sneakers that were found at some of the crime scenes.

"Cops Winced at Feinstein Statement," read the headline of an August 23, 1985, *San Francisco Chronicle* article. L.A. County sheriff Don Block expressed his displeasure with Feinstein's goof during a press conference shown on CBS News. "It places this community in jeopardy because it impedes our ability to go forward fully with the investigation," Sheriff Block said.

In the *Chron*, one unnamed cop called Feinstein's bit of TMI "a buffoon statement."

"There goes the gun into the bay," said another unnamed officer.

And that's almost what happened. According to author Philip Carlo's biography of Ramirez, *The Night Stalker: The True Story of America's Most Feared Serial Killer* (1996), after hearing Feinstein's press conference, Ramirez walked to the center of the Golden Gate Bridge and "dropped the size 11 1/2 Avia sneakers into the water." He kept the gun.

In the days after murdering the Pans, Ramirez shot dice on the streets of the Mission District and listened to Judas Priest cassettes on a boom box in his residential hotel room. He had relocated to San Francisco because things were getting too hot for him in Los Angeles, but things were too hot for him everywhere after the press started calling him the Night Stalker. He felt boxed in by San

Francisco's more crowded streets and thought that the people he knew here were growing suspicious of him. He was right.

Donna Meyers of Lompoc, California, wondered about her friend Rick from El Paso after she heard about the Pan murder. Rick resembled the sketch of the Night Stalker she had seen on TV, and she had met with him in the Bay Area around the time of those murders. Rick gave her some pieces of jewelry to hang onto for him. The jewelry was engraved with what looked like a driver's license number. Meyers called the Lompoc police. She told Sergeant Harry Heidt about the jewelry and gave him the number from the engraving on a gold bracelet. Lompoc police checked the number with the Department of Motor Vehicles. The license belonged to a woman who lived on Baker Street in the Marina. A bracelet and a ring had been stolen from her house.

Heidt contacted the San Francisco police. Homicide investigator Frank Falzon called back and told Heidt that he needed a last name for this "Rick." Meyers didn't know it, but she knew who did. She told police to contact an Armando Rodriguez in El Sobrante. Falzon and other SFPD investigators questioned Rodriguez for hours. He wouldn't talk at first, but he eventually told the detectives that Rick's last name was Ramirez. Police at last knew the name of the Night Stalker.

Los Angeles investigators also had a break in the case when they were able to link a fingerprint found on a Toyota stolen by the Night Stalker to Ramirez using a new computerized fingerprint system. Police had a name and two pieces of evidence connecting him to the Night Stalker murders. They also had a mug shot of Ramirez from a 1984 arrest for suspicion of driving a stolen car. Police issued an all-points bulletin for Ramirez on Saturday, August 30, 1985. Ramirez's face was on the front page of every Sunday paper in California the next morning. On the day that Southern California police officials held a press conference to reveal their suspect for the Night Stalker murders, Ramirez had taken a bus to Tucson, Arizona, to visit his brother. He returned on August 31 unaware that he'd been identified as the Night Stalker.

When he walked into a small liquor store at 8:30 a.m. and saw a newspaper with his picture on the front page, he knew he had to get out of California. He took a bus to East Los Angeles where he tried to steal a fire-engine red mustang but was fought off by Faustino Pinon, 56, who was working on the car.

Ramirez then ran across East Hubbard Street, hit Angelina De La Torre, 28, in the stomach, and tried to snatch her keys as she was getting into her car. According to the *Los Angeles Times*, the woman's husband, Manuel De La Torre, 32, "in a rage chased Ramirez, beating him as he ran with an iron rod."

Three neighbors—Jose Burgoin, 55, and his sons Jaime, 21, and Julio, 17—soon joined in the chase and subdued Ramirez. Many of the East L.A. residents didn't realize they were chasing the infamous Night Stalker. They just knew he was a bad man. The men made Ramirez sit on the curb. When Ramirez tried to stand, De La Torre raised the iron rod over his head daring him to move. When the police finally pulled up, Ramirez said, "Thank God you came."

Clad in black jeans and a Jack Daniel's T-shirt, Ramirez's "dark hair was matted with blood—his scalp gashed by repeated slashing

Photographer: Mike Sergieff; *Los Angeles Herald Examiner* Photo Collection, Los Angeles Public Library

Bruised and scuffed after the people of an East Los Angeles neighborhood rose up against him, serial killer Richard Ramirez, aka the Night Stalker, is escorted to booking by police on September 1, 1985.

blows from a slender steel rod wielded by the enraged De La Torre," reported the *Los Angeles Times*.

Ramirez was convicted on September 20, 1989, of 13 counts of murder, five attempted murders, 11 sexual assaults, and 14 burglaries. That November, he was sentenced to death. Ramirez married journalist Doreen Lioy, one of his many fans, in San Quentin on October 3, 1996. Lioy was drawn to Ramirez because of his "vulnerability," as reported in the *Los Angeles Times*.

In 2009, DNA tests tied Ramirez to the 1984 rape and murder of nine-year-old Mei Leung, giving the Leung family some measure of closure, although genetic testing also revealed that Ramirez might have had an accomplice in that crime. The San Francisco District Attorney's Office issued a statement in 2016 that there was insufficient evidence to charge anyone else in the murder. San Francisco police have also long suspected Ramirez in the killing of master chef Masataka Kobayashi in the restaurateur's Nob Hill apartment on November 13, 1984. The murder of Kobayashi remains unsolved.

The only truth about any number of cold cases that ever came out of Ramirez's mouth was from saliva samples. He never talked, never confessed. The Night Stalker died from blood cancer on June 7, 2013, after serving nearly 28 years in San Quentin.

## CHAPTER 24

# THE SCENE

### THE RESERVOIR'S EDGE

Milpitas, a strip of suburbia sandwiched between the sprawl of San Jose and the butt-end of the Bay, is known mostly for its landfill and the stench that emanates from its marshland at low tide. What little notoriety it had came from *The Milpitas Monster* (1976), a zero-budget creature feature produced by local high school kids featuring "50 tons of living trash on a rampage." The sleepy suburb got the kind of national attention it never wanted, however, when 14-year-old Marcy Renee Conrad's body was found in a ravine near the Calaveras Reservoir on November 5, 1981. But it wasn't that Conrad had been raped and strangled that got the notice of the *New York Times* and, eventually, Hollywood. It was what happened to her afterwards.

Conrad, a ninth grader at Russell Junior High School, was a troubled girl, and she filled notebooks with her vivid poetry. She skipped her afternoon classes on November 3, 1981, and met up with Anthony Jacques Broussard, a hulking 16-year-old from Milpitas

High. Broussard, who went by his middle name, had found his mother dead in the shower as a young child. His close friends said that he'd seemed a little strange after that, but he was considered harmless despite his size. Broussard was anything but harmless on that November afternoon though. He took Conrad back to his house where he raped and strangled her on the couch.

"I was on drugs, LSD," Broussard later claimed, trying to deflect blame. "Marcy had a tendency to mouth off. She was sitting on my lap . . . Basically, what happened, I just grabbed her and she was dead."

After killing Conrad, Broussard drove her half-naked corpse into the hills and dumped her in that tree-lined ravine. A day later, he was hanging out with some friends in an arcade parking lot.

"I just killed Marcy," Broussard boasted.

His friends thought he was joking, so Broussard took them to see the body. Broussard's friends poked Marcy with sticks to make sure she wasn't a mannequin. After they found out she was real, they kept their mouths shut. They didn't tell the cops or their parents. They were stoner kids, or rockers. They were runnin' with the devil and flyin' high again, clad in their peer-approved uniform of denim and black Ozzy concert shirts. These dudes weren't going to snitch, even though one of them used to date Marcy. Instead, they told more of their friends.

"Jacques is a partner of mine," one of Broussard's friends later explained. "He needs help. He's gone wacko, but I wouldn't narc on him."

Shaggy-headed rockers piled into cars and drove up to the hills to see the dead girl. Marcy's ex-boyfriend even brought along his eight-year-old brother. Some of the kids threw rocks at the body, and one girl tore a local rock radio station patch from Marcy's jeans. A close friend of Broussard's covered the body with leaves to help hide the evidence. These viewings went on for two days before someone finally spoke up, setting off a media firestorm fueled by what would now be called hot takes.

"I have never seen a group of people act so callous about death in my 15 years of police work," Sheriff's Sergeant Gary Meeker told the *Washington Post*.

The media blamed a pervasive moral decline, weed, heavy metal, the 1960s, and television for the teens' indifference to the murder of their friend.

"I don't think the kids here are different from anywhere else in the country," John Ellis, a local librarian, told the *New York Times*. "The impact of violence on TV is the same as everywhere else."

One thing that wasn't blamed was race, even though Broussard was Black and Conrad was white. All of Broussard's friends were also white. It turns out many of the teenagers stayed mum simply because they were afraid of being blamed for the crime. For others, it just took a while to set in. One teen later confessed that sudden visions of Marcy's corpse haunted him during class. Broussard was sentenced to life in prison due to the harsh nature of the crime, sparking off the trend in juvenile justice of trying teens as adults. One of Broussard's friends also got three years for covering up the body.

Just six years later, the release of *River's Edge*, a film loosely based on the incident starring a young Keanu Reeves and Crispin Glover, further soured the people of Milpitas on the media. "This movie never should have been made," 19-year-old Terry Dehne, Marcy Conrad's best friend, told director Tim Hunter after a special screening of the film.

"The last thing *River's Edge* needs is to invent more sleazy characters," Glenn F. Bunting wrote in the *Los Angeles Times*, criticizing the addition of an older, sex-doll-loving burnout played by Dennis Hopper. Bunting had covered the murder for the *San Jose Mercury* in 1981. The movie also strayed from reality by casting Daniel Roebuck, a white actor, as the killer.

But hostility towards *River's Edge* didn't extend much beyond Milpitas. Critic Roger Ebert called it "the best analytical film about a crime since *The Onion Field* and *In Cold Blood*." Gary Singh, who covers South Bay neighborhoods for *Metro Silicon Valley* and wore

Slayer shirts back in the day, wrote that the film "depicted San Jose better than anything I'd seen."

"That was my life at that time," Singh added.

Broussard is currently serving out his sentence at the state prison in Soledad. He has been denied parole several times.

## THE GILMAN STREET MUMMY BABY

Jeremy Adkins didn't quite look like a one-time grave robber as he rode up to the courtyard near the Fruitvale BART station on his bicycle. The words "GIVE" and "TAKE" are tattooed across his fingers, crooked and swollen from years of hard jiu-jitsu sparring, but his baggy cargo pants and Evel Knievel bike helmet kept him from looking like the Burke and Hare of the Berkeley punk scene. Adkins once stashed a mummified baby corpse at 924 Gilman Street, the hallowed punk collective that spawned Rancid and Green Day.

"It was something that was dumb, but why not?" Adkins said, recalling the macabre blunder that gave him a kind of East Bay punk infamy. "Like you get a bad idea and instead of a better one coming along, you keep that bad idea all day long and you end up doing it."

At the time of his momentary descent into ghoulishness, Adkins was a spoken word artist performing at Gilman Street under the name Jerme Spew. He even toured with Green Day and opened for Gilman's biggest success story at the American Legion Hall in Napa. His poem "I Miss You Claire" appears on the 2000 spoken word compilation *Less Rock, More Talk* along with monologues by Noam Chomsky and Jello Biafra.

When Adkins wasn't writing or ranting, he and his friends played increasingly strange pranks. They painted a rainbow flag on a friend's front gate over and over again because the guy admitted he was uncomfortable around gay people, and they plugged a TV and VCR into a light pole and watched movies in the middle of a concrete median on Albany's main drag.

"There was plenty for us to do," Adkins explained, "but there was disdain for simply doing what everyone else was doing."

In late January 1992, Adkins and his friends went tromping around Oakland's picturesque Mountain View Cemetery at night. They found what they thought was an open grave but were chased off by security before they could investigate it. They returned the next day (when the cemetery was open) only to find that it was just a water main, but then they discovered an open crypt. In a time before iPhones equipped everyone with a ready flashlight, they couldn't see their way around the old mausoleum that had been there since the 1860s. They returned later that night with flashlights and bags, but no real plan.

"It was goldfish planning," Adkins said. "Obviously we had the idea we might end up taking stuff because we brought bags, but each step was planned after the last step."

Adkins and his accomplices snatched two skulls and some leg bones. On his way out, Adkins picked up what he thought was a tiny skull, but it was "attached to a mummified baby's body." They took the shriveled-up infant and the other bones back to the house at 54th and Shattuck in Oakland where Adkins lived in a double-wide hallway. They put on the band Sleep's first album, which begins ironically with a sludgy dirge titled "Stillborn," while one of the first-time ghouls started cleaning the skulls with a toothbrush that "probably wasn't his," according to Adkins. The other roommates soon found Adkins and company with their ghastly haul and the yelling started.

"The biggest debate wasn't about the corpse at all," author and comedian Bucky Sinister explained, recalling the mood in the East Bay punk scene at the time. "The biggest debate was whether to call the cops."

The cops were called the next morning, but after Adkins had stashed the baby's remains at 924 Gilman, "the one place stupid enough to trust [him] with keys." The police rounded up everyone at the house in Oakland, thinking that there was a fresh corpse there instead of bones that had been interred for 130 years. Police also showed up at 924 Gilman while Rancid was practicing and searched for the child's body. They didn't find her, but Tim Armstrong of Rancid later found her in a Tower Records bag in the sound booth. Armstrong was able to negotiate the return of the girl's body as long as police promised to leave 924 Gilman Street out of any public statements about the crime, and it worked. The *San Francisco Chronicle* article on the desecration said the body was recovered at "a home near Gilman Street in Berkeley."

"It just became a grave-robbing incident and not a punk incident," Andy Asp of Nuisance told Jack Boulware and Silke Tudor in their punk oral history *Gimme Something Better* (2009).

Adkins spent a few weeks in the Santa Rita jail in Dublin, California, and later pleaded out to felony vandalism of a graveyard. Even with almost digging Gilman Street into a grave-robbing scandal, Adkins still worked the door there two years later on the night that Jello Biafra was beaten down by a gang of crusty punks. In more recent years, Adkins channeled his drive for live performance into standup comedy. He did his five minutes at marijuana dispensaries, the Night Light in Oakland and the Comet Club in San Francisco, where he sometimes talked about the mummified baby.

## THE PRINCE OF PORNOBILLY

Joan Rivers was a tough broad from Brooklyn who clawed her way to the top of the comedy business in the late 1950s by working standup gigs in New York's East Village alongside Woody Allen and George Carlin. She became Johnny Carson's go-to guest host on *The Tonight Show* in the 1970s and held her own as she traded barbs with Don Rickles in the '80s. The woman was even felt up by Frank Sinatra backstage at Caesar's Palace in Vegas, and she made it through the media meat grinder when her husband and manager Edgar Rosenberg died by suicide in 1987. By February 1991, she probably thought she had seen it all, but then she had Buck Naked and the Bare Bottom Boys on *The Joan Rivers Show*.

Rivers wore a canary yellow blazer with monstrous shoulder pads as she announced the rock 'n' roll trio that set the standard for weird in the San Francisco music scene. "They play a new form of music called pornobilly," she said and broke out into laughter as she struggled to say the name of their song, "Uncontrollable Flesh."

Through the Jerry Lee Lewis–inspired rock 'n' roll mayhem, Buck strummed his acoustic guitar wearing little more than hot pink cowboy boots, a scarf, and a cowboy hat festooned with American flags and wrapped in a hatband made from a latex gremlin idol. His brother Hector stood up at the drum kit to reveal that his privates were covered only by a bandana fashioned into a hillbilly banana hammock. Guitarist Stinky LePew set himself apart by actually wearing pants.

"It wiggles to the left and it wiggles to the right, it wiggles all day and it wiggles all night," Buck growled as Jewish grandmas in the audience took deep breaths and Jersey girls with lacquered coiffures sat slack-jawed.

But Buck was comparatively reserved during his performance on *The Joan Rivers Show*. In San Francisco clubs such as the Rock & Bowl in the Haight or the Paradise Lounge in South of Market, he added an accessory over his crotch that made his schtick even more outrageous.

"The best thing about the opening song was Buck coming out with the toilet plunger," said George Lazaneo, the band's former tour manager. "So just seeing the look of him strutting out on stage, and the look on the audience's faces was classic, because they didn't know what was going on. There'd be a combination of shock, horror, laughter. It never failed to get a reaction."

"I saw them open for Mojo Nixon once," Bay Area TV personality Webberly Rattenkraft recalled. "[Buck] worked that plunger like a master."

Buck's real name was Phillip Bury. He started the band with his brother Stephen, aka Hector, and guitarist Stinky in Omaha, Nebraska, in 1984. Having outgrown the scene in their home town, they moved to San Francisco, where a bizarre band could find its niche. To make ends meet, Buck and Hector worked as bartenders at the Paradise Lounge, a multilevel nightspot where hard-partying owner Robin Reichert kept a lot of artists and musicians on the payroll.

"At that point of time, if you were in a band, you either had a girlfriend that was a stripper or you worked as a bartender or a bouncer," Lazaneo explained. "You needed a job that provided the flexibility to be able to do shows and be able to rehearse. You couldn't do that working square."

With the flexibility that slinging drinks at the Paradise gave them, Buck Naked and the Bare Bottom Boys mounted a pair of national tours, released an EP, and produced a zero-budget video for an epic piece of bad taste titled "Teenage Pussy from Outer Space," which involved lots of string puppets and papier-mâché planets. By late 1992, they had flummoxed Joan Rivers on national television

Photo: Michael Conen

Philip Bury, better known to Bay Area scenesters as Buck Naked, more than lives up to his stage name at The Omni in Oakland, California, in 1987. He would be murdered in Golden Gate Park's panhandle five years later.

and had the material for their first full-length CD in the can. Buck Naked was primed to unleash his lunacy to the world, but he still couldn't afford to quit working nights.

Early in the morning on Saturday, November 21, 1992, Buck came home to his apartment in the Haight after bartending at the Paradise. Like usual, he took his Rottweiler, Reno, to the Panhandle, a narrow strip of a city park near the much larger Golden Gate Park. As Buck rode his bike and Reno gave chase, a 47-year-old cabbie named Michael Kagan was feeding the pigeons. Known as the "Pigeon Man," Kagan spent $1,000 a month on birdseed. He had gotten into spats with dog owners over the birds and had even threatened to shoot dogs.

When Kagan and Buck had words that morning, the Pigeon Man pulled a revolver out of his bucket of birdseed. He fired three shots, and Buck Naked dropped dead on the grass.

Any notion that Kagan was shooting at the dog was quickly dispelled by the police investigation. "The bullet was way too high," homicide detective and future chief of police Earl Sanders told the *Examiner*. "He meant to shoot the man." Sanders added that Reno "was no threat" and "just a big dog."

Two years later, Kagan's testimony that Buck had swung his bicycle lock at him saved him from a murder conviction, but he was found guilty of manslaughter and sentenced to 16 years in prison, the maximum term allowed. Kagan appealed his conviction to the California Supreme Court but the verdict was upheld.

George Lazaneo organized a successful benefit at the Great American Music Hall to finance the posthumous release of Buck Naked and the Bare Bottom Boys' self-titled album. Through that disc, such raunchy classics as "Bend Over Baby (And Let Me Drive)" and the beautiful simplicity of "Up Your Butt" remained popular selections in the CD juke boxes of San Francisco rock clubs for years until the unlimited choices offered by internet juke boxes made everything the same.

## CHAPTER 25

# UPWARD MOBILITY

### THE CAROLANDS

By the 1980s, the Carolands Mansion was in a state of gothic decay that you'd expect to find in the Deep South, not in an affluent enclave overlooking the San Francisco Bay. Only 20 years earlier, the 110-room Hillsborough chateau was occupied by a European countess and coveted by President Kennedy as the location for a West Coast White House. The house was built for Pullman railcar heiress Harriett Pullman Carolan in 1916. Countess Lillian Remillard Dandini bought the palace for a mere $80,000 in 1950. She died in 1973, leaving the estate to the town of Hillsborough for use as a library and arts center. Hillsborough passed it along to the State of California, and the state couldn't give it away in 1975. The neglect, however, was just a sad prologue to the terrors that took place within the mansion's musty walls 10 years later.

On February 5, 1985, Jeanine Grinsell and Laurie McKenna were driving through San Mateo County's nicer neighborhoods looking for something to do. One of the Burlingame High students had heard that the security guards at Carolands gave unofficial tours, so they headed up the hill. David Allen Raley was the security guard on duty when the girls arrived at the mansion. He was a chubby man with a full beard and an emerging unibrow who had a history of creeping young women out during his little tours. He told one woman how easy it would be to murder someone there, and made others scream their lungs out in a walk-in safe so they would know that no one could hear them. On that Saturday, Raley agreed to give Grinsell and McKenna a tour as long as they parked their car where no one could see it. "Sometimes the guards get sexual favors for doing this," he joked.

By the end of the walk-through, Raley claimed he heard police dogs and demanded that the girls hide in the basement safe so they wouldn't get in trouble. The girls were hesitant. He promised he wouldn't shut the door behind them. They relented and got in the safe. He slammed the thick metal door behind them. Grinsell and McKenna sat in the dark safe for five minutes before they heard him again.

"Laurie," he called out, in an eerie, singsong tone.

He said he'd let them go if they took off their clothes. They stripped down to their underwear only to be handcuffed and led to a workroom. Raley tied McKenna to a workbench and dragged Grinsell away. McKenna sat helpless as she heard her friend's screams echo through the bowels of the mansion. After sexually assaulting both girls, Raley promised to let them go. This promise was only as good as his previous ones. Raley beat Grinsell with his nightstick for several minutes. She somehow survived. He stabbed McKenna in the stomach. She fought back. He stabbed her 34 more times, but she still lived.

Before the end of his shift at 4 p.m., Raley locked the women in the trunk of his 1973 Plymouth and waited for his boss to show up to relieve him. The supervisor didn't get there until 5:15. Raley tut-tutted his boss about being tardy and then drove off with a trunk full of bloody teens. Over an hour later, he got to his house in South San Jose and parked his car in the garage. Grinsell and McKenna were still alive. He gave them a sleeping bag to keep warm and warned them his friend Bob would shoot them if they made a sound. There was no friend Bob.

Raley spent the evening in the house watching TV and playing Monopoly with his sister like it was any normal night in the burbs. McKenna and Grinsell faded in and out of consciousness as they slowly bled out in the trunk. Raley went to check on them several times. His father and sister never got suspicious of what he was doing out there.

The girls were both still alive hours later when Raley drove them out to a rural stretch of Silver Creek Road and dumped them down a ravine. McKenna waited in the cold creek bed at the bottom of the drop for hours, fearing that Raley was still stalking them nearby. It started to drizzle. With her hands cut badly, she climbed up the muddy and trash-strewn embankment using her elbows. She made it to the top of the incline and lay by the side of the road. Three cars passed her without stopping. Finally, two men in a pickup truck stopped and called an ambulance. One of the men tried to hug McKenna; she did not want to be hugged. Laurie McKenna survived her own murder. Jeanine Grinsell did not. She died on the operating table from 41 stab wounds and a fractured skull. Raley was sentenced to death in 1988. He exhausted the last of his appeals in 2014, and currently sits on San Quentin's death row.

The Carolands Mansion was eventually restored to its former grandeur and is now run by a nonprofit foundation. The foundation offers small official tours on Wednesday afternoons that "focus on Carolands' rich historical background and classical architectural traditions."

## PIGSKINS AND CROSSBOWS

NFL teams are modern-day medieval fiefdoms where ruthless barons such as Mark Davis and Dan Snyder preside over helmeted armies culled from the underclass. And no team was more of a game of thrones than the Seattle Seahawks in 1989 when a dispute between co-owners led to an assassination using a weapon favored by the men who guarded Richard the Lionheart.

Mike Blatt was a Stockton-based real estate developer who ruled over vast lands that included apartment complexes in California, Arizona, and Nevada. His Blatt Development Co. oversaw $120 million worth of construction in its first 10 years. He also ran a successful sports agency, but that wasn't enough for him.

In August 1988, Blatt put together a deal to buy the Seattle Seahawks with Florida real estate developer Ken Behring and the Nordstrom family. While his better-known partners held the lion's share of the franchise, Blatt carved out a 10 percent stake in the team. By February 1989, Blatt realized his ambitions as the team's interim general manager. He proclaimed he would "create a dynasty" in Seattle, according to the *Los Angeles Times*.

Blatt's dynastic drive was short-lived. An investigation commissioned by Seahawks minority owner Kenneth Hofmann revealed that Blatt was involved in 31 lawsuits in San Joaquin County. "Mike was getting all the press," Hofmann told the *Los Angeles Times*. "He was walking around like he owned the Seattle Seahawks. That bothered me." By February 22, 1989, Blatt was ousted as Seahawks GM and replaced by former Raiders coach Tom Flores.

Larry Carnegie was responsible for two of the lawsuits that helped cost Blatt control of the Seahawks. Carnegie had worked for Blatt's development company as a broker and property manager. A string of bad business deals caused Carnegie to quit five years later. Carnegie then sued Blatt for $200,000 in unpaid commissions. Blatt countersued for $600,000 over a botched hotel deal.

On February 28, 1989, Carnegie, still in the real estate business, went to meet a potential client at a house he was showing on Tokay Colony Road in Lodi, a Central Valley town that's now part of California's ever-expanding wine-growing country. James Mackey and Carl Hancock, two former college football players, were waiting for Carnegie at the property. Hancock greeted Carnegie outside while Mackey waited inside the garage with a crossbow.

Mackey was supposed to wait until Hancock lured Carnegie into the garage, but the bowman grew nervous. Mackey shot Carnegie while the realtor was standing outside the half-opened garage door. The 16-inch bolt hit Carnegie in the back and plowed through his chest before landing on the lawn.

"I've been shot," Carnegie yelled before collapsing onto the ground.

Carnegie somehow survived. The inept hitmen attempted to smother Carnegie with a sleeping bag right there in the driveway as Denise Brock and Debra Ybarra pulled up to deliver some keys to Carnegie. The women slammed the car into reverse, pulled away, and called the sheriff.

In a panic, Mackey and Hancock dumped their still-living victim into the trunk and sped off, leaving the sleeping bag and the bloody crossbow bolt behind. The duo drove for a while, eventually pulling over to kill Carnegie by strangling him with a rope before dropping the body down a slope a few miles off Highway 101 near Cloverdale. It landed in a much-used garbage dump. The body was discovered the next day.

Besides leaving this trail of evidence and eyewitnesses behind, Mackey had also used his own name when he rented the car used in the crime. Mackey's cousin, John Holmes (not the '70s porn star), was arrested on May 31, 1989, in a case of mistaken identity. Mackey turned himself in a day later, and Hancock was arrested that August.

Mackey and Hancock told authorities that they were hired by Mike Blatt to murder Carnegie, and that Blatt blamed Carnegie for costing him the Seahawks GM position. Mackey and Hancock each received life sentences for the murder and are still in prison today. As for Blatt, two attempts to try him ended with hung juries. He now lives in Sausalito and is part owner of Alta Mira Recovery Programs, a substance abuse treatment center located in a former hotel overlooking the Bay. One can only wonder if Blatt was in the stands when the Super Bowl came to the Bay Area at Levi Stadium in Santa Clara on February 7, 2016, to see the gridiron glory that could have been his.

## 101 CALIFORNIA

High up in the glimmering glass tower at 101 California Street, Pettit and Martin seemed more imposing than it actually was. While it was still one of San Francisco's largest law firms, the economic downturn of the early 1990s had hit it especially hard. But just as business was starting to look up, on July 1, 1993, death got on the elevator in the lobby of 101 California and took it all the way up to Pettit and Martin on the 34th floor. Death came in the form of Gian Luigi Ferri, a stocky middle-aged man filled with blind rage and white-hot hate. In his pocket he carried a four-page hit list combined with a badly spelled, all-caps screed about corporate rape and MSG poisoning at a time before there was a Reddit to post it on. He also brought along two Tec-9 semiautomatic submachine guns, a .45, and a black attaché case heavy with ammo.

Bankruptcy attorney Sharon O'Grady spotted Ferri shortly after he got off the elevator. Just as she squinted at him to see if he belonged there, he fired his Tec-9s into a glass-walled conference room, spraying bullets and glass everywhere.

Attorney Jack Berman and his client Jody Jones Sposato were killed, during a deposition in a sexual discrimination case. Court reporter Deanna Eaves dove under the conference room table to avoid Ferri's gunfire that came in six-shot bursts. She was hit twice but lived.

Ferri turned from the conference room and fired into a nearby office, killing labor law attorney Allen J. Berk, who had just returned from a Scandinavian vacation. Litigation specialist Brian Berger, who had been meeting with Berk, was wounded. Moments later, Ferri made his way down an internal staircase and opened fire on John and Michelle Scully. The young attorneys had met at Gonzaga University in Washington, got married, and moved to San Francisco. Both studied law at USF before joining Pettit. John, a laidback guy from Hawaii, died shielding Michelle with his body. Michelle still took bullets to the chest and shoulder but survived; she was released from the hospital the day after the rampage.

As Ferri fired round after round, an announcement was made over the building's rarely used sound system telling people in the building to lock their doors and stay in place. Lawyers at Boyd and McKay on the 40th floor shoved a couch in front of their office doors, while employees at the Merrill Lynch offices on the 24th floor worked in cubicles with no doors to lock.

Ferri descended to the 32nd floor and then the 31st, shooting more people along the way. Met by a SWAT team on his way down to the 29th floor, Ferri put his .45 to his chin and killed himself rather than shoot it out. By the end of his killing spree, Ferri had murdered eight people and wounded six others. While Ferri named Pettit and Martin in his note, none of his victims were on his list, and Berman and Sposato didn't even work for the firm. Pettit and Martin had represented Ferri in an Indiana land deal that went badly after the firm was already out of the picture. The firm had not heard from him since 1982, nine years earlier.

Following the massacre, Senator Dianne Feinstein authored the Federal Assault Weapons Ban, prohibiting the sale of semiautomatic weapons, like the Tec-9s used at 101 California. President Bill Clinton signed the bill into law on September 14, 1994, after it survived a razor-thin vote in the Senate. The assault weapons ban expired in 2004, despite Feinstein's attempts to renew her bill. She introduced a new assault weapons ban in 2013 following the elementary school shooting in Sandy Hook, Connecticut, but that bill went down in the Senate 60–40, with 15 Democrats who were eyeing reelection bids voting against it. Many of them were defeated by Republicans in the next election cycle anyway.

Pettit and Martin was dissolved in March 1995.

"The tragedy did not cause the problems of the firm, but it certainly made getting over them somewhat more difficult," firm chairman Theodore Russell said during a press conference announcing the closure. "There was a certain sadness that prevailed for a long time."

# CHAPTER 26

# TWO-FISTED LIBERAL

## KAYO

Terence Hallinan was a two-fisted liberal who hailed from a long line of Irish rebels. After a lifetime of fighting the system, he was the last one you'd expect to prosecute perps as district attorney—even in San Francisco—and his past hell-raising had almost prevented him from becoming a lawyer at all.

And it wasn't as though he didn't have the legal pedigree. His father, Vincent Hallinan, was San Francisco's first radical lawyer and the closest thing to a real-life Perry Mason. Vincent's criminal defendants always seemed to go free, and he amassed a large enough fortune from taking on big corporations in personal injury and labor cases to buy a mansion in Marin County. The elder Hallinan began his practice in the 1920s when the Barbary Coast was a living memory, and he was just as likely to spar with opposing counsel with his fists in courthouse hallways as with words before a jury. Vincent had a personal distaste for the American justice system, despite having mastered it, that came from the cynical realization that the entire legal apparatus would pursue an unjust prosecution with even more vigor than it would a just one. With the resulting lack of respect for legal norms, he often flaunted them. In 1939, he and an office assistant were charged with conspiracy to bribe a witness but were acquitted. Vincent served a five-month prison term for contempt in 1950 and did two years for income tax evasion in the mid-1950s.

"I get more honor out of these than any other decoration," Vincent said, referring to the handcuffs that bound him as he was taken to McNeil Island prison in Washington State.

Despite their affluence, Vincent's fame (or infamy, depending on your point of view) didn't always make things easy for his five sons. When Vincent ran for president as an unabashed socialist in 1952 at the height of U.S. anti-communist hysteria, the scions of Northern California's more conservative families bullied his two adolescent sons, Patrick and Terence. The father's very Irish solution to this problem was for the boys to learn the sweet science of boxing. Terence was quick to use his newfound skill set, and getting his skull fractured during a horse-riding accident during a trip to Yosemite National Park when he was 12 didn't exactly help him with anger management issues. Everyone called the boy "Kayo" for a reason.

It was during his dad's two-year stretch in prison that Terence got out of hand. At 17, he and brother Patrick ran three coastguardsmen off the road near Point Reyes, beat them up, and stole a case of beer. A year later, Terence and three of his rowdy pals were asked to leave a Sierra ski lodge near Lake Tahoe for dancing and being too noisy. The teens ganged up on resort owner Kenneth Cotton and beat him down in front of shocked vacationers. With Cotton reeling on the floor, the rowdies piled into their car and were chased into a snowbank by El Dorado County sheriff's officers. Cotton lost two of his teeth from the assault and needed five stitches to close the wounds in his face. He was later awarded $10,000 in damages.

Kayo found a more acceptable outlet for his rage as a light heavyweight on the UC Berkeley boxing team, but still got into scrapes outside the ring. In 1959, 22-year-old Terence was charged with assault after breaking an 18-year-old boy's jaw outside of a bowling alley. He would face up to 10 years in prison if convicted, but his trial ended with a hung jury that leaned towards acquittal. A year later, Kayo picked himself up off the canvas twice during a Golden Gloves semifinal match against Eddie Mendez at what's now the Bill Graham Civic Auditorium. Kayo "stayed in and pitched leather," according to *Examiner* boxing scribe Eddie Muller Sr., but couldn't close the gap from the two knockdowns and lost the bout. This ended his amateur title aspirations and a shot at the 1960 U.S. Olympic team.

After graduating from UC Berkeley in 1960, Terence went from bad trouble to what the late congressman and civil rights hero John Lewis called "good trouble." He was arrested again in 1963, but this time it was for registering Black voters in Mississippi as a member of the Student Nonviolent Coordinating Committee. Those Southern cops beat him for that one. Back in the Bay Area, he kept on protesting. He was arrested six times between 1963 and 1964. He was twice convicted for unlawful assembly and disturbing the peace during sit-ins at racist car dealerships.

Kayo earned his law degree from UC Hastings and passed the bar exam in 1964, but it was his arrests from protesting as much as his thuggish past that led the state bar's committee of examiners to determine he lacked "good moral character." Aided by his dad and white privilege, Terence appealed to the California State Supreme Court and won in a 6–1 decision. He was now a licensed attorney. He still found time to get his head bashed in by riot cops during the student strike at San Francisco State University in 1968—and allegedly shot up heroin with Janis Joplin in her apartment, almost dying from an overdose. He denied that rumor but copped to smoking weed. "I'm a San Francisco guy," he told the *Examiner* in 1995.

Nearly 30 years later, this was the man that the people of San Francisco elected to be their top cop—twice. As the city's most unlikely district attorney, Hallinan was a major player in one of its most bizarre criminal prosecutions and a farcical scandal over Mexican take-out that reverberates to this day. But long before that, Kayo followed in his father's and brothers' leftward footsteps as defense counsel for hippie radicals, violent revolutionaries, and even California's most prolific serial killer.

## THE MACHETE MURDERER

Goro Kagehiro knew that something wasn't right on May 19, 1971, when he found a freshly dug hole on his 20-acre walnut farm in Yuba City, a Central Valley farm town north of Sacramento. At first, Kagehiro thought that someone from the county may have taken some soil samples, but at three feet wide and six feet long, the hole was a bit large for that. It was, however, the right size for a grave.

When Kagehiro drove back to the hole on his tractor in the early evening and found it filled in, he called the sheriff. Deputies didn't have to dig very long before they uncovered the mutilated corpse of Kenneth Whitacre, 40, a drifter from Alameda who had taken up farm work. Whitacre had been raped and stabbed in the chest, and the back of his head had been split open with "a machete or heavy knife," according to Sutter County sheriff Roy Whiteaker.

A few days later, another mysterious mound of dirt was discovered on a neighboring ranch, and authorities soon unearthed the hacked-up body of Charles Fleming, another bindle stiff who worked the fields. Sheriff Whiteaker knew he had something more than a random act of extreme violence on his hands. He had a serial killer.

Whiteaker dispatched his men to scour the countryside for recently dug graves. Deputies discovered several more mutilated corpses on the sandy banks of the Feather River. By May 26, 1971, they had excavated 12 bodies in total. Digging crews smoked cigars to mask the stench. By June 4, 1971, 25 victims had been recovered, all of them men between the ages of 40 and 63, all transient farm workers, and all but one were white. Each man was buried lying on his back with his shirt pulled over his butchered head. The oldest grave found was just six weeks old, making these deaths the result of a recent killing spree rather than years of stealthy carnage. Many of the victims had receipts from Juan V. Corona in their pockets.

Corona was an American success story, immigrating from Jalisco, Mexico, and working his way up from the fields to start his own business that hired out migrant workers to local growers. Corona was married with four young daughters, and Goro Kagehiro had hired laborers from him. Corona had also been diagnosed with schizophrenia by a state mental hospital in 1956, and he was the last person seen with several of the victims.

Police arrested Corona at his beige stucco home in the early morning hours of May 26, 1971. Searching the house, police found a post-hole digger with blood and human hairs on the blade, an 18-inch "bolo machete" with possible bloodstains, and some articles of bloody clothing. They also found a work ledger bearing 17 of the murdered men's names. A few hours later, two of Corona's young daughters were seen waiting for their school bus "apparently unaware of what happened," according to a UPI story.

On January 18, 1973, a Solano County Superior Court jury of 10 men and two women found Juan Corona guilty of slaying 25 itinerant farm workers. Corona's wife and oldest daughter wept as Judge Richard E. Patton took 28 minutes to read the verdict. Corona pressed his fingers against the defense counsel table until his knuckles turned white.

In 1978, the California Courts of Appeal threw out Corona's conviction after Terence Hallinan successfully argued that Corona's previous defense team was incompetent. At Corona's second trial in 1982, Hallinan argued that Corona's dead brother, Natividad, was the actual killer and had planted evidence on the victims to frame Juan. Hallinan made a case that Natividad was homosexual and suffered from tertiary syphilis that drove him to "insanity and maniacal rage." With the prosecution's mountain of evidence linking Juan to the victims and the murder weapons, alongside testimony that Natividad was in Mexico at the time of the murders, the jury didn't buy Hallinan's theory. Juan Corona was reconvicted of his crimes after a trial that lasted seven months and cost $5.1 million, then the most expensive trial for a single defendant in Californian history.

Corona was denied parole eight times and lost the sight in his left eye after barely surviving a stabbing attack in 1973 at the California Medical Facility in Vacaville. By the time he died on March 4, 2019, he'd spent 48 years in prison.

## BANE AND HERA

Diane Whipple was terrified of "those dogs," and she wasn't the type who scared easily. She was a lacrosse player and coach at St. Mary's College in the East Bay. Whipple could take care of herself in most situations, but those dogs were different—a combined 250 pounds of snarling fury named Bane and Hera. They were Presa Canarios, a brindled Spanish mastiff mostly bred as guard or attack dogs. Whipple did everything she could to avoid them in the halls of the apartment building she lived in at 2398 Pacific Avenue in San Francisco with her partner, Sharon Smith, but keeping away was nearly impossible.

The dogs lived in an apartment across the hall from Whipple's with their owners Robert Noel and Marjorie Knoller, an aging pair of hard-nosed attorneys. Noel and Knoller never apologized when their pack lunged at children or bowled over old ladies in and around their Pacific Heights apartment. And nobody ever filed any complaints either, even after the dogs bit a man in June 2000 and chomped on Whipple's hand in December 2000. Noel's and Knoller's legal backgrounds made them nearly as imposing as their living Cerberus.

A little over a month later, on January 26, 2001, the moment that Diane Whipple feared finally happened. She had come home with some groceries when Bane savagely tore into her in the hall outside of her sixth-floor apartment. A neighbor heard the dogs barking but dared only to look through the peephole to see Whipple's body on the floor with groceries strewn everywhere. The neighbor called 911.

Police arrived six minutes later and found Whipple lying face down on a blood-soaked carpet. She was nearly stripped naked with bite marks all over her body. A SWAT team officer with EMT training couldn't stop the blood from gushing out of deep wounds in her neck. Whipple died sometime after paramedics got her out of the building. It was just five days before her 34th birthday.

When police questioned Marjorie Knoller, her sweatsuit and hair were smeared with Whipple's blood. Knoller told the cops that the dogs were in her apartment. She never asked how Whipple was. Bane was put down shortly after being taken to the shelter, but Noel and Knoller refused to give permission for Animal Care and Control to euthanize Hera.

"They move on Hera and they will have the fight of their lives on their hands," Noel later wrote.

The strange case got even stranger when it came out Noel and Knoller had formed a partnership to breed Presa Canarios with Paul "Cornfed" Schneider, a leader of the Aryan Brotherhood serving a double life sentence in the supermax state prison at Pelican Bay. They called their enterprise Dog O' War kennels, and hyper-aggression was a feature, not a bug. Things got weirder still when it was found that the attorneys had legally adopted Schneider and exchanged pornographic letters with him that involved the dogs. Knoller called one of the animals her "certified lick therapist."

At the time, Terence Hallinan was in his second term as San Francisco district attorney. After first being elected in 1995, Kayo had enacted the kinds of reforms that the Defund the Police and Black Lives Matter movements clamored for 20 years later. He fired 14 veteran prosecutors to diversify his staff and took steps to keep from empaneling all-white juries, even though it may have cost him some convictions. He also avoided nonviolent three-strikes cases to keep from sending petty crooks to prison for life, and diverted nonviolent offenders into rehab programs instead of jail, which cost him still more convictions during that era when his fellow Democrats espoused "tough on crime" rhetoric.

While Hallinan went easy on nonviolent crimes, he refused to plea down violent ones. With public pressure mounting as the lurid details of the dog-mauling case emerged, Hallinan went for a murder conviction, instead of lesser manslaughter charges. He staffed his legal team with lead prosecutor James Hammer, an openly gay former Jesuit, and Kimberly Guilfoyle, a young assistant district attorney who was often defined by her appearance in the local press. A February 9, 2001, Matier and Ross column in the *Chronicle* described her as "the legal eyeful" and a "former lingerie model." The columnists went on to dish on Guilfoyle's TV offers and speculated if "her beau," Supervisor Gavin Newsom, "will get offered a co-starring role."

"If they're looking for looks, these two up-and-comers have certainly got 'em," the item concluded, reading as if it had been written by Hedda Hopper 50 years earlier.

Not to be outdone in the media department, Knoller went on *Good Morning America* and blamed the victim. "Ms. Whipple had ample opportunity to go into her apartment," Knoller told Elizabeth Vargas. When asked if she bore any responsibility for the attack, Knoller replied, "Not at all."

At a time when California prosecutors had trouble securing murder convictions in high-profile cases (think O.J. Simpson and Robert Blake), Hammer and Guilfoyle convinced the jury that Knoller was guilty of second-degree murder, a verdict that has withstood several appeals. Robert Noel, who was in court in Sacramento at the time of the mauling, was found guilty of involuntary manslaughter and was released in 2003.

Guilfoyle and Newsom were married in December 2001 but divorced a little over three years later. Something about seeing the underbelly of liberal high society may have driven Guilfoyle to the dark side, however. She joined conservative propaganda machine Fox News in 2006, and she is now dating Don Trump Jr. The politics of her ex and her current beau couldn't be more different, but the hair remains the same.

## FAJITAGATE

The scandal that shook San Francisco's criminal justice establishment in the first decade of the 21st century started with a greasy bag containing some strips of grilled flank steak, a few tortillas, and maybe some guacamole. The incident was quickly named Fajitagate, because all political scandals have to have "gate" in the name since Tricky Dick Nixon and the break-in at a certain hotel in 1972. For a brief moment though, it looked like this controversy named for assemble-yourself tacos could bring down the San Francisco Police Department. It ended the political career of the city's activist district attorney instead.

Adam Snyder and his pal Jade Santoro were walking back to their cars at 2 a.m. on Wednesday, November 20, 2002. Snyder had just finished his bartending shift at the Blue Light Bar on Union Street in Pacific Heights and was carrying a bag of fajitas that he'd ordered from his bar's kitchen before last call. When they got to their cars at Union and Laguna Streets, they ran into a trio of young white men with buzz cuts and broad shoulders who looked like they'd definitely closed down some other pub. One of the men demanded that Snyder fork over the fajitas. Snyder thought he was joking, but it wasn't long before fists, feet, and beer bottles started flying. One man put Snyder in a chokehold and dragged him down Union Street, while the other two stomped Santoro into the pavement.

After the beatings that left Santoro with a broken nose and a gash in his head that had to be stapled shut, the men piled into a pickup truck and sped away. Snyder was clearheaded enough to get their license plate number and call 911. The police arrived and were taking Snyder's statement when the truck carrying the fajita snatchers passed by the crime scene.

"That's them! That's them!" Snyder cried.

"There they go right there," Santoro said. "Go pull them over! Those are the guys who kicked our ass!"

The men in the pickup truck turned out to be off-duty cops David Lee, Matt Tonsing, and Alex Fagan Jr. Earlier that evening, they had joined 100 other cops at the House of Prime Rib to celebrate Fagan's dad, Alex Fagan Sr. He'd been made SFPD's second-in-command by Mayor Willie Brown despite his arrest in 1990 for brawling with highway patrol officers and his 30-day suspension in 2000 for getting into two car accidents driving back from a Giants game. After the celebration, Lee, Tonsing, and Fagan Jr. kept the party going at the Bus Stop, a sports bar on Union and Laguna Streets.

After the attack, Snyder was never allowed to identify the suspects, and none of the officers were arrested or even questioned. The urinalysis tests to determine how much beer they'd swilled were delayed for hours, which rendered them useless. And the SFPD's internal investigation into the matter wasn't that much better. Investigators were prevented from interviewing officers or reviewing phone and disciplinary records. In January 2003, Lieutenant Joe Dutto, who'd been leading the police investigation, was transferred to the vice squad. "You can read between the lines," he said.

City leadership went into damage-control mode. The city's first Black police chief, Earl Sanders, likened critics of the police probe to those who persecuted Christ, and Willie Brown blamed the victims by calling the attack "mutual combat."

But Terence Hallinan didn't get the talking points. After a lifetime of confrontations with police that sometimes left him beaten and bloody, the old rabble-rouser couldn't resist the opportunity to bring the whole system down. In February 2003, Hallinan submitted a blank indictment form to the grand jury, which was returned with indictments against not only the alleged attackers but also several members of SFPD's top brass, including Chief Sanders, Fagan Sr., and Deputy Chief Greg Suhr (whose future turn as police chief would end in controversy after several police shootings and a racist text scandal).

But Hallinan should've known how this story would end from his days as a young bruiser with a well-connected father. His case

National Lawyers Guild

A bloody Terence Hallinan confronts San Francisco riot cops after reportedly having his head caved in by a billy club during the Strike at San Francisco State College (now University) in 1968.

against the SFPD's higher-ups fell apart, and he dropped charges against Sanders in March 2003. The stymying of the investigation into the beating was more the department's standard operating procedure in cases involving their own than any kind of organized conspiracy that could be prosecuted. The city's first Black mayor had appointed its first Black police chief but the force hadn't changed all that much since Chief Biggy was fished out of the Bay a century earlier. As for the off-duty cops at the center of Fajitagate, they were all acquitted, although a civil jury later found that Fagan Jr. and Tonsing had both committed battery against Snyder and Santoro, awarding the victims $41,000.

Hallinan's overreach in the Fajitagate scandal mortally wounded his 2003 bid for reelection. With Hallinan not only going after the police brass but the heads of other city departments, outgoing Mayor Brown—along with the restaurant lobby and big-money donors—got behind the candidacy of his protégé and former lover Kamala

Harris, a Black woman with Jamaican and Indian parents and former assistant district attorney who would crank up the criminal prosecutions without reversing all of Hallinan's reforms. They were all liberal Democrats after all, but things were a whole lot easier without Kayo handing out indictments and punching real estate developers in front of Izzy's Steakhouse. With a campaign that was fined for breaking fundraising limits, and scary mailers that showed a shirtless man holding a gun in one hand and flashing gang signs with the other, Harris won the runoff by 13 points and was positioned for bigger things.

After losing his last race, Hallinan returned to private practice and specialized in medical marijuana cases. He ended his legal career in 2014 after some minor but unethical creative accounting resulted in a 90-day suspension. When he died on January 17, 2020, his successor—by then a United States Senator—issued a statement.

"California has suffered a terrible loss with the passing of Terence Hallinan," Senator Harris said. "He was a fighter who dedicated his life to pursuing justice and serving the people of San Francisco. He will be greatly missed."

Just a year later, Kamala Harris became the first woman, African American, and Asian American to be sworn in as vice president of the United States of America.

## CHAPTER 27

# THE TECHNOLOGICAL DIVIDE

The Lehigh Permanente Quarry on the edge of Cupertino's aggressively tree-lined suburbs stood as a holdover from a time when orchards and mining drove the South Bay's economy, before anyone thought of calling the place Silicon Valley. Just four miles south from this still-functioning monument to the Bay Area's rapidly dwindling working class was Apple—formerly Apple Computer—not only the richest company in Cupertino, but the world. On October 5, 2011, death swept across Cupertino's sea of single-family homes, top schools, and shopping malls both large and small. By the end of that bloody Wednesday, the reaper had claimed a trio of veteran quarrymen and the town's most famous son in a separate pair of tragedies that united the old polluting cement plant with the $1.3 trillion iPhone leviathan.

Shareef Allman, a 49-year-old truck driver, showed up incensed to a 4:15 a.m. safety meeting at the quarry that day. He was mad that his union shop steward wasn't going to represent him and his bad safety record anymore; that he had been moved from the day shift to nights; and about the $10 he chipped in for a coworker's going away party. But when Allman first entered the trailer where the meeting was held, he said hi to everyone like nothing was wrong, grabbed a cup of coffee, and then left for a couple of minutes. He came back with a .40 caliber handgun and a .223 caliber assault rifle and shot two rounds into the ceiling.

"You think you can fuck with me?" he raged, and then fired on colleagues he'd worked with for many years.

"Everyone was jumping under the table," quarry worker Mike Ambrosio told the *Mercury News*. "Some sitting at the table were shot in the stomach." Ambrosio was shot in the arm but survived by playing dead.

Working at the Permanente Quarry was a family affair, and Allman's bullets hit workers bound by blood as well as profession. Allman killed Ambrosio's cousin, Manuel Piñon, 48. Piñon's brother Jerry had just finished his shift moments before the shooting started. Longtime safety leader John Vallejos, 51, died in that trailer, while his brother Jesse was among the six left wounded. Mark Munoz, 59, was the third worker killed that morning. He had trained many of the other victims in their jobs and was looking forward to his retirement in three years.

After the smoke cleared, Allman fled the blood-soaked trailer and the quarry. He ditched his brown Mercury sedan and four guns at an Arco station, and tried to take a woman's car at gunpoint from a Hewlett-Packard parking lot at 7 a.m. The woman refused. Allman shot her. She survived, and Allman melted away into the suburbs again.

A few miles south down the Peninsula, Apple cofounder Steve Jobs was nodding in and out of consciousness in his English-country-style manse in Palo Alto. Jobs was the globally beloved prophet of the computer age and the beneficiary of dubiously backdated stock option and offshore tax schemes that swelled his net worth by billions. Jobs's life was a modernized Horatio Alger story complete with a rise where he cofounded the biggest company in the world in that nearly apocryphal garage that wasn't quite in Cupertino but close enough. He then fell from high-tech paradise and rebounded with a spectacular comeback that surpassed MacArthur's return to Leyte and Elvis's '68 Comeback Special all rolled into one. After retaking the helm of Apple in 1997, Jobs liberated us with his iPhones and iPads while tethering our eyes to handheld flatscreens. With his combination of ego, drive, and uncanny design sense, Jobs was able to disrupt the music and telephone industries almost simultaneously, but he was still mortal. He was now dying from pancreatic cancer, and didn't have much time left.

That October 5, he said his goodbyes to longtime Apple employees over the phone and said what he could to his family gathered at his side. Sometime during that already tragic morning for Cupertino, Jobs uttered a verbal triptych, thrice chanting, "Oh wow," before succumbing to permanent unconsciousness.

Steve Jobs died at 3 p.m. while the 215-pound Allman eluded capture as bands of militarized police clad in army surplus cammies combed through every backyard and carport searching for him. Schools and businesses were on lockdown. Streets were closed. Apple employees, unaware that their day was about to get worse, could only look at the hillside quarry through their HQ's western windows as they and everyone else in Cupertino were ordered to shelter in place.

At the apartment complex where Allman lived in San Jose, he was known as a community and religious activist who worked with at-risk African American youth. He even had his own show called *Real 2 Real* on San Jose's public access channel where he interviewed gospel singers and celebrities such as Damon Wayans and Mr. T. However, like so many other mass shooters, Allman also had a history of domestic violence. His ex-wife, Valeri Allman, got a restraining order on him 20 years earlier, alleging that Allman had beaten her several times during their three-year marriage.

Allman wrote and self-published a book decrying domestic abuse titled *Amazing Grace*. "I've struggled from childhood, to man, to be the best that I am," he wrote in the book's foreword. "I had a very disheartened childhood. I felt unloved and hurt, and that hurt feeling turned into hate. Hate for the drugs that my mother used and hate for my father for the women he used and abused."

Negativity was also a frequent topic on Allman's talk show. "When you're a negative person, I don't care how good your day was, let one negative thought come to mind, it'll mess up your whole day," he said in an episode still available on YouTube. "I tell people I'm in negative recovery, so don't call me telling me your problems."

Allman spent his whole life trying to outrun the hate that consumed him. He turned to God and the church, but it didn't stop him from buying guns.

Apple CEO Tim Cook announced Jobs's death with a press release at 4:55 p.m., issued from Cupertino while Allman was still at large and nearby. The imminent danger of a mass shooter emerging from Apple's well-tended shrubbery and unloading his clip didn't stop Jobs's admirers from flooding Cupertino to mourn their dead techie king. A group of computer science students left an Apple logo made from tea candles on the pavement as others scrawled their condolences in chalk on the walkway. "You were loved! You will be missed!!!" read one missive written inside of a red heart. The news crews working out of their satellite trucks pivoted from the quarry killings to the reaction to Jobs's passing, while broadcasts juxtaposed archival video of Jobs in his trademark black turtleneck holding up a new iPhone with Allman talking to Jesse Jackson on his public access show.

Thankfully, the escalation of tragedy that could have happened never materialized. Allman was found hiding behind parked cars on the 900 block of Lorne Way in Sunnyvale at 7:30 a.m. the next morning. He took his own life during a shootout with three young deputies. In the following days, hundreds of coworkers and family members packed the Oak Hill Cemetery chapel to say their goodbyes to slain quarry worker Manuel Piñon, while Jobs's memorial was a smaller affair at Stanford University attended by a few billionaires along with Bill Clinton and Al Gore. As for Allman, the spot where he ended it all was barely a block away from where Apple soon built its new spaceship-like campus, a pharaonic monument to Steve Jobs's memory, if not his earthly remains.

Arne Müseler / www.arne-mueseler.com

An aerial view of Apple's new spaceship-like HQ, a monument to Steve Jobs erected nearly on the site of where Shareef Allman killed himself after murdering several of his coworkers.

## CHAPTER 28

# A REAL FIXER-UPPER

Real estate agent Cheryl Bower stood in the sunlit living room of the Queen Anne Victorian at 152 Fourth Avenue in the Richmond District, greeting potential buyers with a well-polished cheeriness.

"Do you know the history of the house?" she asked as my wife, Rosemary, and I inspected a shallow "decorative" fireplace that was no longer suitable for burning things, if it ever had been. We told her we did. Bower let us know that a "disclosure packet was available."

The words "disclosure packet" formed an oft-repeated refrain coming from Bower during the open house on Sunday, July 29, 2015. Phrases like "mummified corpse" or "dead body" were never uttered by Bower or any of the wannabe buyers with dreams of scooping up the property for anything close to its $928,000 asking price. Almost everyone there had seen the *Chronicle* and *SFist* stories detailing how cleanup crews and firemen had pulled 300 jars of urine and a long-dead body out of the house—almost.

"Who lived here? Who lived here?" a little girl of about seven with sandy blonde hair asked repeatedly as she and her parents made their way through the row house's tiny rooms.

"A lady lived here, and now we've answered your question," the girl's exasperated mother replied.

An older woman with long gray hair made a speedy retreat when she found out she had strayed into the "hoarder house." "Oh my God," she said, before scrambling down front steps that bowed almost to the point of breaking with even the lightest footfall.

But she was the only one deterred from going farther. Several brave real estate speculators wanted to see the attic, even though it was only accessible through a rectangular opening in the ceiling of one of the closets. Fortunately for the safety of all concerned, the home stagers employed by Zephyr Real Estate didn't leave a stepladder behind.

Built in 1904, this little house in the avenues not only withstood years of neglect, but also the great earthquake and conflagration of 1906 that leveled the San Francisco of the Gold Rush and Barbary Coast. Archibald and Anna Mae Ragin bought the place on June 29, 1954, after securing a loan for $7,500. If people still put down 20 percent back then, it means the home's asking price was under $10,000. After Archibald died in 2000, Anna lived in the house with the couple's daughter, Carolyn Ragin, a retired Pac Bell worker. The Ragins stopped paying their county property tax in 2006.

Sometime after that, the neighbors stopped seeing Anna Mae around the house. When Anna Mae shuffled off this mortal coil, Carolyn either didn't notice or couldn't let go. Carolyn continued living in the house with what was left of her mother as liens piled up for unpaid garbage bills and property taxes, until the County Assessor's Office filed a notice to sell the property to claim $1,651.28 in back taxes. The home was foreclosed on. The city cleanup crews were summoned, and they found a true house of horrors.

"The police captains I've spoken with tell me this is the worst case of hoarding they have ever seen," Supervisor Eric Mar told the

Photo: Bob Calhoun

The "Mummy House" on Fourth Avenue in the Richmond District where Carolyn Ragin lived for several years with the decaying remains of her long-dead mother. The Victorian sold for over $1 million when it hit the market in 2015.

*Chron* in April when Anna Mae's remains were discovered alongside rooms filled with rat-infested trash piled up to the ceiling. According to several news reports, Carolyn was taken to a hospital to undergo psychiatric evaluation as professional cleaners continued to excavate the detritus from the Ragin family home.

A fresh coat of paint on the walls and a good floor-scrubbing couldn't quite chase away the smell of toxic mold and urine from the corners of the bedroom and kitchen during the open house. In the bedroom, a large square about the size of a bed was cut out of the flooring, revealing boards even more worn and ancient underneath. Bower claimed not to know why the floor had been removed, but we could all take a wild guess.

"I'd start brand new," Bower advised. "Take it down to the studs."

In the backyard, another real estate agent named Adam directed foot traffic, which included a well-to-do-looking white couple wearing pullover shirts with the logos of Northeastern colleges; a young bearded dad hauling his baby around in one of those detachable car-seat carriers; and a pair of elderly Chinese men.

"This is going to be a pretty popular house," Adam explained, "so I'm just helping out."

The middle-aged man in a Middlebury sweatshirt congratulated Adam like he was the CEO of a company that had just launched an IPO on the NASDAQ. "It's going to do real well," the Middlebury alum said. "It's a real diamond in the rough."

The two men agreed that the house, which had last sold for something like $9,375, could go for as much as $2.5 million after being fixed up.

As we were about to leave, I prodded my wife, Rosemary, to ask if there had been any paranormal activity in the house.

"The house doesn't feel creepy," Bower said evasively. "If there were ghost stories, we could probably charge more for it."

It's only been a couple of months. There will be ghost stories. Just give it time.

## CHAPTER 29

# THE LAST DAYS OF TOM GUIDO

The bad news traveled through Facebook the way that bad news always does now. "Just talked to a reporter for the *San Francisco Chronicle*," Beth Allen posted on January 9, 2019. "She wanted to talk to me about Tom Guido, and said that he'd died and that the coroner's office and his 'family'—a nephew—have talked to her and confirmed his death."

An outpouring of grief came from the aging Bay Area punks and retro rockers who remembered Guido in the 102 comments that followed.

"What a character that guy was," Barry Ward from the trucker-punk band Crosstops posted.

"Tom Guido was such an incredible part of the fabric of my youth and the San Francisco music scene," Kitty Chow wrote.

"Some of my best days in SF were at those shows," concurred Janette Lopez, front woman of Mad Mama and the Bona Fide Few.

Guido was the possibly the weirdest club owner that the San Francisco music scene ever produced, which was quite a feat considering the milieu. Beth Allen met him in the 1990s when her punk band the Loudmouths played the Purple Onion, a North Beach nightspot that he transformed into an underground outpost for punky garage rock bands such as the Phantom Surfers, the Count Backwards, and 3 Stoned Men. At first Allen hoped that news of Guido's death was just a rumor—that it wasn't true. But the confirmation came with an *Examiner* article later that afternoon. Guido wasn't just dead. He'd been murdered.

Police responded to reports of a man jumping out a window of the Weller Hotel at 908 Post Street at around 5:45 p.m. on Monday, January 7, 2019, and they also found a bloody Guido inside one of its apartments. Guido had been stabbed in the neck and head. He was rushed to the hospital. He didn't make it. The Medical Examiner's Office recorded Guido's death as an unusual homicide. The man who jumped from the window died in the hospital two days later. Police chief Bill Scott referred to the jumper as a suspect in Guido's

Photo: Michael Day

Purple Onion proprietor Tom Guido attempts to throw everyone out of his nightclub as a totally nude Christian "Regal" Goltry, drummer of the punk band. The Jack Saints, tries to warm up behind a well-placed snare drum.

murder, but it was days before they released his name. Word traveled fast, but autopsies still took time.

"Leave it to Tom to go out so dramatically," Allen said in a later interview. "No dying in his sleep or anything boring like that."

With her raven hair and arms covered with tattoos, Allen kept on gigging long after the Loudmouths played their last show at the Purple Onion in 1996. But even with all her bands that followed—the Meat Sluts, the McCools, the Jaded Fucks, the Wastedeads, and the Womentors—her thoughts turned back to that strange scene in North Beach 20 years earlier. She launched a website called Tom Guido's Purple Onion over a year before the tragedy to preserve a moment of San Francisco music history that might otherwise go overlooked. "Tom always reminded me of the actor Crispin Glover," she said. "He had this nasally, whiny voice and '60s bob haircut with bangs. He was erratic, slightly unhinged, and so funny!"

Entering the Purple Onion at 140 Columbus Avenue was like descending into a subterranean cavern, but the place had a cachet in

Photo: Brian Archer

The Loudmouths onstage at the Purple Onion in 1994. Left to right: Jay Loudmouth, Dulcinea Loudmouth, Pete Loudmouth, and Beth Loudmouth.

the early 1960s when the Smothers Brothers recorded a live album there, before they had transitioned from a square folk comedy duo into antiwar shit-disturbers that got booted off network television. Comedian Phyllis Diller—with her 1950s housewife gone horribly wrong schtick—and even Barbra Streisand got their starts there. It was still a cave, but it was a classy cave. Things were different by the 1990s when Guido took over. He was obsessed with the '60s, but not the one where Babs and Diller commanded the stage while your Nixon-voting parents or grandparents guzzled vodka gimlets. Guido's version of that decade was one glimpsed through Roger Corman druggie and biker flicks with soundtracks by Davie Allan and the Arrows. It was a '60s that never quite existed, but Guido did everything he could bring it to life through the sheer force of his off-kilter personality.

And the San Francisco music scene of the time had produced several bands that reenforced Guido's aesthetic. The female-fronted Loudmouths played thrash odes to Tura Satana, the Amazonian star of Russ Meyer's top-heavy cult curiosity *Faster, Pussycat! Kill! Kill!* (1965). The Phantom Surfers wore Lone Ranger masks and interspersed their surf instrumentals with one-liners that could've gone over at an open mic during the venue's standup heyday. The Rip Offs wore nylon stockings over their faces like perps in a *Streets of San Francisco* episode. And filling out the scene were the Count Backwards, 3 Stoned Men, the Trashwomen, the Bobbyteens, Mens Club, the Groovie Ghoulies from Sacramento, the Bomboras from Los Angeles, and many more bands that never got much further than a couple of shows in Guido's retro basement. And all of them took a mid-'60s fuzztone vibe and infused it with punk angst that fit the dinginess of a Purple Onion in decline.

Anthony Bedard, former booker of the now defunct Hemlock Tavern, met Guido in 1990 when the future impresario was hosting a DJ night around San Francisco called Club Fuzz, and the two became friends. "He was the ringmaster," Bedard said. "He was literally doing every job at the club. He was running from stamping

Photo: Michael Day

An especially impish-looking Tom Guido on stage with the Phantom Surfers at his North Beach nightspot, the Purple Onion, in the mid-1990s.

somebody's hand at the door, over to the bar to sell a drink, over to the stage to, you know, to interrupt the band."

Interrupting bands was Guido's thing, and musicians played the Purple Onion with the terror that Guido would throw them off its tinsel-lined stage halfway through their sets. Christian Goltry was the drummer for the Jack Saints, a shock rock band whose front man, Mike Desertt, paid homage to GG Allin and wrestling legend Ric Flair by carving his head open with broken beer bottles while a sometimes totally nude Goltry held down the beat. Their bloody and frantic stage show often compelled Guido to join the action, leading to even more pandemonium. "[Guido] would sometimes interrupt our set and grab the microphone and tell someone that they had to leave the club," Goltry recalled. "This would sometimes go on for minutes at a time. I have to admit it was fun to hear his whiny angry voice shouting over the microphone to get the fuck out of this club!"

The Jack Saints even included a rough recording of one of Guido's extended rants on their 2000 *Rock and Roll Holocaust* album as its closing track, "Live Riot at the Famous Purple Onion 1997." For nearly six minutes, Guido yells at people to get out over the random sounds of feedback as the Jack Saints struggle to set up their amps. "You're out. Out! Out! Get out!" Guido screams like a power-mad Andy Kaufman as voiced by Crispin Glover while wigged out on peyote laced with mescaline. "I'll close the place! And you're out too and your buddy is too! You pushed me! You pushed me! You can have your fucking five bucks back! Out! Talk to Maurice. Get your money back. Out! Out!

"You're killing punk rock! You! You pushed me, man. Don't do that. I don't care anymore. Out! Out! Out!"

By the midpoint of the fracas, somebody gets on the mic and demands to see Goltry's cock. Goltry obliges to a smattering of cheers and polite clapping. "I'm sorry you attract assholes," Guido says to the Jack Saints before telling Goltry that he's "hung like a cricket."

Sometime after Guido introduces the bands and it sounds like the show is finally going to start, somebody in the crowd hauls off and slugs Guido.

"That guy just punched me over there! Show's off! Get the fuck out of here, asshole! The club is closed! You ruined it, fuck boy!"

"Kill him! Kill Him!" Guido growls as his voice drops down an octave. "You want me to go kill somebody in front of you? Well . . ."

The audience responds with chants of "Kill! Kill! Kill!" And by the end of the track, it's unclear if the Jack Saints actually played the show or not.

But Goltry recalled all the chaos fondly, even when after the show Guido charged his drum kit and sent a cymbal crashing into his chest. "His actions were a spectacle but it was I think entertaining at times," Goltry said. "I hope he knew how much we loved him."

"[The Purple Onion] was always on the verge of falling apart, especially in the later years," Bedard said. "I mean that club really did have an arc." By 1998, "it really kind of came off the rails." Bedard's band, the Icky Boyfriends, played Guido's grand opening of the North Beach nightspot in 1993, but by the late 1990s, bands would show up to play and Guido "wasn't even there or he had locked himself in the club and he wouldn't open the doors." The last shows that Guido put on at the Purple Onion came in December 1999. The Roofies played there on December 10, with Dolly Dearest headlining the following night, and then it was over.

After the Onion, Guido never had such a forum again, but he was still a performance artist, no matter where he ended up. He was spotted at clubs and shows, and sometimes seen getting thrown out of them. For a time, he lived in an apartment above Mad Dog in the Fog, an Irish pub on Haight Street, before he succumbed to couch surfing and homelessness. By 2016, a nonprofit called North Beach Citizens set him up with a room in the Tenderloin, a stretch of prime real estate adjacent to the Financial District that is overseen by several nonprofits dedicated to helping people like Guido stay in the city—much to the chagrin of real estate speculators looking to build yet more luxury condos and office towers. Guido's room was in the Weller Hotel above the UN Market, a liquor store on the corner of Post and Hyde Streets. Guido became a regular at the market and befriended its 29-year-old manager, Frank Khalil.

"He came to the store, I'd say, at least 10 times a day," Khalil recalled. "I talked to him on a daily basis." Guido helped Khalil stock the shelves and swept up the cigarette butts from in front of the store. He went on lunch runs to Subway or McDonald's when Khalil was stuck behind the cash register, and even fed his cat and cleaned her litter box. "He loved my cat, Cocoa," Khalil said. And through all the self-imposed chores, Guido never stopped with his mile-a-minute patter, just like he was throwing someone out of the Purple Onion.

"He had a joke about everything," Khalil said. "You can ask him 10 trivia questions, and he'll answer all 10 of them. He really knows. He's a smart guy."

Even as Guido's scruffy brown bob gave way to a close-cropped silver mane, customers in the store still recognized him from the '90s music scene and treated him like a local celebrity. A woman with a dog once came into the store just to see him. Khalil told Guido to turn around and say hi to her.

"And he bends down to the dog and he says, 'Hi, my name is Tom' to the dog instead of the lady," Khalil recalled, still laughing about it. "And that's how funny he was."

While living at the Weller, Guido also became friends with Michael Dodd, another of the hotel's residents who struggled to stay housed in a city that had become increasingly unforgiving to people living on the margins. Dodd was much younger than Guido, but the two were drinking buddies who knocked back tallboys of malt liquor together at least five days a week, according to Khalil. While Guido was affable even in his lowest moments, Dodd was often sullen and kept samurai swords on the walls of his apartment. On Dodd's still live Facebook page, you can click through public-facing photos of him posing with friends, smiling with horses, and holding a black-and-white tuxedo cat. There are also several mobile uploads from 2013 of him wearing a neck brace and lying in a hospital bed. In what would be his final posts during the early morning hours of Monday, January 7, 2019, Dodd complained of punishing headaches.

"I have migraines like crazy and I don't feel right damn this sucks I played football I played soccer I played snowboarding too many hits to my head!" Dodd posted at 2:57 a.m. that morning. "I'm trying to tell you I'm afraid now."

At 3:11 a.m., he followed up with a thread about needing to get to sleep. "I time [sic] I told you about whatever things going on it's time for me to go to sleep," he wrote. "I'm going to die in this chamber but you need to find the chamber to where they could put you away and sleep."

Hours passed until around 5 p.m. that evening when Guido came into the UN Market and bought two beers—one for him and one for Dodd. "He was just the same, same goofy funny guy," Khalil recalled. "He was so happy; he was taking the beers up to Michael's room."

After ringing up the beers, Khalil left the store to take an extended smoke break. Shortly after he returned 45 minutes later, Dodd jumped out one of the hotel's second story windows. Somebody called to Khalil and he rushed out of the market to see Dodd lying on the pavement.

"Michael, what are you doing, man?" Khalil shouted, as Dodd lay broken on the sidewalk, his life ebbing away. "Wake up, Michael! You stupid man! You jumping out the window! Wake up, Michael! You stupid man! What are you doing?! You crazy?"

Paramedics came two minutes later and stretchered out Dodd. When police found Guido in Dodd's blood-soaked apartment, they performed CPR, but he was near dead from several cuts to the head and neck. "When I seen them carry out his body, they had his face covered because, uh, it was, I guess a very bad image," Khalil said.

Both men were taken to Chan Zuckerberg San Francisco General Hospital. Guido died later that night. Dodd died two days later. Officers found an unsheathed samurai sword in the apartment that presumably served as the murder weapon. According to investigators, Guido and Dodd had gotten into an argument before Dodd hacked at his friend and jumped out a window. Whatever they argued over, nobody knows.

When asked if there was anything more to Guido and Dodd's relationship than a mutual appreciation for Hurricane Malt Liquor, Khalil couldn't answer. "I think only a couple of people know the real, real truth," Khalil said. "The only people that really know are Tommy and Michael."

In the days following Guido's death, Khalil and the employees of the UN Market struggled to keep their corner of the Tenderloin clean through the sadness.

"We've been trying to do it since he left and nobody can do it like Tom, believe it or not," Khalil said, speaking of Guido in the present tense like he'd be coming back some day. "He pays attention to all the little cigarette butts and stuff like that. I've cried over a dozen times already."

The UN Market was so lively when Guido was there, but after his death, Khalil found himself alone with the constant electric hum of the beer and wine coolers that line the store's walls. "The store is very, very quiet," he observed. "I've never heard so much refrigeration in my life before. All I hear is refrigerators."

And the loss hit just as hard in the city's music scene. "[Guido] was such a sweet guy," Bedard said and then took a long pause. "I think he really did so much for people and really created so many good times for people and made so much good music happen. And then for him to go out that way, that's the worst.

"That's the worst part of it all."

My mom saw a young Barbra Streisand perform at the Purple Onion sometime in the very early 1960s, when everything was still like the '50s, before Bill Graham and his unwashed hippie mob went and ruined El Patio by turning it into the Fillmore West. My weird rock band played the Purple Onion in late 1996, just as Tom Guido's reign over the club began its relative decline. But when my mom heard that I'd played the Onion, she thought my musical career was really taking off. After all, I sang on the same stage as *Barbra Streisand*! The best singer since *Judy Garland*! I must have been on my way to superstardom and sold-out engagements at the International Hotel in Vegas like Elvis. My mother hadn't set foot in San Francisco in years, if not decades, and the Onion was still a class joint in her mind.

"The place has changed a little," I said to keep her from thinking that an appearance on *The Tonight Show* was just around the corner for me. The Purple Onion as a pathway to network late-night shows went out with Jack Parr.

My band in the 1990s (and later) was Count Dante and the Black Dragon Fighting Society. I was Count Dante, an identity I pilfered from a kung-fu huckster whose ads touting his pamphlet of *World's Deadliest Fighting Secrets* were inescapable in the pages of mid-1970s Marvel Comics. I wore sequined kimonos and did high kicks on stage.

My band wore less spectacular karate gi. The Purple Onion seemed like a place we should play, so I sent our demo tape to Tom Guido. I called him during his office hours to follow up. Even someone like Guido had to be together enough to keep office hours and answer phone calls back in those ancient times before a band could just tweet a link to its SoundCloud at bookers. He gave us an opening slot somewhat begrudgingly. I couldn't tell if he'd listened to our cassette or not, but it really didn't matter. On November 9, 1996, we opened for the Vaticans and 4 Nurses, two bands I have no recollection of.

It was the same night as Mike Tyson's first fight against Evander Holyfield, a long-anticipated bout that was delayed as Iron Mike served three years in the Indiana Youth Center near Plainfield, Indiana, for raping a young woman named Desiree Washington in 1991. As we waited to go on, I wandered over to Mr. Bing's, a dive bar on the corner of Columbus and Pacific Streets about a block and a half from the Onion. Mr. Bing's showed the fight on the analog TV that hung above its triangular bar because they did not give a fuck about pay-per-view licensing. If I had to take a guess, the broadcast was probably pirated as well.

I joined the spillover crowd on the sidewalk and watched the fight through the window. We all cheered like we were at the MGM Grand in Las Vegas as Holyfield knocked out Tyson in the 11th round in a stunning upset. It was all I could talk about when I got back to the club, but nobody seemed to care. In the rematch in 1997, Tyson bit off a piece of Holyfield's ear; that probably would have gotten a rise out of club goers.

The band went on. I did my kicks and my schtick. Guido watched us from the side of the stage, which was really more like a one-foot drum riser that we all stood on. He looked bemused, but he did not interrupt our set and make us march back up the club's 24 cold steps to Columbus Street. When we were done, he said, "More '60s!" like he was giving us advice after an audition. "You gotta be more '60s."

His bartender—or I should say the guy in the corner who sold you cans of Hamm's bought at the Foods Co. on Folsom Street—liked us though, so we came back for two more shows. At our last show there in February 1997, Guido had warmed up to me, at least a little. He told me about this party he'd been at where some dude had vibed him the wrong way.

"I thought of you," Guido said, "and I started kicking him!" He demonstrated a couple of really high kicks for me with a couple of '60s *Man from U.N.C.L.E.* karate chops thrown in.

"My God," I thought, "I'm inciting Tom Guido to violence."

That was the last time I thought I'd seen him. After he was killed, however, and newspapers ran more recent pictures that showed him with shorter silver hair, I realized that I had seen him after that. There were a few nights that I had sat down the bar from him at the Edinburgh Castle Pub, two and a half blocks away from where it had ended for him. I just hadn't recognized him without his trademark mid-1960s bob hairdo that was all the rage in the hippie episodes of *Gomer Pyle, U.S.M.C.*, and *Lost in Space*. He was just another denizen of the Castle, grabbing a pint on one of the sometimes-trendy bar's off nights when it reverted back to being the dive it was always meant to be.

By the time Tom Guido died in early 2019, the once swinging corner of North Beach where he held court had grown so much quieter. The Purple Onion's subsequent owners tried to bring the club back to its standup comedy glory but had to close it down in 2012, leaving behind another San Francisco building painted gentrification gray. Caesar's Italian Restaurant, an old-school macaroni joint where the bar was long and waiters still wore tuxes, closed earlier that same year. Just a half a block away on Kearney Street, the Lusty Lady, America's only employee-owned and unionized strip club, closed shop in 2013 when its landlord, local strip club magnate Roger Forbes, refused to renew the lease. After tasting the ambrosia of controlling the means of production, the soon-to-be-unemployed strippers held a funeral procession for the Lusty Lady, carrying a pink bejeweled coffin along Columbus and Kearney Streets past what had so recently been the Purple Onion.

And joints within a three-block radius of Guido's 1990s fiefdom kept on closing, or threatening to. Sexual misconduct allegations against its superstar chef co-owner and mounting overdue bills shut down Tosca Cafe in July 2019 after 100 years of serving boozy cappuccino across the street from City Lights Books. The place is supposed to reopen, but the days when beat cops could mingle with old beatniks went out when a $48 chicken dish was added to the menu.

Mr. Bing's Cocktail Lounge was sold in 2016. The new owners removed the old triangular bar that once pushed barflies to the walls of the corner building and cleared out the basement—where illicit mahjong games had been probably going on since the days of the original Barbary Coast—to make way for high-end party rentals. Celebrity chef and Emmy-winning travel show host Anthony Bourdain visited Mr. Bing's for his show *The Layover* in 2012. Upon hearing about the changes coming to the old dive, he lamented, "Just another day in the death spiral . . . Another good and noble thing, in this case, a fine drinking establishment, ground under the slow, inevitable, pitiless forward motion of the Terrible Wheel. It will consume us all in the end." Bourdain killed himself in 2018.

But there were still some dives left in the old neighborhood, and a memorial for Tom Guido was held on February 2, 2019, at Kell's Irish Pub at 530 Jackson Street around the corner from where the Purple Onion once was. Bands cobbled together from the wreckage of other bands jammed in the basement while Tony Bedard and several others lined up to give their eulogies by the main bar upstairs. Frank Khalil even showed up and looked like the youngest one there (because he probably was).

As Khalil eased his way into the packed bar, he grinned from ear to ear at the site of so many people there to pay tribute to his good friend. And the aging scenesters—myself included—were just as happy to see him. Not only did Khalil give us the closure we needed by telling us what happened above his store on that grim evening three weeks past, but he also let us know that Guido's legacy continued beyond the Purple Onion and the 1990s. The kookiness of Tom Guido had enduring appeal.

While Kell's was there when we needed it in 2019, a lot of places weren't, or didn't stick around for much longer. San Francisco lost over 400 restaurants that year along with the bars attached to them, and 2018 hadn't been all that kind to diners and watering holes either. Whether the closures were rumored or all-too-often real, somebody would post the inevitable *SFGate*, *SFist*, or *SF Weekly* article about the loss to their Facebook feed.

> Polk Street's Hemlock Tavern Will Close in Early October
>
> Lucky 13 Will Close, Be Demolished for Apartments
>
> SF's Edinburgh Castle Bar Is Up for Sale: Will a New Owner Continue the Legend?
>
> The Elbo Room to Close after Decades in the Mission
>
> La Victoria, Legendary SF Mexican-Owned Bakery, to Close Tuesday
>
> The Bay Area Mourns the Closure of Oakland's 91-year-old Mexicali Rose
>
> Goodbye, Paradise Lounge

And things kept getting worse with COVID-19. Slim's—the live music club founded by Boz Scaggs where Count Dante twice backed Canadian metal god Thor—closed down in March 2020. In August, it was announced it would be replaced by something called YOLO. The new owners promised that their new entertainment venture would have "no live band[s] like what Slim's had," as if to turn everyone's stomachs. In June 2020, the *Bay Area Reporter* spilled the beans that the Stud, San Francisco's oldest queer bar, was shutting down its longtime location at Ninth and Harrison Streets. The property owners couldn't even wait for the end of Pride Month to paint the building a sickly beige color, covering up a multicolored mural that spelled out "Queer Trans Spaces" that had been there for three years. A few days later, somebody painted "BLACK LIVES MATTER" and "WE WILL NOT BE ERASED" along with a pink triangle across the front of the former nightspot where queer disco legend Sylvester once performed. The owners of the Stud hope to reopen in a new spot, so maybe all is not quite lost.

And with the creative destruction starting long before the pandemic, Facebook and the other tech companies that moved fast and broke the fuck out of everything had all caused this on some level. But their walls, feeds, and timelines have become the delivery system for our collective sorrows. Nobody knows how many joints will be left when we can again leave our hovels without fear of coughing up the pink mist and dying, but it's a pretty safe bet that boarded-up storefronts will be the norm by the time this is published and we have Zoomed our last funeral until the next pandemic hits.

It is also certain that some new art and music scene will prosper in all those vacant retail spaces as even well-capitalized real estate investment trusts get desperate enough to rent to collectives of weirdos again post COVID-19—credit scores be damned. And this art scene born of the wreckage of late-stage capitalist greed and staggering civic neglect will be earthshaking, groundbreaking, and totally lit as these things always are and must be. However, I cannot say that I will recognize whatever-it-is for what-it-is.

But if I am still cool enough to speak with young artists by the year 2026, and they tell me about their new scene and all the boundaries that they are pushing, I will say, "You missed it when Tom Guido owned the Purple Onion in the 1990s, man.

"You missed the real San Francisco."

I will carry on this tradition.

# ACKNOWLEDGMENTS

Before I can get on with thanking anybody else, I must thank my editors at *SF Weekly*: Jeremy Lybarger, Chris Roberts, Nuala Bishari, and Peter Lawrence Kane. They gave me the freedom to explore the darkest corners of the Bay Area's history, and no story idea was ever too weird or obscure for them. If anything, the weirder and more obscure the better. I can never express how much I appreciate that. This work would not exist without their editorial guidance and *SF Weekly* itself, a vital and shit-disturbing institution that the city cannot do without. For those in and around San Francisco, please read the *Weekly* on the regular and buy your gummies from the dispensaries that advertise in it.

I am also so glad to be working with Michael Holmes and ECW Press again. Michael was my editor on *Beer, Blood and Cornmeal*, so that makes this the second book of weird San Francisco stories that he has helped bring to life. Thank you for believing in me and my book, Michael.

After reading *Beer, Blood and Cornmeal* and my following book, *Shattering Conventions*, my uncle on my mother's side, Dan Williams, sent me detailed notes on my efforts. He was an English teacher and also a devout Catholic, so he advised that I write Shakespearean sonnets to strengthen my prose and also expressed concerns for my eternal soul. It was all very sweet. Along with the critiques, he told me I had "the gift." Uncle Dan passed away in November 2016; this will be my first book where I won't get one of those notes. I will miss the advice and concern, and hope my prose has gotten a little bit better. I did a lot more rewriting this time, even if I haven't attempted to craft a sonnet.

A big thanks to all the people who were nice enough to take time out of their lives to read chapters for me. I owe all of you, but none more than my wife, Rosemary, who has read these gruesome yarns over and over again for years now, and had the indignity of sharing me with Patty Hearst for several weekends. "I feel like she's the other woman," she said, but then copyedited my essay on her and every iteration of it. She also read, like, a gazillion versions of the Dan White essay, which I started in April 2019 but didn't finish until February 2020. With both undertakings, she endured me talking about them through so many dinners and breakfasts as I struggled to work out the oddest details of so much depressing shit. I love you so much, Tiger Mama. You have all of my best ideas.

Bill Cane has been a teacher to me since high school, even though I never took his English class back then. His reading of this manuscript gave me the encouragement I needed to get to the finish line. Thanks also go to Bob Barnett—another student of Bill's who I don't think was in his English class either. Bob's ideas made the Dan White and Al Capone chapters a whole lot better. David Henry Sterry read the book when it was maybe two-thirds finished and gave some indispensable advice on how to close it. Special thanks to Loudmouth Beth for fact-checking the last chapter, and to Barry Ward for giving me the lowdown on several local crimes. Eddie Muller, Alia Volz, and Alan Black were also gracious enough to read some sections of the book and gave me their much-needed input. And Greg Franklin was often the recipient of stray paragraphs delivered through whatever instant messaging app we're using this week, just as he was with BBAC. I thank you all.

Big thanks go to Dana Smith and everyone at the Daly City History Guild for all their support and help with the chapter on my mother and the murder of August Norrie. I don't know anyone who works for Archive.org, but the research for so many of these stories would have been a whole lot harder without all of the materials that they make freely available. It is such a great resource. Please support it. Anthony Oertel was a huge help with all matters concerning San Francisco's hoodlums through his Frederick Bee History Project website (frederickbee.com). He has also been so generous with story suggestions—many of which I still hope to tackle someday. And special thanks to Lisa Hesselgesser of the Berkeley Public Library, every librarian at the San Francisco Public Library who helped me untangle spools of microfilm over the years, and the librarians at the Bancroft Library at UC Berkeley who gave me access to the *San Francisco Examiner* photograph archive.

An extra thanks goes to Peter Hartlaub of the Chron for taking the time to locate and scan crucial and otherwise impossible to find images of Penny Bjorkland. And while I am name-checking a current San Francisco journalist, I should also mention Carolyn Anspacher, Charles Raudebaugh, Paul Avery, Warren Hinckle, Art Hoppe, Maitland Zane and so many other—and all-too often uncredited—reporters who wrote for the *Chron*, *Ex*, *San Mateo Times*, *San Jose Mercury*, and *Oakland Tribune* during the last century. Without their work, this book would not exist.

And lastly but not leastly thanks to my former colleagues at UC Berkeley for putting up with all the murder stories, and to my new colleagues at Climate Leadership Initiative for giving me the space to finish this thing.

# SELECTED BIBLIOGRAPHY

## BOOKS


Asbury, H. (2002). *The Barbary Coast*. Thunder's Mouth Press.

Barton B. (1990). *The Secret Life of a Satanist: The Authorized Biography of Anton Szandor LaVey*. Port Townsend, WA: Feral House Press. Retrieved from books.google.com.

Bean W. (1968). *Boss Ruef's San Francisco: The Story of the Union Labor Party, Big Business, and the Graft Prosecution*. University of California Press. Retrieved from archive.org.

Berry-Dee C. (2011). *Cannibal Serial Killers: Profiles of Depraved Flesh-Eating Murderers*. Ulysses Press.

Boulware J., Tudor S. (2009). *Gimme Something Better: The Profound, Progressive, and Occasionally Pointless History of Bay Area Punk from Dead Kennedys to Green Day*. Penguin Group.

Brechin GA. (1999). *Imperial San Francisco: Urban Power, Earthly Ruin*. Berkeley, CA: University of California Press.

Carlo P. (2006). *The night stalker: The life and crimes of Richard Ramirez*. Pinnacle.

Coblentz SA. (1957). *Villains and Vigilantes: The Story of James King, of William, and Pioneer Justice in California*. New York: T. Yoseloff. Retrieved from archive.org.

Cowan RO., Homer WE. (1996). *California Saints: A 150-Year Legacy in the Golden State*. Bookcraft Pubs. Retrieved from rsc-legacy.byu.edu/pt-pt/archived/california-saints-150-year-legacy-golden-state/chapter-11-pacific-mission.

Didion J. (1979). *The White Album (1968–78)*. Simon & Schuster.

Dolan EF. (1967). *Disaster 1906: The San Francisco Earthquake and Fire*. New York: J. Messner. Retrieved from archive.org.

Dudman J., Scollins R. (1988). *The San Francisco Earthquake*. Bookwright Press. Retrieved from archive.org.

Duke TS. (1910). *Celebrated Criminal Cases of America*. San Francisco: The James H. Barry Company. Retrieved from archive.org.

Fallon M. (2016). *Dodgerland: Decadent Los Angeles and the 1977–78 Dodgers*. University of Nebraska Press. Retrieved from books.google.com.

Farrell H. (1992). *Swift Justice: Murder and Vengeance in a California Town*. New York: St. Martin's Press.

Gentry C. (1967). *Frame-Up: The Incredible Case of Tom Mooney and Warren Billings*. New York: Norton. Retrieved from archive.org.

Gong EY. (1930). *Tong War! The First Complete History of the Tongs in America*. New York: N.L. Brown.

Graysmith R. (1999). *The Bell Tower: The Case of Jack the Ripper Finally Solved . . . in San Francisco*. Washington, DC: Regnery Publishing.

Guinn J. (2014). *Manson: The Life and Times of Charles Manson.* Simon & Schuster.

Guinn J. (2017). *The Road to Jonestown: Jim Jones and Peoples Temple.* Simon & Schuster.

Hearst P. (1988). *Patty Hearst: Her Own Story.* New York: Avon Books. Retrieved from archive.org.

Hammer R. (1975). *Playboy's History of Organized Crime.* Chicago: Playboy Press.

Hanhardt C. (2013). *Perverse Modernities: Safe Space: Gay Neighborhood History and the Politics of Violence.* Duke University Press Books.

Hooper P. (Ed). (1882). *Illustrated History of Plumas, Lassen & Sierra Counties with California from 1513 to 1850.* San Francisco: Fariss & Smith. Retrieved from sites.rootsweb.com/~cagha/history/sierra/sierra-criminal-annals.txt.

Jentz T. (2006). *Strange Piece of Paradise.* Farrar, Straus and Giroux.

Jones C., Dawson J. (2001). *Stitching a Revolution: The Making of an Activist.* Harper One.

Kamiya G. (2013). *Cool Gray City of Love: 49 Views of San Francisco.* Bloomsbury.

King G. (2000). *Sharon Tate and the Manson Murders.* Barricade Books.

Lee B. (1999). *Chinese Playground: A Memoir.* Rhapsody Press.

Lunde DT. (1976). *Murder and Madness.* San Francisco: San Francisco Book Company, Inc.

Lunde DT., Morgan J. (1980). *The Die Song: A Journey into the Mind of a Mass Murderer.* New York: W. W. Norton & Co Inc.

Manson C., Emmons N. (1986). *Manson in His Own Words.* New York: Grove Press.

Mills J. (1979). *Six Years with God: Life Inside Rev. Jim Jones's Peoples Temple.* MBR/Investments Inc.

Newton H. (1973). *Revolutionary Suicide.* New https://archive.org.

Newton M. (2009). *The Encyclopedia of Unsolved Crimes.* Facts of File, Inc. Retrieved from books.google.com.

Pearlstein RM. (1986). *Lives of Disquieting Desperation: An Inquiry Into the Mind of the Political Terrorist.* (Publication No. 8618381). [PhD dissertation, University of North Carolina at Chapel Hill]. Retrieved from ProQuest.

Pepin E., Watts L. (2005). *Harlem of the West: The San Francisco Fillmore Jazz Era.* Chronicle Books.

Quinn A. (1994). *The Rivals : William Gwin, David Broderick, and the Birth of California.* Crown Publishers. Retrieved from archive.org.

Roldan G. (1996). *Activities of the Ku Klux Klan in Kern and Los Angeles Counties, California, During the 1920s.* (Publication No. 1381395). [Master's thesis, California State University, Fresno]. Retrieved from ProQuest.

Sanders E. (2016). *Sharon Tate: A Life.* Da Capo Press. Retrieved from books.google.com.

Schreiber B. (2016). *Revolution's End: The Patty Hearst Kidnapping, Mind Control, and the Secret History of Donald DeFreeze and the SLA.* New York: Skyhorse Publishing.

Shilts R. (2005). *Conduct Unbecoming: Gays and Lesbians in the U.S. Military.* St. Martin's Griffin. Retrieved from books.google.com.

Sides J. (2009). *Erotic City: Sexual Revolutions and the Making of Modern San Francisco.* Oxford University Press. Retrieved from books.google.com.

Toobin J. (2016). *American Heiress: The Wild Saga of the Kidnapping, Crimes and Trial of Patty Hearst.* New York: Doubleday.

Uris J., Uris L. (1975). *Ireland: A Terrible Beauty*. Doubleday.

Walsh JP. (1982). *San Francisco's Hallinan: Toughest Lawyer in Town*. Presidio Press. Retrieved from archive.org.

Ward DA. (2009). *Alcatraz: The Gangster Years*. Berkeley, CA: University of California Press.

Weiss M. (1984). *Double Play: The San Francisco City Hall Killings*. Reading, MA: Addison-Wesley Pub. Co. Retrieved from archive.org.

## AUDIO-VISUAL MEDIA

Bibb P., Schneider R. (Producers) and Maysles A., Maysles D., Zwerin C. (Directors). (1970). *Gimme shelter* [Film]. USA: Maysles Films.

Butler R. (1999). Neighborhoods: The Hidden Cities of San Francisco - The Fillmore. [Film]. KQED.

C-SPAN. (Nov. 3, 1976). *President Ford Concession Speech*. [Video]. c-span.org/video/?153625-1/president-ford-concession-speech.

Fruit Punch Collective. (May 23, 1979). Reaction to Dan White verdict. KPFA. Retrieved from archive.org.

Hitchcock AJ. (1958). *Vertigo* [Film]. Alfred J. Hitchcock Productions, Paramount Pictures.

The Jack Saints (2000). Live Riot at the Famous Purple Onion 1997. *Rock and roll holocaust* [Album]. Scooch Pooch Records.

KPIX Eyewitness News. (Oct. 28th, 1967). Shooting of Oakland police officer John Frey. [Video]. Retrieved from diva.sfsu.edu/collections/sfbatv/bundles/206883.

Longworth K. (Aug. 11, 2015). Charles Manson's Hollywood, Part 12: The Manson Family on Trial. [Audio podcast episode]. In *You Must Remember This*. Panoply.

Morris E. (Director). (2013). *The Unknown Known.* [Film]. History Films. Moxie Pictures. Participant Media.

Oscars. (March 30, 2015). The streaker: 1974 Oscars. [Video]. YouTube. Retrieved from youtu.be/EWBc-ir6IFM.

Petrelis M. (2014). Dan White's audio confession after killing Harvey Milk & George Moscone. Retrieved from soundcloud.com/michael-petrelis/dan-whites-audio-confession.

Prior D. (2007) *This is Zodiac Speaking* [Film]. Dreamlogic Pictures.

ShareefAllmanTV2. (Nov. 11, 2011). Shareef Allman words Of inspiration R.I.P Dad & Jessy mamas duh. [Video]. Youtube. Retrieved from youtu.be/xcDzXehGrRo.

TwainHarteFam. (2008). Buck Naked on Joan Rivers Show, part 1 of 2. [Video]. Youtube. Retrieved from youtube.com/watch?v=EBqqApNzgoo.

TwainHarteFam. (2008). Buck Naked on Joan Rivers Show, part 2. [Video]. Youtube. Retrieved from youtube.com/watch?v=jmJtiQKsvWw.

Van Dyke WS. (1936) *San Francisco* [Film]. Metro-Goldwyn-Mayer.

## INTERVIEWS

Jeremy Adkins (interview, June 9, 2017).

Beth Allen (Facebook Messenger interview, Jan. 10, 2019).

Charles Baker (phone interview, Aug. 3, 2017).

Tony Bedard (phone interview, Jan. 10, 2019).

Karen Blackstock (phone interview, Aug. 4, 2016).

Christian "Regal" Goltry (Facebook Messenger interview, Jan. 10, 2019).

Jeff Guinn (phone interview, March 17, 2017).

Patrick Hallinan (phone interview, July 22, 2017).

Frank Khalil (phone interview, Jan. 11, 2019).

Paul Krassner (email interview, May 9, 2019).

George Lazaneo (phone interview, May 4, 2020).

Al Nalbandian (phone interview, May 19, 2016).

Joel Selvin (phone interview, Aug. 4, 2016).

## PUBLIC DOCUMENTS

City and County of San Francisco. (Aug. 8, 1966). Coroner's register: Record of death: Charles Sullivan.

County of Solano, Office of Sheriff. (Dec. 20, 1968). Offense report. Retrieved from zodiackiller.com/LHRPR19.html.

Federal Bureau of Investigation. (1978-1979). Jonestown Part 168 of 287. Retrieved from vault.fbi.gov/jonestown/jonestown-part-168-of-288/view.

People v. Newton (Crim. No. 7753. Court of Appeals of California, First Appellate District, Division Four. May 29, 1970). Retrieved from law.justia.com/cases/california/court-of-appeal/3d/8/359.html.

People v. Raley (Superior Court of Santa Clara County, No. 99021, Jun 18, 1992). Retrieved from https://law.justia.com/cases/california/supreme-court/4th/2/870.html.

People v. Szeto (Crim. No. 21523, Supreme Court of California, Feb. 11, 1981). Retrieved from LexisNexis.

People v. Sully (Crim. No. 25590. Jul 11, 1991). Retrieved from law.justia.com/cases/california/supreme-court/3d/53/1195.html.

San Francisco Police Department. (Jan. 7, 2019). Incident report.